WANTING WAR

WANTING
WAR

Why the Bush Administration Invaded Iraq

JEFFREY RECORD

POTOMAC BOOKS, INC.
WASHINGTON, D.C.

Library of Congress Cataloging-in-Publication Data
Record, Jeffrey.
  Wanting war : why the Bush administration invaded Iraq / Jeffrey Record.
    p. cm.
  Includes bibliographical references and index.
  ISBN 978-1-59797-437-0 (hardcover : alk. paper)
  1. Iraq War, 2003– —Causes. 2. Cold War—Influence. 3. Bush, George W. (George Walker), 1946– —Political and social views. 4. Military planning—United States—History—21st century. 5. United States—Military policy—21st century. 6. United States—Politics and government—2001–2009. I. Title.
  DS79.764.U6R436 2010
  956.7044'31—dc22

                                                                    2009040571

Printed in the United States of America on acid-free paper that meets the American National Standards Institute Z39-48 Standard.

Potomac Books, Inc.
22841 Quicksilver Drive
Dulles, Virginia 20166

First Edition

10 9 8 7 6 5 4 3 2 1

Contents

Preface

I wrote this book because the U.S. invasion of Iraq made no sense to me. There was never any convincing evidence that Saddam Hussein's Iraq had anything to do with the 9/11 terrorist attacks or that he was an ally of al Qaeda. And there was no evidence that the Iraqi dictator would have been undeterrable even had he acquired nuclear weapons. Saddam Hussein was homicidal, not suicidal. Even before the invasion it became apparent to me that the George W. Bush administration wanted war with Iraq and wanted it for multiple reasons—some stated, others not—that had little or nothing to do with Saddam Hussein's alleged possession of weapons of mass destruction and collaboration with al Qaeda. A loose combination of sometimes contradictory arguments and expectations, none of them sufficient to justify war, propelled the administration into Iraq. Indeed, my research led me to conclude that the Iraq War was more about the United States than it was about Iraq. More specifically, the war was about the hubris of seemingly irresistible American military power.

I am indebted to the Air University's fabulous Muir S. Fairchild Research Information Center and to the Air War College for providing me the research opportunities and time to write this book. I am also indebted to several colleagues for their helpful comments and suggestions, especially Dr. Christopher Hemmer and Dr. Alexander Lassner at the Air War College in Montgomery, Alabama; and Dr. W. Andrew Terrill and Dr. Steven Metz at the U.S. Army's Strategic Studies Institute in Carlisle, Pennsylvania.

ONE

INTRODUCTION:
A MYSTERIOUS WAR

The conviction that Saddam Hussein was an imminent threat to America and therefore necessitated removal by force began as a kind of communicable agent to which some in the administration had great resistance and others not. Its host bodies belonged to, among others, Vice President Dick Cheney; his chief of staff, I. Lewis "Scooter" Libby; Deputy Secretary of Defense Paul Wolfowitz; and Douglas J. Feith, undersecretary of defense for policy. The agent resided in these four men, and in lesser hosts, well before September 11. But after the attack on America, the contagion swept through the Beltway and insinuated itself into the minds of many—including the White House national security adviser and the president of the United States.

—Robert Draper,
Dead Certain: The Presidency of George W. Bush[1]

President Bush did a great favor for bin Laden when he followed the war on terrorism with the invasion of Iraq, which created a failed state in the middle of the Islamic world and provided a breeding and training ground for more terrorists. . . . There has probably been no more profound self-fulfilling prophesy than the President's declaration of Iraq as the center of the war [on terrorism]; prior to the invasion and the U.S. occupation, there was virtually no terrorism in Iraq and certainly no safe haven there for terrorists.

—Melvin A. Goodman,
Failure of Intelligence: The Decline and Fall of the CIA[2]

The United States is headed into the eighth year of an exceptionally frustrating war whose consequences so far have been largely injurious to America's long-term national security. Preoccupation with that war understandably has obscured the original decision to launch it. That decision, moreover, cannot be repealed, and the controversies surrounding it offer little instruction to those grappling with the political and military challenges confronting the United States in Iraq today. Knowing the way into Iraq offers little guidance for extrication. However wrongheaded the decision to invade Iraq may have been—and I believed then and still do that it was a historic strategic blunder—the situation and the policy choices in Iraq today are different than they were in 2002–2003. Failure to think through the potential consequences of invading Iraq is hardly an excuse to ignore the likely consequences of an abrupt and unconditional withdrawal. At present, under the terms of a status of forces agreement concluded with the Iraqi government on November 17, 2008, the United States is committed to withdraw *all* of its military forces from Iraq by December 31, 2011. President Barack Obama is also committed to removing all U.S. combat forces from Iraq by the late summer of 2010.

Regardless of when and how America leaves Iraq, it is critical that Americans understand how the United States came to invade and occupy Iraq, if for no other reason than to better inform future discussion of whether, when, and how to employ U.S. military power. Understanding how we got into Iraq may help avoid additional disastrous wars. If, in fact, the decision to invade Iraq was, as most Americans now believe, a horrible mistake, then it is imperative that the decision be analyzed for the purpose of improving the judgment of future national security decision makers.

The Iraq War is the third unnecessary war into which the United States has stumbled since 1945, a record that suggests a dismal inability to learn from past mistakes. Indeed, in the aftermath of these three wars neither Congress nor the White House sponsored a formal bipartisan inquiry, such as the 1945 Joint Committee on the Investigation of the Pearl Harbor Attack (the so-called Pearl Harbor Commission) or the 2002 National Commission on Terrorist Attacks upon the United States (also known as the 9/11 Commission), to examine the causes of the associated calamitous White House decisions. It would seem that such inquiries are reserved for situations in which enemy action caught the United States unprepared as opposed to circumstances in which U.S. action invited defeat. This situation must change. Most of America's wars have been wars of choice, not necessity; and these bad choices, which have resulted in large and unnecessary losses of blood and treasure, merit official inquiry. Conducting formal investigations has been the practice in Israel, and it should be the practice in the United States today as well.

Since 1945, the first unnecessary war was the Harry S. Truman administration's war with China in Korea (1950–53), which the United States recklessly provoked by attempting to forcefully reunify the Korean Peninsula following Gen. Douglas MacArthur's September 1950 landing at Inchon and his routing of the North Korean army. (The administration's initial decision in June 1950 to repel North Korea's aggression and restore South Korea's territorial integrity was separate from its subsequent choice to cross the 38th Parallel and push deep into North Korea. The first entailed war with North Korea, the second with China.) The second unnecessary war stemmed from the Lyndon Johnson administration's 1965 decision to intervene directly in the Vietnam War, a decision that produced a decade of bloody and stalemated military operations culminating in an American defeat.[3]

And the third, of course, is the present war in Iraq. Just as the Korean and Vietnam wars before it, the Iraq War has had exceptionally adverse foreign policy consequences for the United States. Though the war's outcome remains unknown, so far it has alienated friends and allies around the world;

exposed the limits of American military power for enemies to see and exploit; raised the prospect of an Iraq syndrome that could weaken U.S. foreign policy for decades; soured civil-military relations to the point where retired generals have publicly indicted their former civilian superiors for arrogance and incompetence; depleted U.S. land power and retarded recapitalization of U.S. air and naval power; weakened the dollar in international currency markets; inflated the national debt by as much as $2 trillion; contributed to record-high crude oil prices; encouraged Russian and Chinese strategic hostility; vindicated, to millions of Muslims, al Qaeda's story line about American imperial ambitions in the Middle East; aided and abetted the electoral victories of Hamas in Palestine and Hezbollah in Lebanon; transformed Iraq into a recruiting and training ground for Islamist terrorism; promoted the expansion of Iranian power and influence in the region; encouraged Iran to accelerate its quest for nuclear weapons; and enabled the probable establishment of a Shiite-dominated regime in Baghdad aligned with Tehran that could undermine Saudi Arabia and other Sunni Arab states with significant Shiite minorities. An April 2008 National Defense University study summarized the damage:

> Globally, U.S. standing among friends and allies has fallen. Our status as a moral leader has been damaged by the war, the subsequent occupation of a Muslim nation, and various issues concerning the treatment of detainees. At the same time, operations in Iraq have had a negative impact on all other efforts in the war on terror, which must bow to the priority of Iraq when it comes to manpower, materiel, and the attention of decisionmakers. Our Armed Forces—especially the Army and Marine Corps—have been severely strained by the war in Iraq. Compounding all of these problems, our efforts there were designed to enhance national security, but they have become, at least temporarily, an incubator for terrorism and have emboldened Iran to expand its influence throughout the Middle East.

The study went on to conclude that despite the surge in U.S. forces in 2007, "the outcome of the war is in doubt" and that "[s]trong majorities of both Iraqis and Americans favor some sort of U.S. withdrawal," even though "the only thing worse than an Iraq with an American army may be an Iraq after the rapid withdrawal of that army."[4]

To be sure, the U.S. invasion and occupation of Iraq removed a brutal dictator from power and opened the door to the possibility of enduring positive political and economic change in Iraq. But to argue that the world is better off without Saddam Hussein is to ignore the cost side of the Operation Iraqi Freedom's ledger. A democratic Iraq never qualified as a vital American security interest before the United States invaded in 2003. It was desirable, yes, but vital, no. Further, the blood and treasure costs and the adverse strategic consequences of the Bush administration's enterprise in Iraq, so far, have greatly outweighed the benefits. Ultimately, of course, the balance sheet could change, but as of this writing, when the United States seems buried in an avalanche of liabilities, it is hard to see how the United States could transform its strategic investment in Iraq into a net asset. The substantial military progress, beginning in 2007, that flowed from new U.S. approaches to counterinsurgency and from American forces' exploitation of al Qaeda's alienation of key Sunni Arab tribes in Anbar Province was not matched on the Iraqi side by political progress at the national level. The Kurds' de facto independence in northern Iraq has effectively partitioned the country, and Baghdad's willingness and ability to integrate the Sunni Arab community into Iraq's unfolding new political order remains highly questionable. Final judgment on the wisdom of the gamble in Iraq must wait on what happens in Iraq *after* the United States departs. (Two years separated the withdrawal of U.S. military power from Indochina and the collapse of South Vietnam.)

————————

The unnecessary wars in Vietnam and against the Chinese in Korea merit brief review here because as with the Iraq War, their eras' policymakers made decisions based on faulty assumptions, wishful thinking, and ignorance of local history and culture, all of which combined to produce unexpectedly unpleasant outcomes. As precedents for the Iraq War, the Korean and Vietnam decisions also underscore the recurrence of dangerous miscalculation in the use of force as a phenomenon of post–World War II American statecraft. That the Iraq intervention followed the Vietnam intervention, which followed the Korea intervention, suggests the absence of a political learning curve as well as the probability of another disastrous intervention by some future administration.

There were alternative courses of action in Korea, Vietnam, and Iraq. The Truman administration could have halted U.S. forces at the 38th Parallel, restoring South Korea's territorial integrity and avoiding war with China. The Johnson administration could have cut its losses in Vietnam (as Richard Nixon's administration did, finally, in 1973), sparing both Vietnam and the United States eight years of war. And the Bush administration need not have made its war with Iraq a self-fulfilling prophecy; instead, it could have remained focused on al Qaeda's destruction and Afghanistan's reconstruction while continuing to contain a militarily toothless Saddam Hussein. Yet in each case, alternatives to war were rejected.

The 38th Parallel decision was made on the twin assumptions that sending U.S. forces into North Korea for the avowed purpose of regime change in Pyongyang would not provoke Chinese intervention and that in any event Mao Zedong's People's Liberation Army (PLA) would not contest the advance of MacArthur's forces. The possibility of Chinese intervention was dismissed in large measure because the administration had low regard for the PLA's fighting power and because Truman and his secretary of state, Dean Acheson, knew next to nothing about Mao and failed to imagine how the Chinese might regard the establishment of U.S. military power along China's Yalu River border with North Korea. Truman, Acheson, and MacArthur all believed that U.S. military power was irresistible in Inchon's wake and that the Chinese would be mad to intervene. Thus, in the weeks following Inchon, they were self-insulated from growing evidence, including verbal warnings from Beijing, of imminent Chinese intervention. Indeed,

MacArthur pressed on to the Yalu even after the forces under his command began capturing PLA soldiers deep in North Korea. Thus, the decision to cross the 38th Parallel transformed a quick and decisive victory over the North Korean army, one that would have ensured the reestablishment of South Korea's territorial integrity, into a much larger, longer, bloodier, and, as it turned out, indecisive war with China.

The White House assumed that China would accept at face value the administration's declarations that the United States did not seek war with China. In addition, it simply could not imagine that the Chinese Communists, against whom the United States had backed Chiang Kai-shek's Nationalist government, might regard a U.S.-occupied North Korea, which had served as Japan's invasion corridor into China's industrial heartland, as an unacceptable strategic threat. "When assessing Communist China's own intentions," observes Shu Guang Zhang, "U.S. strategists simply did not believe that the Chinese would intervene. From [the American] perspective, U.S. actions did not affect Chinese security interests."[5] Notwithstanding a recently concluded Sino-Soviet mutual defense treaty, Secretary of State Acheson believed that China had much more to fear from Soviet domination of mainland northeast Asia than from an American military presence in Korea. Acheson argued, "It would be sheer madness for the Chinese to enter the Korean War."[6] (Nine years earlier, Acheson, then assistant secretary of state for economic affairs, had declared that "no rational Japanese could believe that an attack on us could result in anything but disaster for his country.")[7]

The Truman administration's military optimism stemmed from its ignorance of the PLA. China's military reputation in 1950 was one of more than a century's worth of humiliation and defeat at the hands of Western powers and Japan. In all Asia, only the Japanese had inflicted significant defeats on Western adversaries, but that was because Japan had converted itself into a modern industrial state and had adopted Western military practices. China remained a poor and backward state, and MacArthur certainly did not view the PLA as anything out of the ordinary for the Chinese. On the contrary, as John Stoessinger observes, he "had a curious contempt for the

Chinese soldier," mistakenly equating "the thoroughly indoctrinated, well-disciplined Communist soldier of 1950 with the demoralized Nationalist soldier of 1949."[8] MacArthur (and the rest of the senior American military leaders) knew practically nothing about the new and different army Mao had fashioned in northern China during the 1930s and 1940s. The Pentagon's assumption was that the PLA was probably no better or worse (though much larger) than the vanquished, conventional, vehicle-heavy North Korean army. It did not recognize that the PLA's divisions were much lighter and better disciplined or that they relied on unconventional off-road infiltration and "hugging" tactics, night operations, and superb camouflage, all of which minimized the impact of American airpower.[9]

At the famous meeting between Truman and MacArthur on Wake Island on October 15, 1950, a month after Inchon, the general assured Truman that the chances of a Chinese intervention were low and that if the PLA did intervene he would crush it with airpower. When Truman asked him directly about what the chances of a Chinese intervention were, MacArthur replied:

> Very little. Had they intervened in the first or second months it would have been decisive. We are no longer fearful of their intervention.... The Chinese have 300,000 men in Manchuria. Of these probably not more than 100–125,000 are distributed along the Yalu River. Only 50,000 or 60,000 could be gotten across the Yalu River. They have no air force. Now that we have bases for our Air Force in Korea, if the Chinese tried to get down to Pyongyang, there would be the greatest slaughter.[10]

At the time MacArthur made these assertions, six PLA armies comprising eighteen infantry divisions and totaling at least 180,000 men were but two days away from crossing the Yalu (at night and completely undetected). Ten days later, on October 25, the PLA struck advancing United Nations (UN) forces and then abruptly broke contact, luring MacArthur farther north. By November 24, the day MacArthur launched his final dash to the Yalu, a total of thirty PLA divisions and 300,000 men had been deployed to Korea.[11]

The decision to cross the 38th Parallel, though horribly wrong, may have been militarily and politically irresistible. The late David Halberstam believed that "[b]ecause the Communists had started the war . . . , because so many Americans had already died in Korea, and because the commander in chief in the field had always wanted to go north, the decision was essentially foreordained."[12] But MacArthur's decision to rush his overextended and exposed forces on to the Yalu *after* encountering the PLA in North Korea and *against* the express wish of the Joint Chiefs of Staff (JCS)—namely, that MacArthur halt and consolidate his forces along North Korea's relatively narrow neck just north of Pyongyang—set the stage for the greatest American military defeat of the twentieth century.

Of the American military miscalculations of the twentieth century, Douglas MacArthur's decision to send his troops all the way to the Yalu stands alone. (Vietnam was a *political* miscalculation and the chief architects of it were civilians.) All sorts of red flags were there for him, flags that he chose not to see. So it was that his troops, their command split, their communications often dangerously weak, the weather worsening by the day, pushed north, while the Chinese watched and patiently waited for them on the high hills, already preparing to block the narrow arteries of retreat or escape.[13]

The Vietnam decision was made on the assumption that the loss of South Vietnam to the Communists would spark the loss of the rest of Southeast Asia (the so-called domino theory) and invite a third world war by undermining the credibility of U.S. security commitments worldwide. Policymakers were convinced that an American failure to fight in Vietnam would invite further Communist aggression in Southeast Asia as well as demoralize U.S. treaty allies elsewhere. Some also viewed Vietnam as a test of America's ability to defeat guerrilla-style "wars of national liberation." Still others saw the Vietnamese Communists as stalking horses for Chinese imperialism.[14]

President Dwight Eisenhower was the first to publicly espouse the theory that served as a principal rationale for American intervention in Vietnam. At a press conference in August 1953, he described the consequences of a Communist victory in what was still French Indochina, warning: "If Indochina goes, several things happen right away. The Malayan peninsula would scarcely be defensible . . . all India would be outflanked . . . [and] how would the free world hold the rich empire of Indonesia? So you see, somewhere along the line this must be blocked. It must be blocked now."[15] In April 1954, just before the French garrison at Dien Bien Phu fell, he compared Burma, Thailand, Malaya, and Indonesia to a row of dominoes. France's defeat in Indochina, he said, would involve

> broader considerations that might follow what you would call the "falling" domino principle. You have a row of dominoes set up, you knock over the first one, and what will happen to the last one is the certainty that it will go over very quickly. So you could have a beginning of a disintegration that would have the most profound influences.[16]

Closely related to the domino theory was his administration's fear of the consequences of reneging on the U.S. commitment to South Vietnam's defense. Vietnam was part of a worldwide network of U.S. defense commitments, and abandoning one of them would place all the others in jeopardy by encouraging further Communist aggression and would demoralize allies. Indeed, the issue of reputation, driven by the still vividly remembered repercussions of the Anglo-French appeasement of Nazi Germany during the 1930s, was central to the Johnson administration's reasoning about

South Vietnam.[17] As Secretary of State Dean Rusk put it in a 1965 CBS Television News interview,

> The fact is that we know we have a commitment. The South Vietnamese know we have a commitment. The Communist world knows we have a commitment. The rest of the world knows it. Now, this means that the integrity of the American commitment is at the heart of this problem. I believe that the integrity of the American commitment is the principal structure of peace throughout the world . . . if our allies, or more particularly, if our adversaries should discover that the American commitment is not worth anything, then the world would face dangers of which we have not yet dreamed.[18]

The Johnson administration thus viewed the stakes in Vietnam in terms of the perceived consequences of *non*intervention—i.e., of American *in*action. Vietnam was a Cold War struggle, a test of American resolve in containing the spread of Communism. It mattered little that Vietnam had no intrinsic strategic value to the United States or that it might be impossible to establish a viable non-Communist political order in the southern half of the artificially divided country. Completely missing from this picture was a recognition of the overpowering presence of Vietnamese nationalism, the indigenous political roots of the war, the military skill and tenacity of the Vietnamese Communist forces, and the limited utility of the American way of war in Indochina's strategic and operational setting. U.S. officialdom knew next to nothing about Vietnam's history and culture and only a little more about the fighting power of Vietnamese Communists than it had of Chinese Communists. Moreover, while there was scant confidence in a quick victory, it was beyond the imagination of the White House and Pentagon that so materially weak an enemy could defeat the United States. The Vietnamese defeat of the French in Indochina did not impress the Johnson administration. After all, the French were fighting a colonial war, the U.S. military in 1965 was much more powerful than the French had been in 1946–54, and the successful U.S. defense of South Korea seemed to argue strongly for the feasibility of South Vietnam's defense.

Both the administration's conception of the war as simply another case of international Communist aggression and its assumption of America's military irresistibility virtually guaranteed its failure of imagination. As former defense secretary Robert McNamara lamented in retrospect,

> We failed to ask the most basic questions: Was it true that the fall of South Vietnam would trigger the fall of the rest of Southeast Asia? Would that constitute a grave threat to the West's security? What kind of war—conventional or guerrilla—might develop? Could we win it with U.S. troops fighting alongside the South Vietnamese? Should we not know the answers to these questions before deciding whether to commit troops? It seems beyond all understanding, incredible, that we did not force ourselves to confront such issues head-on.[19]

Perhaps the worst failure of all was the administration's inability to grasp that what the United States considered a limited war was for the Vietnamese Communists a total war. Put simply, the Communists had a far greater stake in the war's outcome than did the United States; thus, they were prepared to make far greater sacrifices proportional to their resources than were the Americans. That U.S. policymakers simply did not grasp this decisive asymmetry in the two sides' will to win, which in turn guaranteed a persistent underestimation of the enemy, was evident in their repeatedly expressed awe over the enemy's staying power. (Against the Americans, who withdrew from Vietnam after losing 58,000 military dead, the Vietnamese Communists incurred 1.1 million military dead.)[20] In 1965, U.S. ambassador to South Vietnam (and former chairman of the JCS) Maxwell Taylor marveled, "The ability of the Vietcong continuously to rebuild their units and make good their losses is one the mysteries of this guerrilla war. We still find no plausible explanation of the continued strength of the Vietcong. . . . Not only do the

Vietcong units have the recuperative power of the phoenix, but they have an amazing ability to maintain morale."[21] A year later, McNamara remarked to an acquaintance, "I never thought [the war] would go like this. I didn't think these people had the capacity to fight this way. If I had thought they could take this punishment and fight this well, could enjoy fighting like this, I would have thought differently at the start."[22] Rusk later confessed: "Hanoi's persistence was incredible. I don't understand it, even to this day."[23] Even Gen. William Westmoreland, the American commander in South Vietnam, conceded that America's leaders "underestimated the toughness of the North Vietnamese."[24] He seemed to complain, "Any American commander who took the same losses as General Giap, would have been sacked overnight."[25]

No less an obstacle to American success than the Vietnamese Communists' fighting power was the Saigon regime's lack of it. The Republic of Vietnam (RVN), or South Vietnam, was essentially an American Cold War creation. Established in the wake of France's defeat in Indochina and with the 1954 Geneva agreement's temporary division of Vietnam into a Communist north and a non-Communist south, the republic lacked legitimacy from the start. Ruled by the devoutly Catholic dictator Ngo Dinh Diem during its first eight years and subsequently by a parade of coup-making generals—Duong Van Minh, Nguyen Khanh, Nguyen Cao Ky, Nguyen Van Thieu—during its remaining twelve years, the RVN was completely dependent on American diplomatic and economic largesse. Permeated with venality and officered predominately by generals and colonels who had fought *for* the French, the RVN was never in a position to challenge the Vietnamese Communists' nationalist credentials or (even with massive U.S. assistance) to create an effective military counterweight to the People's Army of Vietnam and the forces of the National Liberation Front. The U.S. client-regime in Saigon was fundamentally unsalvageable, a reality that virtually guaranteed a Communist victory once the United States disengaged its military forces from Indochina. The Nixon administration's policy of "Vietnamizing" the war, which was driven by collapsing domestic public support for continued U.S. intervention and (one suspects) an unspoken recognition that the war was unwinnable at any acceptable moral or material cost, rested on the vain hope that South Vietnam's armed forces could somehow succeed where American forces had failed. All the hand-wringing over self-imposed restrictions on the use of U.S. force in Indochina ignores not only the inevitability of an American military drawdown in Vietnam but also the fatal disparity in fighting power between the Vietnamese Communists and the South Vietnamese regime.

The Iraq decision was likewise based on a host of false assumptions, much wishful thinking, and a profound ignorance of Iraqi history and culture. The decision reflected many failings, including a gross overestimation of the stakes in Iraq, overconfidence in U.S. military power, obliviousness to potentially negative consequences, poor reasoning by historical analogy, and an inability to imagine how others might perceive American actions. The George W. Bush administration presented both a worst-case scenario of the Iraqi threat that went far beyond the evidence and a best-case picture of the potential consequences of a U.S. invasion of Iraq. It assumed that the Iraq War would be short and decisive, that U.S. forces would be welcomed as liberators, that the Iraqi state would remain intact, that democratic governance would naturally arise from the ashes of Baathist tyranny, that war costs would be minimal, and that Iraq's reconstruction would be self-financing. The administration dismissed or failed to anticipate the difficulties inherent in Iraq's forcible political transformation. It did not imagine the possibility of an Iraqi insurgent reaction to an American occupation, and, worse still, it applied a measure of military force grossly insufficient to achieve its ambitious military and political objectives in Iraq.

What motivated the disastrous Korea, Vietnam, and Iraq decisions? Korea and Vietnam are relatively easy to explain. Both were Cold War decisions by Democratic presidents who feared the domestic political consequences of not acting. Truman and Johnson believed, rightly or wrongly, that the strategic stakes were high in Korea and Vietnam, respectively. Both believed that America's resolve to resist totalitarian aggression was being tested, just as Hitler had tested the Western democracies in the 1930s, and that a failure to fight was tantamount to the disastrous appeasement policies of that decade. As Democrats, moreover, Truman and Johnson were leaders of a political party that during the 1940s and 1950s had been subjected to brutal Republican charges of being "soft" on Communism both at home and abroad. Such Republican politicians as California congressman Richard Nixon, California senator William Knowland, Wisconsin senator Joseph McCarthy, and Nevada senator Pat McCarran accused the Democratic White House of "giving away" Eastern Europe to Joseph Stalin at the Yalta Conference in 1945, "losing" China to the Communists in 1949, and tolerating Communist infiltration of the State Department (the infamous Alger Hiss case) and the Manhattan Project (Klaus Fuchs, David Greenglass, and others). Having lost the last five presidential elections and taking advantage of the dismay caused by the onset of the Cold War, the unexpected Communist takeover of China, and the abrupt loss of America's atomic monopoly just four years after Japan's surrender, the Republicans deliberately fanned a Red Scare in the late 1940s and early 1950s that placed the Democrats (and détente-minded Republicans) on the defensive for the remainder of the Cold War. Republicans were particularly critical of Truman's policy of containment, which they regarded as tantamount to appeasement of Communist expansion in Eastern Europe and Asia. In their view, the United States should not accept Communist territorial gains but rather seek to roll them back. Nixon, a savage critic of the Truman administration and soon to be vice president under Dwight Eisenhower, condemned what he termed the "Dean Acheson Cowardly College of Communist Containment."[26]

Against this domestic backdrop the Truman administration made its decision to cross the 38th Parallel. At the time Republicans and Democrats alike roundly applauded the decision. To have halted at the 38th Parallel after Inchon and the North Korean army's collapse would have dismayed many Democrats and infuriated Republicans, including the headstrong and politically ambitious MacArthur. Barring Chinese intervention, which both Acheson and MacArthur dismissed, the Truman administration stood to reverse Communist gains and win an enormous Cold War victory that could void the Republican indictment of Truman's foreign policy. Reunifying Korea under Western auspices would also promote Japan's security as well as check Soviet and Chinese ambitions in East Asia. Just weeks before, the question was whether U.S. forces could retain a foothold in South Korea; now, with MacArthur seemingly infallible, all of Korea seemed within easy reach. To have halted arbitrarily at the 38th Parallel (or some line north of it) would have left the North Korean government and its remaining army forces intact, free to invade South Korea another day. In short, there seemed to be every reason to press on and no reason to stop.

"For five years," notes Robert Beisner, Acheson's best biographer, "the administration had been on the defensive in Asia, internationally and domestically. In a state of euphoria after Inchon, it succumbed to the galloping optimism that nearly killed sober analysis of the risks lying ahead . . . the state department presumed total victory." Besides, he continued,

> MacArthur's feats and the chance to wipe out Kim [Il-sung]'s regime were simply too exhilarating to resist. A clear-cut reduction in the acreage of world communism could do wonders to smother McCarthy and other Republicans. With each statement about Korean reunification and each approval of expanded military orders, Truman with Acheson's unvoiced approval closed the escape routes, leaving them only the chancy course northward.[27]

Gary Hess, in his assessment of the decision to cross the 38th Parallel, cites four underlying assumptions. First, stopping at the parallel or simply restoring the status quo "would renew the instability of the Korean peninsula,"[28] a judgment surely vindicated by history. Acheson argued that the 38th Parallel had no political validity and that advancing UN forces could not be expected "to march up to a surveyor's line and stop."[29] Second, "U.N. movement into North Korea offered a unique opportunity to achieve a victory over communism," undermining "the impression that communism was the wave of the future."[30] Third, a decisive victory would "enhance the purpose of the United Nations by punishing North Korea for its aggression and the hardship that its army had inflicted upon South Koreans."[31] (In 1950 there were still high hopes for the United Nations as an effective collective security organization, and the U.S. forces were fighting in Korea, as they would not again until 1991 against Iraq, under UN authorization.) Finally, "the military conquest of North Korea did not seem to risk a larger war."[32] Though a few within the administration—notably Paul Nitze, head of the State Department's Policy Planning Staff, and George Kennan, Nitze's predecessor and the intellectual godfather of containment—believed that crossing the 38th Parallel risked Soviet or Chinese intervention or both, Truman, Acheson, and the Joint Chiefs of Staff rejected their views.[33] Even in retrospect, the 38th Parallel decision seems politically and militarily irresistible, notwithstanding its calamitous consequences.

Dread of a domestic political backlash was also a prime motivator for Lyndon Johnson's 1965 decision to escalate the U.S. military intervention in Vietnam. Though he believed in the domino theory and the argument that the credibility of U.S. security commitments worldwide was at stake, Johnson was not optimistic about a decisive U.S. military victory in Vietnam. But he was convinced that "if I got out of Vietnam and let Ho Chi Minh run through the streets of Saigon, then I'd be doing exactly what [Neville] Chamberlain did. . . . I'd be giving a fat reward to aggression."[34] Johnson believed that his presidency, which included his ambitious Great Society domestic social agenda, was at stake in Vietnam. As a young senator and later as majority leader in the Senate, he had witnessed firsthand the Republicans' brutal soft-on-communism assaults on the integrity of such impeccable patriots as Acheson and George Marshall during the wave of anti-Communist hysteria that swept the country after China's fall and the Soviet Union's first atomic bomb test. Ceding yet more Asian real estate to Communism without a fight would be politically suicidal. Truman had "lost" China, but Johnson was not about to lose Southeast Asia or be the first U.S. president to lose a war. Furthermore, a Johnson administration perceived as not allocating sufficient resources to defeat Communism in Vietnam would provide opponents of the Great Society, which included hostile southern committee chairmen in the Senate, the perfect argument against proceeding with costly social and economic reforms at home. To avoid being accused of appeasing Communism, he had to fight in Vietnam, but he would not let the war devour his domestic programs. As he told Doris Kearns (now Doris Kearns Goodwin) after he left the White House,

> Conservatives in Congress would use [the war] as a weapon against the Great Society. You see, they'd never wanted to help the poor or the Negroes in the first place. But they were having a hard time figuring out how to make their opposition sound noble in a time of great prosperity. But the war. Oh, they'd use it to say they were against my programs, not because they were against the poor—why, they were just as generous and charitable as the best of Americans—but because the war had to come first.[35]

Fear of the domestic political consequences of not acting to prevent the spread of Communism abroad plagued all Democratic presidents during the Cold War, and though this fear was but one factor in the decisions for military intervention in Korea and Vietnam, it was a powerful if negative motivator. Republicans condemned Franklin Roosevelt for the Yalta sellout of Eastern Europe, Truman for losing China, John F. Kennedy for being soft on Fidel Castro's Cuba, and Jimmy Carter, who once proclaimed that Americans had an "inordinate fear" of Communism, for being indifferent to the Soviet military threat. Republican presidents, in contrast, were more or less immune to such charges. Eisenhower could "lose" Tibet, northern Vietnam, and Cuba to Communism, but he was a war hero untainted by the foreign policies of the two Democratic administrations he had served as a senior military officer. Nixon could pursue détente with the Soviet Union and open diplomatic relations with "Red" China (for which a Democratic president would have been mercilessly pilloried—by Richard Nixon himself, among others), but his anti-Communist credentials were impeccable. So were those of Ronald Reagan, who exploited a widespread perception of America's relative military decline vis-à-vis the Soviet Union to defeat Carter in 1980.

George W. Bush was the first post–Cold War Republican president. As such, he suffered no perceived domestic political imperative to use force overseas. The spread of Communism was no longer an issue, and he was the leader of a political party whose toughness on national security issues was largely taken for granted. In situations where the case for action was less than self-evident, he did not have to worry about the domestic political consequences of not acting. On the contrary, in the case of Iraq, the Bush administration had to work hard to convince a majority of the American electorate that major military action against that country *was* necessary. Indeed, there is every reason to believe that it would not have had more public support for an invasion of Iraq even after 9/11 if the White House had remained focused on destroying al Qaeda and had refrained from linking Saddam Hussein to al Qaeda and 9/11.

In Korea, the Truman administration responded to a Communist attack on South Korea. In Indochina, the Johnson administration responded to an escalating Communist war to take over South Vietnam. In Iraq, however, the George W. Bush administration responded to the *possibility of an imagined future attack* by a nuclear-armed Saddam Hussein.

Though the Iraq War has (so far) claimed far fewer American lives than either the Korean or Vietnam wars, it has lasted longer than World War II and almost as long as the U.S. combat intervention in Vietnam and has become as controversial as the Vietnam War. Americans have been treated to an avalanche of finger-pointing over who is responsible for the war and its consequences. The blame games between Democrats and Republicans, hawks and doves, military leaders and their civilian superiors, and Congress and the executive branch seem headed for extra innings. What Americans deserve, however, is a reasoned, dispassionate debate over why and how the

United States found itself in a bloody and protracted war in a country that posed no uncontainable threat to the United States. They deserve a critical, no-holds-barred examination of the motivations and assumptions behind the Bush administration's decision for war. That judgment led to our current predicament in Iraq, and understanding it could prevent disastrous future decisions.

Why the United States invaded Iraq in the first place is perhaps the most perplexing of many confounding questions about the Iraq War. It is likely to bedevil historians for decades to come. "It still isn't possible to be sure—and this remains the most remarkable thing about the Iraq War," observed George Packer in *The Assassins' Gate*, his bestselling indictment of America's misadventure in Iraq. "It was something some people wanted to do. Before the invasion, Americans argued not just about whether a war should happen, but for what reasons it should happen—what the real motives of the Bush administration were and should be. Since the invasion, we have continued to argue, and will go on arguing for years to come."[36]

John Mearsheimer and Stephen Walt are no less stumped:

> [The] decision to overthrow Saddam Hussein even now seems difficult to fathom.... [I]n the aftermath of 9/11, when one would have expected the United States to be focusing laserlike on al Qaeda, the Bush administration chose to invade a deteriorating country that had nothing to do with the attacks on the World Trade Center and the Pentagon and was already effectively contained. From this perspective, it *is* a deeply puzzling decision.[37]

Even before the invasion, Brent Scowcroft, the former national security adviser to President George H. W. Bush, warned in a *Wall Street Journal* op-ed entitled "Don't Attack Saddam" that an invasion of Iraq would be both a diversion from and an impediment to the war against al Qaeda. He felt "our preeminent security policy . . . is the war on terrorism," which a war with Iraq "would seriously jeopardize" because the unpopularity of an attack on Iraq would result in a "serious degradation in international cooperation with us against terrorism."[38]

U.S. Army War College analyst Steven Metz contends:

> No one other than those very close to President Bush and privy to private discussion fully understands why he chose to make America's conflict with Iraq a central part of the war on terrorism. [Saddam] Hussein certainly supported some terrorist movements and may have had some ties to al Qaeda, but he was not a central cog in global terrorism. His demise in itself did not decisively damage . . . al Qaeda, America's primary enemy. The assertion that Hussein *could* provide weapons of mass destruction is technically true, but there is no evidence that he intended to do so. Plus, this argument is made even more implausible by the fact that the use of weapons of mass destruction provided to terrorists by Hussein could probably be traced back to Baghdad, thus leading to the certain demise of his regime. In all of his evil behavior, Hussein had never shown himself to be suicidal.
>
> Rather than being built on clear, linear logic or a "smoking gun," the administration's case for war was like a courtroom argument where a number of facts, none of which were convincing in isolation, were, when combined, held to constitute a valid rationale.[39]

Echoing Metz, Jacob Weisberg has characterized "the case for war" as "a jumble," with Cheney and Donald Rumsfeld focused on "preventing what Saddam might do to the United States" and the neoconservatives concentrated on "what getting rid of him might do *for* the United States"— i.e., "pulling the plug on his toxic regime would transform the sick political culture of the Middle East."[40] By the summer of 2002, "the neocon and non-neocon justifications were converging in an overdetermined conclusion. They all thought there were so many good reasons for regime change that it didn't matter which ones any particular official emphasized."[41]

This book examines the question, why did the United States invade Iraq in 2003? This book offers neither a narrative of events nor an assessment of the myriad U.S. misjudgments and policy mistakes in post-Baathist Iraq for America's military and political performance in Iraq has been extensively and impressively treated elsewhere. The book also does not seek to assign blame to individual policymakers. There is plenty to go around: virtually the entire American foreign policy establishment, including its congressional and media components, supported the decision for war. That decision, however, can no more be repealed than can the decision to invade Iraq with insufficient forces to seize control of the country or the decision to disband the regular Iraqi army. Finally the book proposes neither changes in U.S. policy in Iraq nor ways to extricate the United States from Iraq. (As noted the United States, by agreement with Iraq, is pledged to withdraw all its military forces from that country by the end of 2011, but that agreement could be altered by mutual consent.) The fate of the American gamble in Iraq awaits events over which the United States may have little control. That said, two observations are in order. First, U.S. military progress against the Iraqi insurgency is no substitute for an Iraqi political resolution of the profound ethno-sectarian divisions and revenue-sharing issues that threaten the country's very integrity; and second, the American electorate has never displayed unlimited tolerance for continued major U.S. military intervention in an ill-considered, protracted war for the purpose of simply avoiding defeat.

Wanting War: Why the Bush Administration Invaded Iraq identifies and critically assesses the reasons, motivations, and perceived imperatives that convinced the Bush White House that the United States had to forcibly remove Saddam Hussein from power even if it meant invading and occupying Iraq. What were the ends that the invasion of Iraq was designed to serve, and how well grounded were they in reality? What did the administration hope to accomplish in Iraq, and how realistic were those hopes? Was Iraq the only target of the invasion, or was the invasion aimed at other audiences? Did political ideology contribute to the decision for war, and if so, how? To what extent did arrogance, ignorance, misperception, and wishful thinking shape the reasons for war? Was the administration internally united on the reasons for war, or were multiple agendas at play?

Chapter 2, "The Neoconservative Imprint," explores the influence of neoconservatives and neoconservative ideology on the decision for this war. Neoconservative ideology embraced an aggressive foreign policy based on a willingness to use preventive force to advance American political values overseas and to defeat emerging challenges to U.S. military freedom of action, especially hostile states seeking weapons of mass destruction (WMDs). It was the foreign policy to which the newly elected George W. Bush, untutored and relatively disinterested in international affairs, converted after the 9/11 attacks. Neoconservatives who populated key positions in the Bush administration had been gunning for Saddam Hussein's regime in Iraq long before the 9/11 attacks and saw the attacks as an opportunity to expand the war against al Qaeda into a war of regime change in Iraq. Within hours of the attacks, neoconservatives within and outside the administration began pressing hard for a military assault on Iraq, even as a substitute for regime change in Afghanistan. The vision of a free, prosperous, and democratic Iraq that would ignite the political transformation of the Middle East was a neoconservative vision.

Chapter 3, "Bogus Assumptions, Wishful Thinking," addresses the Bush administration's "selling" of the Iraq War on the grounds that Saddam Hussein was an ally of al Qaeda's (which suggested the probable Iraqi complicity in the 9/11 attacks) and that Iraq was on the verge of acquiring nuclear weapons, which it would happily transfer to Osama bin Laden. Clearly, the administration established a worst-case scenario that implicated an Iraqi threat far beyond the available evidence and in violation of simple common sense (while downplaying the risks, costs, and consequences of invading Iraq), and it did so for the purpose of mobilizing public and congressional opinion. It remains unclear, however, whether George W. Bush and other top administration officials really believed in the threat they postulated; perhaps they simply wanted to believe it, or perhaps it was a case of imaginations run wild. Aside from the issue of evidence and common sense, which supported treating Iraq as a strategic nuisance rather than as an urgent threat, the Pentagon's invasion plan was completely insensitive to the leading rationale for the war, which demanded the swift seizure and securing of Iraq's hundreds of suspected WMD sites. This apparent oversight suggests that the real reasons for war lay elsewhere—i.e., beyond the political mobilization issues of Saddam's alleged alliance with al Qaeda and near-acquisition of nuclear weapons.

Chapter 4, "The Reasons Why," identifies and examines the propellants for war. Behind the decision for war lay a mélange of arguments, motives, hopes, and expectations: completing the "unfinished business" of the 1991 Gulf War; demonstrating a willingness to use American military power and use it unilaterally; asserting the principle of preventive military action; intimidating Iran, North Korea, and other rogue states; transforming the Middle East by establishing a model democracy in Iraq for other Arab states to emulate; creating an Arab client-state alternative to Saudi Arabia; eliminating an enemy of Israel; vindicating the Pentagon's "revolutionary" employment of force; sustaining the reestablishment of an "imperial" presidency; and ridding the world of evil. None of these reasons alone was sufficient to justify war. Together, however, they seemed to make a convincing case, especially given the assumption that a war with Iraq was going to be a low-risk and low-cost enterprise. Further, beyond removing Saddam Hussein from power, war proponents were not united on the war's purpose. Different proponents had diverse reasons for going to war and various expectations of what the war would accomplish. The war was the product of a coalition of arguments, some of which were unrelated and even incompatible with one another.

Chapter 4 offers the book's central thesis—namely, that the decision to invade Iraq was, at bottom, *more about the United States than about Iraq.* Specifically, *the invasion was a conscious expression of America's unchecked global military hegemony that was designed to perpetuate that hegemony by intimidating those who would challenge it.* The invasion represented power exercised first and foremost for its own sake. It was a show of force and, above all, a demonstration of the will to use it. Iraq was targeted because, unlike the other states in the "axis of evil"—namely, Iran and North Korea—Iraq was both helpless and friendless. The invasion offered the perfect opportunity to jettison once and for all the strictures of the Weinberger-Powell Doctrine, the agonizing over the use of force seen in the 1990s, and the traditional American aversion to preventive war. The 9/11 attacks made preventive war possible, and Iraq provided the irresistible test case. The decision to invade Iraq was the neoconservatives' dream come true. It was the realization of a United States forcefully committed to the perpetuation of its post–Cold War, global, conventional military supremacy and no longer prepared to accept restraints on its freedom of action by treaties or allies.

This explanation for the Iraq War is consistent with the "realist" theory of international relations, which holds that power unchecked is power exercised. The Soviet Union's collapse dissolved the East-West balance of power and ushered in the reality of global American hegemony and the irresistible temptation to exploit it. That the Bush administration did so in the name of ridding the world of evil and bringing freedom and democracy to the Middle East is quintessentially American in that it reflected a long-standing tenet of national idealism, but it does not alter the reality that some measure of American strategic overreach was virtually inevitable once the United States became the world's sole remaining superpower. Sooner or later, the United States was bound to succumb to the temptations of its military primacy,[42] although not necessarily to the degree to which the Bush administration misused it after the 9/11 attacks. Notwithstanding the U.S. experience in Vietnam, Lebanon, and Somalia, it is tragic that neither the Bush White House nor the neoconservatives understood that conventional military supremacy—i.e., the ability to crush another state's armed forces in regular warfare—is of limited effectiveness and even counterproductive against a determined non-state foe practicing irregular warfare. Indeed, the conventional military supremacy of the United States drove America's ene-mies to adopt terrorism, guerrilla warfare, and other forms of irregular combat.

The final chapter, "Consequences: An Iraq Syndrome?" examines the great irony of the Iraq War, which has demonstrated the limits of U.S. military power in both defeating irregular enemies and forcing political change overseas. Above all, the war has also demonstrated the limits of the American electorate's tolerance for the neoconservatives' costly and ambitious foreign policy pretensions. Even worse for the neoconservatives is the likelihood that the Iraq War, just as the Vietnam War before it, will usher in an era of American strategic timidity. The Vietnam War exerted a chilling effect on the use of U.S. forces overseas. Post-Vietnam presidents were markedly hesitant to use force and exceptionally sensitive to incurring casualties even to the point where "force protection" assumed a higher value than the mission that the force was employed to accomplish. The Pentagon, led by Secretary of Defense Caspar Weinberger and later by JCS chairman Gen. Colin Powell, propounded a use-of-force doctrine that called for military intervention only on behalf of vital interests and in circumstances that virtually guaranteed military victory. By implication, the doctrine ruled out coercive diplomacy and the use of force to defend or promote American values. Neoconservatives came to detest the Weinberger-Powell Doctrine precisely because it called for exceptional caution in using force and because it was indifferent to the muscular promotion of American political values overseas.

The coming years, however, promise a revival of exceptional caution in American statecraft. The Iraq War, which was not only unnecessary but also bungled in execution, has seemingly vindicated John Quincy Adams's famous warning about hitching American power to moral crusades abroad. Responding in 1821 to calls for American intervention on behalf of a Greek revolt against Turkish rule, Adams declared: "Wherever the standard of freedom and independence has been or shall be unfurled, there will [America's] heart, her benedictions and her prayers be. But she does not go abroad in search of monsters to destroy. She is the well-wisher to the freedom and independence of all. She is the champion and vindicator only of her own."[43]

TWO

THE NEOCONSERVATIVE
IMPRINT

The defeat in Vietnam led to a preoccupation with first regaining and then maintaining American military power. This was as true for the careers of Richard Cheney, Donald Rumsfeld and Paul Wolfowitz as it was for Colin Powell and Richard Armitage. The pronounced emphasis upon military perspectives to foreign policy problems was the principal distinguishing feature of the team that came to power in the [George W.] Bush administration.

—James Mann,
Rise of the Vulcans: The History of Bush's War Cabinet[1]

[T]he success of American military technology during the 1990s created the illusion that military intervention would always be as clean or cheap as the Gulf or Kosovo wars. The Iraq War has clearly demonstrated the limits of this form of light, mobile warfare; it can defeat virtually any existing conventional military force, but it provides no special advantages in fighting a prolonged insurgency. [Precision-guided munitions] cannot distinguish between insurgents and noncombatants or help soldiers speak Arabic. Indeed, the very model of a professional, all-volunteer military that was established in Vietnam's waning days works only for short, high-intensity wars.

—Frances Fukuyama,
America at the Crossroads: Democracy, Power, and the
Neoconservative Legacy[2]

Why did President George W. Bush order the invasion of Iraq? It is especially curious given the absence, during the run-up to the invasion (and since), of any evidence of either Iraqi complicity in the al Qaeda attacks of 9/11 on the World Trade Center and the Pentagon or an operational relationship between al Qaeda and the Baathist regime in Baghdad. To be sure, momentum for a war with Iraq had existed before 9/11 and even before President George W. Bush took office as "hawks" were scattered throughout the halls of Congress and national security bureaucracy during the 1990s.[3] But a war against Iraq in response to 9/11 was strategically nonsensical.

Douglas Feith, who served as undersecretary of defense for policy during George W. Bush's first term, claims that in the wake of the 9/11 attacks, "[w]e could not define the enemy with precision with any short, clear formulation." Iraq, however, "was on the minds of many Administration officials" who shared "a common assumption . . . that a global war on terrorism would, at some point, involve some kind of showdown with Iraq."[4] He also recounts his agreement with Donald Rumsfeld's judgment, expressed three days after the 9/11 attacks, that the U.S. response to the attacks should be a "sustained, broad campaign" against targets well beyond al Qaeda and the Taliban regime in Afghanistan. Rumsfeld's injunction, "Don't over-elevate the importance of al Qaida,"[5] indicated that the war on terrorism was going to be a general one against all purveyors of terrorism and not just against those who aided, abetted, and perpetrated the 9/11attacks.

Afghanistan's link to 9/11 was self-evident. The attacks were planned in Afghanistan by a resident terrorist organization that enjoyed a geographic and ideological sanctuary in Afghanistan courtesy of the Taliban regime in Kabul. Afghanistan was al Qaeda's central hideout, and the Taliban was comprised of al Qaeda's ideological soul mates. In the wake of 9/11, no president could have refused military action against Afghanistan.

In contrast, the Bush administration simply asserted Iraq's connection to 9/11 for the purpose of mobilizing public and congressional support for a war that otherwise would have been a hard and perhaps impossible sell. Indeed, policymakers and commentators who had been gunning for Saddam

Hussein even before the Gulf War of 1991 successfully converted public rage over the al Qaeda attacks into a war to bring down the Iraqi dictator.[6] They transformed the reality of Osama bin Laden as an avowed enemy of "apostate" secular regimes in the Middle East into the fantasy of bin Laden as an operational ally of Saddam Hussein. President Bush and other war proponents repeatedly spoke of al Qaeda, Saddam, and 9/11 in the same breath. As the president declared in September 2002, "You can't distinguish between al Qaeda and Saddam when you talk about the war on terror. . . . I can't distinguish between the two, because they're both equally as bad, and equally as evil, and equally as destructive."[7] (By this reasoning the United States should have declared war on Hitler *and* Stalin in December 1941.) Thus, Saddam Hussein was suddenly depicted as a crazed, undeterrable dictator just months away from acquiring nuclear weapons and gleefully handing them over to bin Laden. Public and congressional support for an invasion of Iraq simply could not be mustered absent a deliberate conflation of Saddam Hussein and al Qaeda into a single terrifying threat. Richard A. Clarke, the former counterterrorism czar for both the Bill Clinton and George W. Bush administrations, believes that

> any leader whom one can imagine as President on September 11 would have declared a "war on terrorism" and would have ended the Afghan sanctuary by invading. Almost any President would have stepped up domestic security and preparedness measures. Exactly what did George Bush do after September 11 that any other President one can imagine wouldn't have done after such attacks? In the end, what was unique about George Bush's reaction to terrorism was his selection as an object lesson for potential state sponsors of terrorism, not a country that had been engaging in anti-U.S. terrorism but one that had not been, Iraq.[8]

Why did Bush pick Iraq? Largely because of key neoconservatives and their allies. Indeed, it is impossible to explain the road from 9/11 to the invasion of Iraq without recognizing the tremendous influence of neoconservative opinion, both inside and outside the administration, on the Bush White House.[9] Accurately if colorfully described by Alan Weisman as "that rowdy collection of former liberal Democrats, Wilsonian globalists, and Trotskyites who soured on the New Left for its wimpy, weak-kneed response to the adventurism of the Soviet Union, and for its aversion to the use of military force regardless of consequences,"[10] the neoconservatives had a ready explanation for the 9/11 attacks, provided the intellectual justification for the war, and persuaded President George W. Bush, a former Texas governor untutored in foreign policy and ignorant of the Middle East, that the global assault on al Qaeda had to include regime change in Iraq. The neoconservatives moreover reinforced the president's predisposition to see the world in terms of good versus evil and to view the use of military power as the decisive determinant of relations among states.

There never was a neoconservative cabal or conspiracy to subvert Bush's foreign policy. Bush did not even have a well-formulated foreign policy before 9/11, and there was nothing secret about the neoconservatives or their views. The leading neoconservatives were public intellectuals who openly associated with each other and published extensively on foreign policy. They shared a combative ideology about the nature of the world and America's role in it, an ideology to which Bush, Cheney, and Rumsfeld were instinctively disposed, especially after 9/11. These neoconservatives were not bashful about pushing their views on non-neoconservative policymakers; exhortation was their stock-in-trade. In effect, the neoconservatives constituted an ideological interest group that sought to influence the formulation and execution of U.S. foreign policy, and influence it they did. In *America Alone: The Neo-Conservatives and the Global Order*, a 2004 definitive assessment of neoconservative ideology and its influence on post-9/11 U.S. foreign policy, Stefan Halper and Jonathan Clarke persuasively assert:

> The situation of unending war in which we find ourselves results in
> large part from the fact that the policies adopted after 9/11, the initial

strike against the Taliban aside, were hardly specific to that event. Unlike the policy of containment that evolved in direct response to Soviet moves in Central and Eastern Europe and involved radical new thinking on the part of those involved, the post-9/11 policy was in fact grounded in an ideology that existed well before the terror attacks and that in a stroke of opportunistic daring by its progenitors, has emerged as the new orthodoxy. The paper trail is unambiguous. Minds were already made up. A preexisting ideological agenda was taken off the shelf, dusted off, and relabeled as *the* response to terror....

In neo-conservative eyes, the Iraq war was not about terrorism; it was about the pivotal relationship between Saddam Hussein and the assertion of American power. Hussein provided, in effect, the opportunity to clarify America's global objectives and moral obligations. His continued survival in power was a metaphor for all that had gone wrong with American foreign policy since the Soviet collapse in the sense that the first Bush administration's Realpolitik and Clinton's wishful liberalism had left the Iraqi dictator in power. Iraq was now the arena in which to demonstrate the crucial tenets of neo-conservative doctrine: military preemption, regime change, the merits of exporting democracy, and a vision of American power that is "fully engaged and never apologetic."[11]

President Bush's post-9/11 receptivity to the neoconservative agenda was manifest in the administration's provocative September 2002 *The National Security Strategy of the United States of America* (*NSS*), which embraced regime change in rogue states, aggressively promoted democracy, viewed American military supremacy as a given, and, in a stunning departure from traditional U.S. foreign policy norms, asserted the right to launch preventive wars to protect national interests. Before turning to that pivotal document, however, an understanding of neoconservative foreign policy ideology is in order.

Andrew Bacevich convincingly argues that six core propositions define "the essence of the neoconservative persuasion." The first is that "evil is real," and the second is that "for evil to prevail requires only one thing: for those confronted by it to flinch from duty."[12] The foundation of these propositions was the Anglo-French appeasement of Hitler in the 1930s, an event to which neoconservatives constantly refer as the starting instruction on foreign policy. Indeed, neoconservatives have never hesitated to invoke the so-called Munich analogy as an argument for preventive military action, and they routinely compared Saddam Hussein to Adolf Hitler, notwithstanding the absence of convincing historical parallels.[13] "Appeasement" is the neoconservatives' preferred characterization of a reluctance to use force in the face of evil, and they have not hesitated to denounce as "appeasers" those who have opposed or expressed doubt about the wisdom or feasibility of neoconservative-proposed military action.

The third proposition is that "American ideals define America's purpose, to be achieved through the exercise of superior American power."[14] For neoconservatives, American values and strategic interests are inseparable. Spreading democracy abroad is the paramount strategic interest, and the United States should not hesitate to use its global military primacy to clear away dictatorships and other obstacles to democracy. The next proposition is an "appreciation for authority" stemming from the neoconservatives' hatred of the New Left's counterculture and political radicalism of the 1960s.[15] They despised liberal Democrats who turned against the Vietnam War and succumbed to political correctness at home. The fifth is that "the United States after Vietnam confronted a dire crisis" with "unspeakable consequences"—i.e., that America had not only lost the will to win the Cold War but also, under the guidance of Richard Nixon and Henry Kissinger and later Jimmy Carter, had actually sought to appease the Soviet Union via the mechanism of détente.[16] And the sixth is that "the antidote to crisis is leadership," as exemplified by Ronald Reagan's determination to win the Cold War once and for all.[17]

Neoconservatives fancy themselves as an intellectual elite that best knows what America can and should do in the world, and they once regarded Reagan as an ideal vehicle for promoting their global agenda. They believe in a global American hegemony that is inherently benevolent and that it is America's destiny to reshape the world in America's image. For neoconservatives, the Vietnam War was a noble cause betrayed by weak-kneed politicians, a defeatist press, and a subversive antiwar movement. Except for Reagan, the post-Vietnam Cold War presidents stood guilty of accepting strategic nuclear parity with the Soviet Union and its despised associated doctrine of mutual assured destruction. And until George W. Bush's experience after 9/11, these post–Cold War presidents lacked the imagination and courage to exploit America's unprecedented global military hegemony.

For neoconservatives, military power is not only the basic currency of international politics but also the central vehicle for advancing American political values overseas. Military victory, by sweeping away tyranny, lays the foundation for democratic revolution; thus, the United States converted Germany and Japan from dictatorships to democracies, and thus America's superior military competitiveness contributed mightily to Communism's collapse in the Soviet empire. America's global, conventional military superiority, moreover, is irresistible. Even after seven years of war in Iraq, the neoconservatives' confidence in U.S. military irresistibility is little shaken; indeed, they give scant recognition to the inherent limits of conventional military power in unconventional political and operational settings.

The term "neoconservative" first appeared in the 1950s and referred to a group of largely Jewish and Catholic intellectuals who were once captivated by the ideals and promises of Communism and Socialism but were later disenchanted by the Soviet state's brutal totalitarianism. These intellectuals, many of them New Deal Democrats, became hard-line Cold Warriors and supporters of U.S. intervention in the Vietnam War. After the war, they gravitated to the Democratic Party's conservative wing, which was led by Senator Henry "Scoop" Jackson, a hawk on the Vietnam War and a steadfast friend of Israel. Many subsequently became followers of President Reagan, who in his first term discarded détente with the Soviet Union and favored uncompromising hostility to Communism around the world.

Neoconservatives strongly supported the Reagan-sponsored U.S. military buildup of the 1980s and now believe that it was instrumental in pushing the Soviet Union toward collapse. Reagan remains the neoconservative presidential model, although during his second term his embrace of arms control with the Soviet Union and talk of a world without nuclear weapons ran counter to the neoconservatives' commitment to confrontation and military superiority.[18]

Indeed, central to neoconservative ideology is the perpetuation of America's post–Cold War, global military supremacy via—if necessary—unilateral preventive military action against rising potential enemies, especially so-called rogue states seeking to acquire nuclear weapons. Neoconservative intellectuals, many of them Jewish, sympathetic to the Likud Party's imperial security ambitions for Israel, and haunted by the consequences of appeasing Hitler in the 1930s, have provided the core of the neoconservative construct of the world and America's role in it. The neoconservative agenda also commands support, in varying degrees, among the broader conservative community, including the Republican Party and its Christian Right base. Indeed, the first George W. Bush administration was populated by prominent neoconservatives and other proponents of perpetual American military primacy, including the vice president and his staff, the secretary of defense, the deputy secretary of defense, and the head of the Defense Policy Board (DPB). Together with such influential neoconservative commentators as Robert Kagan, William Kristol, Charles Krauthammer, and Lawrence Kaplan, these individuals provided both the intellectual and policy foundations of President Bush's post-9/11 foreign policy.

The neoconservative vision of America's present role in the world traces its origin to the Soviet Union's collapse, which neoconservatives believed made the world safe for an ambitious, forward-leaning foreign policy reliant on force to rid the world of tyranny and to promote the spread of democracy. The neoconservatives sought "nothing less than the transformation of world politics" via a "policy that proposes to use military supremacy aggressively, unilaterally and, in such cases as Iraq, to attempt to impose [democratic] governance," observes Edward Rhodes.[19] The policy's premise, long and deeply rooted in American political thought, is that the security of the United States is ultimately assured only in a world of democracies—that is, a world rid of totalitarianism, autocracy, and terrorism. A democratic world would be a peaceful world because, as neoconservatives believe, as did Woodrow Wilson, democracies do not fight each other. But a democratic peace is not inevitable. Achieving it requires an activist American foreign policy based on military primacy and a willingness to use force to ensure the ultimate triumph of American political values. Neoconservatives also believe people around the world aspire to these values but do not prevail everywhere because of persistent tyranny, especially in the Middle East.

For neoconservatives, as well as for President George W. Bush after 9/11, tyranny and terrorism are moral evils that the United States is obligated to destroy. "Wherever we carry it, the American flag will stand not only for our power, but for freedom," the president declared in his June 2002 speech to West Point's graduating class. He continued,

> Our nation's cause has always been larger than our nation's defense. We fight, as we always fight, for a just peace—a peace that favors human liberty. We will defend the peace against threats from terrorists and tyrants. . . . And we will extend the peace by encouraging free and open societies on every continent. Building this peace is America's opportunity and America's duty.[20]

President Bush later elaborated:

> Freedom is the non-negotiable demand of human dignity; the birthright of every person—in every civilization. . . . Throughout history, freedom has been threatened by war and terror; it has been challenged by the clashing of wills of powerful states and the evil designs of tyrants; and it has been tested by widespread disease and poverty. Today, humanity holds in its hands the opportunity

to further freedom's triumph over all these foes. The United States welcomes our responsibility to lead in this great mission.[21]

A seminal neoconservative document was the 1992 *Defense Planning Guidance*, written for then–Secretary of Defense Dick Cheney by then–Pentagon analysts Paul Wolfowitz (who later served the George W. Bush administration as deputy secretary of defense) and I. Lewis "Scooter" Libby (who later became Vice President Cheney's chief of staff). The guidance called for establishing America's military primacy over Eurasia by preventing the rise of any hostile power capable of challenging that primacy. It also endorsed a policy of preventive disarmament of rogue states seeking to acquire weapons of mass destruction. The document, leaked excerpts of which provoked sharp condemnation on Capitol Hill, was never translated into policy because President George H. W. Bush was defeated for reelection in 1992.

During the 1990s, however, the neoconservative vision remained very much alive in such think tanks as the Hudson Institute, the Center for Security Policy, and especially the American Enterprise Institute. The *Weekly Standard*, the opinion magazine edited by William Kristol, became a major vehicle for the exposition of the neoconservative vision, as did the *National Interest*, *Commentary*, and the *New Republic*. The neoconservatives, also known as "democratic imperialists" for their willingness to coerce others to adopt liberal political values, were united in their condemnation of the George H. W. Bush and Clinton administrations' foreign policies. They criticized the former for its "narrow realism," the latter for its toothless idealism, and both for their failure to exploit U.S. military primacy in the post-Soviet world.[22] They also pummeled Bush and especially Clinton for deference toward and reliance on the United Nations, the North Atlantic Treaty Organization (NATO), and other formal multilateral institutions that traditionally had served to legitimize America's use of force. Neoconservatives believe that America's power is inherently and self-evidently legitimate by virtue of America's political values. "[W]e are not just any hegemon," wrote

Charles Krauthammer in the *Weekly Standard.* "We run a uniquely benign imperium. This is not mere self-congratulation; it is manifest in the way others welcome our power."[23] They also hold that the United States should not hesitate to exercise its power unilaterally, if necessary. For neoconservatives, the mission defines the coalition, not vice versa. In the words of one observer, "America's global power must not be challenged. The US reserves for itself the right to decide who might be its enemies and how they are to be dealt with. No other nation can be permitted to challenge its primacy."[24]

In 1997 leading neoconservative intellectuals and their past and future allies in government, including Cheney, Wolfowitz, and Rumsfeld, founded the Project for a New American Century (PNAC). Dedicated to increasing defense spending, challenging "regimes hostile to our interests and values," and promoting political and economic freedom abroad, it also accepted "responsibility for America's unique role in preserving and extending an international order friendly to our security, our prosperity, and our principles." In its "Statement of Principles," the PNAC declared that "the United States stands as the world's preeminent power," but it also asked: "Does [it] have the vision to build upon the achievements of past decades? Does it have the resolve to shape a new century favorable to American principles and interests?" The statement lamented that "we seem to have forgotten the essential elements of the Reagan Administration's success: a [strong] military . . . a foreign policy that boldly and purposefully promotes American principles abroad; and national leadership that accepts the United States' global responsibilities." The statement concluded: "Such a Reaganite policy of military strength and moral clarity may not be fashionable today. But it is necessary if the United States is to build on the successes of this past century and to ensure our security and our greatness in the next."[25]

The neoconservatives' agenda and critique of the George H. W. Bush and Clinton administrations appeared in a seminal 2000 book, *Present Dangers: Crisis and Opportunity in American Foreign and Defense Policy.* Edited by Robert Kagan and William Kristol, it contains essays by such neoconservative luminaries as Reuel Marc Gerecht, William Schneider,

William J. Bennett, Donald Kagan, Wolfowitz, and Richard Perle (whose essay "Iraq: Saddam Unbound," attacked Clinton's policy toward Iraq and called for Hussein's forcible removal). In their introductory essay, "National Interest and Global Responsibility," Kagan and Kristol summarized the case for a foreign policy based on America's global military primacy. The "present danger," in their view, was that

> the United States, the world's dominant power on whom the maintenance of international peace and the support of liberal democratic principles depend, will shrink from its responsibilities and—in a fit of absent-mindedness, or parsimony, or indifference—allow the international order that it created and sustained to collapse. Our present danger is one of declining military strength, flagging will and confusion about our role in the world.[26]

With the demise of the Soviet Union, America's global task "ought to have been obvious. It was to prolong this extraordinary moment and to guard the international system from any threats that might challenge it. This meant, above all, preserving and reinforcing America's benevolent global hegemony." Instead, they wrote, the 1990s witnessed America's failure to finish off Saddam Hussein after the Gulf War; to check the growth of Chinese military power and imperial ambitions (as America's "response to China's aggressive behavior at home and abroad has . . . been one of appeasement"); and to shun "confronting the moral and strategic challenges" of dealing with "evil regimes." Kagan and Kristol felt, instead, that "the United States tried to do business with them in pursuit of the illusion of stability."[27]

In their view, "a fundamental change in the way our leaders and public think about America's role in the world" was required. Specifically, what was needed was "a foreign policy based on American hegemony, and on the blending of principle with material interest," which in the long run would "mean fewer, not more, overseas interventions than under the 'vital interest' standard" because "a forward-leaning conception of the national interest would emphasize early action before crises erupt." The primary tool of such a forward-leaning foreign policy would be an "America capable of projecting force quickly and with devastating effect to important regions of the world," which would enable the United States to "set about making trouble for hostile and potentially hostile nations, rather than waiting for them to make trouble for us." Sustaining this capacity for preventive war against "smaller powers seeking to acquire weapons of mass destruction and missiles to launch them at American forces, at our allies and at the American homeland" would require robust antimissile defenses. Thus, antimissile defenses would serve not only to protect Americans but also to prohibit target states from deterring U.S. military action against *them*.[28]

Kagan and Kristol then proceeded to denounce the "idea, common to many foreign policy minimalists and commerce-oriented liberals alike, that the United States can 'do business' with any regime, no matter how odious and hostile to our basic principles." Such regimes, in their view, deserved removal by one means or another, be it a U.S.-sponsored insurgency or an outright American invasion. It was "absurd" and "self-defeating" not to have finished off Saddam Hussein in 1991, for example, and those "who caution against the difficulties of occupying and reforming such [defeated tyrannical] countries . . . may wish to reflect on the American experiences in Germany and Japan—or even the Dominican Republic and Panama."[29] The call for Saddam Hussein's forcible overthrow became a neoconservative mantra during the 1990s and culminated in the U.S. invasion of Iraq in 2003. For neoconservatives the defiant Iraqi dictator's very survival represented an embarrassing strategic defeat for the United States. As David Wurmser summed up in his 1999 book, *Tyranny's Ally: America's Failure to Defeat Saddam Hussein*, which featured a foreword by Richard Perle,

> Strategic defeat of the U.S. policy on Iraq will have far-reaching consequences. As the Gulf War signaled America's determination to remain globally engaged, so the resurrection of Saddam could be read as a signal of America's retreat into isolationism. The world's

leaders, both those who benefit from and those who are obstructed by America's power and purpose, will draw the appropriate conclusions and craft appropriate policies. We will lose allies and embolden enemies.[30]

Kagan and Kristol closed their "national interest" essay by condemning restrictive use-of-force doctrines—read as the Weinberger-Powell Doctrine—and American foreign policy thinkers, or "realists," who defined "the 'national interest' as consisting of a grid of ground, sea lanes, industrial centers, strategic choke-points and the like." This narrow, materialistic definition of interest was "foisted upon our foreign policy establishment by 'realists' in the middle of the century," and it should be supplanted by a foreign policy based on "[h]onor and greatness in the service of liberal principles."[31]

For Wolfowitz, in his essay "Statesmanship in the New Century," "the core of American foreign policy is . . . the universalization of American principles." He wrote, "Nothing could be less realistic than the version of 'realism' that dismisses human rights as an important tool of foreign policy." In his view, citing the triumph of democracy in the Philippines, "[d]emocratic change is not only a way to weaken one's enemies, it is also a way to strengthen our friends."[32] Indeed, for neoconservatives a democratic Middle East was the ultimate goal of regime change in Iraq. Neoconservatives not only subscribed to the "democratic peace" theory; they also believed the United States could establish democracy in Iraq and that Iraq's example would provoke the fall of other tyrannical dominoes in the region. In their preinvasion book, *The War over Iraq: Saddam's Tyranny and America's Mission*, Kristol and Kaplan declared,

> Iraq's experience of liberal democratic rule . . . could increase pressure already being felt by Teheran's mullahs to open that society. Iraq's model will be eyed warily by Saudi Arabia's theocrats to the south. . . . Meanwhile, Iraq could even replace Saudi Arabia as the key American ally and source of oil in the region. A democratic Iraq

would also encourage the region's already liberalizing regimes—such as those in Qatar, Morocco and Jordan—to continue on their paths to democracy.[33]

In September 2002 Wolfowitz told Bill Keller of the *New York Times*,

You hear people mock [the idea of a democratic Iraq] by saying that Iraq isn't ready for Jeffersonian democracy. Well, Japan isn't Jeffersonian democracy, either. I think the more we are committed to influencing the outcome, the more chance there could be that it would be something quite significant for Iraq. And I think if it's significant for Iraq, it's going to cast a very large shadow, starting with Syria and Iraq, but across the whole Arab world, I think.[34]

"Would Saddam's removal set the [Middle East] region aflame?" asked Richard Perle before the invasion. "It seems at least as likely that Saddam's replacement by a decent regime would open the way to a far more stable and peaceful region. . . . A democratic Iraq would be a powerful refutation of the patronizing view that Arabs are incapable of democracy."[35]

George W. Bush, characteristically, had no doubts. "Iraqi democracy will succeed," he declared in a November 2003 speech to the National Endowment of Democracy, "and that success will send forth the news, from Damascus to Tehran—that freedom can be the future of every nation. The establishment of a free Iraq at the heart of the Middle East will be a watershed event in the global democratic revolution."[36]

The election of George W. Bush in 2000 ushered the neoconservatives into power, and by the time Bush ordered the invasion of Iraq in 2003 he had become a de facto neoconservative. Of the twenty-five founding members of the Project for a New American Century, ten entered the new administration: Cheney, Libby, Rumsfeld (secretary of defense), Wolfowitz (deputy secretary of defense), Perle (the DPB chairman), Paula Dobriansky (undersecretary of state for democracy and global affairs), Peter Rodman (assistant secretary of defense for international security affairs), Zalmay Khalilzad (special envoy to the Middle East and later ambassador to Iraq), Elliott Abrams (National Security Council [NSC] staff member responsible for Middle East policy), and Eliot Cohen (a DPB member). Other neoconservatives who were not PNAC founders also assumed key positions. Prominent among them were Feith (undersecretary of defense for policy) and John Bolton (undersecretary of state for arms control and international security and, later, ambassador to the United Nations).[37]

The neoconservatives' influence was evident in President Bush's wholesale embrace of their foreign policy ideology and language in the wake of the 9/11 terrorist attacks on the World Trade Center and the Pentagon. And that espousal, in turn, was manifest in numerous presidential speeches but most significantly in the pivotal foreign policy document of his presidency and, indeed, of perhaps any presidency since Harry Truman's[38]—the 2002 publication of *The National Security Strategy*.

Neoconservatives are wont to suggest that Bush arrived at a neoconservative foreign policy on his own. But to believe that assertion is to ignore the reality of a 9/11-shocked foreign policy novice not given to contemplation but desperate for the very ready-made explanation and course of action the neoconservatives were more than happy to supply. It also ignores Bush's arrival at the White House as a self-avowed realist who was critical of Clinton's interventions in Haiti and the Balkans because they were not firmly anchored in threatened vital U.S. security interests. In a November 1999 speech, Bush declared that "a President must be a clear-eyed realist," a statement that reflected the foreign policy approach of his father's administration and of former secretary of defense Cheney. Until 9/11 the Bush White House did not take the al Qaeda threat seriously; on the contrary, the president displayed a general disinterest in foreign policy, certainly when compared to his keen interest in such domestic issues as tax cuts, educational reform, deregulation, government support of faith-based charities, expanded oil drilling in Alaska, and federally restricted funding for stem cell research. Further, he did not support significant increases—and certainly not of the magnitude the service chiefs and the neoconservatives wanted—in defense spending. (During the 2000 election campaign Al Gore had called for a larger five-year defense spending plan than Bush had proposed.) He moreover registered no noteworthy departure from his predecessor's policies toward Iraq, Iran, and North Korea; indeed, Kaplan and Kristol complained that Bush "proceeded to water down even the demands that the Clinton team had imposed on Iraq."[39]

Then came 9/11, which immediately transformed Bush into a foreign policy president and prompted him, over the following months, to endorse the neoconservatives' vision of the world and America's role in it. "Bush the realist became a zealous Wilsonian," observes Robert Litwak.[40] As Kaplan and Kristol approvingly recounted, "Bush transformed himself from a realist following in his father's footsteps to an internationalist touting America's ideals as sincerely and forcefully as Harry Truman, John Kennedy, and Ronald Reagan before him."[41] The blunt assessment of the prestigious London-based International Institute for Strategic Studies is that

> the events of September 11 2001 provided hawks, including those of "utopian" persuasion, with the opportunity to push Iraq to the top of the agenda. They successfully exploited the belief in the upper tier of the government immediately after the attacks that there was a better than even chance that Iraq had been involved, and the more broadly held concern that Baghdad might in the future supply WMD to terrorists. In bureaucratic terms, this resulted in the insertion of a single provision, at the end of a presidential guidance document otherwise dedicated to the government's response to 11 September, instructing the military to prepare for war with Iraq.[42]

Neoconservative White House speechwriter (and coiner of the "axis of evil" phrase) David Frum, in his 2003 memoir of the impact of 9/11 on President Bush, traced the transformation of Bush's thinking from realism to idealism with respect to the war on terrorism. This change was reflected in Bush's broadening conception of the source of the terrorist challenge to include the absence of democracy in the Middle East. Traditional U.S. policy had favored stability over justice, but the "pursuit of stability in the Middle East had brought chaos and slaughter to New York and Washington. Bush decided that the United States was no longer a status quo power in the Middle East."[43]

Iraq quickly began moving to the center stage in the Bush White House, with Rumsfeld and Wolfowitz pushing hard. Within hours after the attacks, Iraq popped up in White House Situation Room discussions. The apparent assumptions, unsupported by any hard evidence, were that no terrorist organization could possibly have carried out such spectacular actions on its own—i.e., without rogue state support—and that Saddam Hussein's Iraq was the probable state sponsor. Expecting to attend meetings focused on al Qaeda, "I walked into a series of discussions about Iraq," recalls Richard Clarke, the Bush White House's counterterrorism director.

> At first I was incredulous we were talking about something other than getting al Qaeda. Then I realized with almost a sharp physical pain that Rumsfeld and Wolfowitz were going to try to take advantage of this national tragedy to promote their agenda about Iraq. Since the beginning of the administration, indeed well before, they had been pressing for war against Iraq.[44]

When Clarke said that the focus should be on Osama bin Laden and al Qaeda, Wolfowitz countered that the main threat was Iraqi terrorism. "I said, that's interesting, because there hasn't been any Iraqi terrorism against the United States," Clarke later recounted to a British newspaper interviewer.

> There hasn't been any for 8 years [since Saddam Hussein's alleged attempt to assassinate former president George H. W. Bush in Kuwait in 1993]. And [Wolfowitz] said something derisive about how I shouldn't believe the CIA [Central Intelligence Agency] and

FBI [Federal Bureau of Investigation], that they've been wrong. And I said if you know more than I know, tell me what it is, because I've been doing this for 8 years and I don't know about any Iraqi-sponsored terrorism against the U.S. since 1993. . . . He said bin Laden couldn't possibly have attacked the World Trade Center. . . . One little terrorist group like that couldn't possibly have staged that operation. It must have been Iraq.[45]

Later, on the evening of September 12, Clarke encountered President Bush in the Situation Room, and it was obvious to him that Bush, who had also talked to Wolfowitz, wanted to believe that Saddam Hussein was involved in the attacks. Even though Clarke declared that "we have looked several times for state sponsorship of al Qaeda and not found any real linkages to Iraq," Bush insisted that Clarke look again. "See if Saddam did this. See if he is linked in any way," charged Bush.[46]

Kenneth Pollack, an Iraqi expert formerly with the CIA and NSC staff and author of the influential 2002 book, *The Threatening Storm: The Case for Invading Iraq*, identified the Iraq hawks within the administration as a

group led by Deputy Secretary of Defense Paul Wolfowitz and a number of others in the offices of the Secretary of Defense and Vice President. This band had an almost excessive fixation on getting rid of Saddam's regime. . . . From day one, they urged an aggressive regime change strategy relying on the INC [Iraqi National Congress, an exile group led by Ahmed Chalabi] and U.S. air power to topple Saddam. Their dogma was that the Iraqi regime was the root cause of nearly every evil to befall the United States (from Arab-Israeli violence to international terrorism), while the Iraqi people were waiting to rise up against Saddam and would do so if the United States demonstrated it was serious about overthrowing him.[47]

For Cheney, Rumsfeld, and Wolfowitz, remembers Clarke, Iraq was "the most dangerous thing in national security . . . an idée fixe, a rigid belief, received wisdom, a decision already made and one that no fact or event could derail."[48]

President Bush gave legendary journalist Bob Woodward cooperative interviews about the 9/11 attacks. According to Woodward's account of the administration's first reactions to the attacks (an account that Bush has not disputed), at an NSC meeting immediately afterward both Rumsfeld and Wolfowitz argued unsuccessfully for an American military response that included an assault on Iraq.

> Rumsfeld raised the question of Iraq. Why shouldn't we go against Iraq, not just al Qaeda? he asked. Rumsfeld was speaking not only for himself when he raised the question. His deputy, Paul D. Wolfowitz, was committed to a policy that would make Iraq a principal target of the first round in the war on terrorism. . . . Rumsfeld was raising the possibility that they could take advantage of the terrorist attacks to go after Saddam immediately.[49]

Thus, from the start, neoconservatives inside the administration's upper reaches were prepared to lump together Iraq and al Qaeda into an undifferentiated terrorism threat and to use the al Qaeda attacks as the fulcrum for a war on Iraq that would finish off Saddam Hussein once and for all.

Secretary of State Colin Powell opposed the Rumsfeld-Wolfowitz option and persuaded the president to focus on al Qaeda first. "Any action needs public support," he argued. "It's not just what the international coalition supports: it's what the American people want to support. The American people want us to do something about al Qaeda."[50] Clarke added, for good measure: "Having been attacked by al Qaeda, for us now to go bombing Iraq in response would be like our invading Mexico after the Japanese attacked us at Pearl Harbor."[51] According to Powell biographer Karen DeYoung, the proposed Rumsfeld-Wolfowitz option made it "clear to Powell that some of his colleagues were trying to use the events of September to promote their own policy obsessions and settle old scores."[52]

At another NSC meeting at Camp David on September 15, by which time the focus was on coercing the Taliban to turn over the al Qaeda leadership or face regime change in Afghanistan, Wolfowitz again raised the issue of Iraq. When National Security Adviser Condoleezza Rice asked whether those at the meeting

could envision a successful military operation beyond Afghanistan . . . Wolfowitz seized the opportunity. Attacking Afghanistan would be uncertain. He worried about 100,000 American troops bogged down in mountain fighting six months from then. In contrast, Iraq was a brittle, oppressive regime that might break easily. It was doable. He estimated there was a 10 to 50 percent chance Saddam was involved in the September 11 terrorist attacks. The U.S. would have to go after Saddam at some time if the war on terrorism was to be taken seriously. . . .

But Bush had strong reservations about attacking Iraq. . . . He was concerned about two things, he said later. "My theory is you've got to do something and do it well and that . . . if we could prove that we could be successful in [the Afghanistan] theater, then the rest of the task would be easier. If we tried to do too many things—two things, for example, or three things—militarily, then . . . the lack of focus would have been a huge risk.

Bush's other concern was one he did not express to his war cabinet but that he would later say was part of his thinking. He knew that around the table were advisers—Powell, Cheney, Wolfowitz—who had been with his father during the Gulf War deliberations. "And one of the things I wasn't going to allow to happen is, that we weren't going to let their previous experience in this theater become a rational course for a new war. In other words, he didn't want them to use the war on terror as an excuse to settle an old score."[53]

Neoconservative pressure on the White House was unrelenting. On September 20, just nine days after the 9/11 attacks, more than three dozen leading neoconservatives and their like-minded political allies on Iraq published an open letter to President Bush that endorsed al Qaeda's destruction and urged the president to target other hostile groups and states as well. The letter suggested that Iraq might have provided assistance to the 9/11 perpetrators but insisted that "even if evidence does *not* link Iraq directly to the attack, any strategy aimed at the eradication of terrorism and its sponsors must include a determined effort to remove Saddam Hussein from power." The letter then warned that "[f]ailure to undertake such an effort will constitute an early and perhaps decisive *surrender* in the war on international terrorism."[54] Thus, for the neoconservatives even after 9/11, Iraq—not al Qaeda—remained the leading prize in the amorphous war on terrorism.

Exactly when President Bush decided on waging the war remains unclear. Most of his post-9/11 national security team regarded a regime change war against Saddam Hussein as feasible, desirable, and even inevitable. The unexpectedly quick, cheap, and seemingly decisive U.S. destruction of the Taliban regime in Afghanistan certainly encouraged action. Did not 9/11 demand a bigger and more dramatic payback than what transpired in Afghanistan? Why not take advantage of Americans' continuing demand for vengeance by knocking off other hostile regimes? With Osama bin Laden continuing to elude justice, why not take down Saddam Hussein? Would he not be a much easier mark than he was in 1991?

In March 2003 *Time* published a long account tracing the post-9/11 evolution of Bush's thinking on Iraq as influenced increasingly by neoconservative argumentation. In *Time*'s report, in March 2002, or six months after 9/11, the president poked his head into Rice's office as she met with senators and heard them discussing the possibilities of dealing with Iraq through the United Nations or a coalition of U.S. allies in the Middle East. Bush declared to the startled senators, "Fuck Saddam. We're taking him out."[55] In early July 2002 Rice told the State Department's Richard Haass that Bush had "made up his mind" to go to war absent some major capitulation by Saddam Hussein.[56]

A post-invasion *Financial Times* account concluded that Bush had decided on war no later than December 2002, when he was confronted with Saddam Hussein's 12,000-page declaration regarding charges that Iraq still possessed WMDs. The declaration seemed to be nothing more than a tedious obfuscation, leading the president to conclude that the Iraqi dictator had made a strategic decision not to cooperate. "There was a feeling that the White House was being mocked," according to one National Security Council source. "A tinpot dictator was mocking the president. It provoked . . . anger inside the White House. At that point, there was no prospect of a diplomatic solution."[57] Certainly by that point—indeed, even months before—Bush had made it clear that he would settle for nothing less than Hussein's departure from power, which made war inevitable unless the dictator fled Iraq or died.

———

The terrorist attacks of 9/11 and a receptive president combined to permit the translation of the neoconservatives' ideology into established U.S. foreign policy, the major tenets of which were laid out in the White House's 2002 *National Security Strategy*. The document is a symphony of neoconservative themes, objectives, and language. The universality of core American political values, the presence of evil regimes, the need to perpetuate America's global military primacy, the confidence in force as an instrument of overseas regime change, the imperative of democratic expansion, and the embrace of preventive war are all there. What quickly became known as the "Bush Doctrine" consisted of the *NSS* and key antecedent presidential pronouncements, including Bush's speeches before a joint session of Congress on September 20, 2001, and before the Warsaw Conference on Combating Terrorism on November 6, 2001; his State of the Union address on January 29, 2002; his remarks before the student body of the Virginia Military Institute on April 17, 2002; and his speech to the graduating class at the U.S. Military Academy at West Point on June 1, 2002. By the fall of 2002 the administration had in place a clear, declaratory use-of-force policy whose objective was stated in the title of the *NSS*'s chapter 5: "Prevent Our

Enemies from Threatening Us, Our Allies, and Our Friends with Weapons of Mass Destruction."[58]

The *NSS* opens by declaring the universality of American values, a key tenet of neoconservative ideology:

> The great struggles of the twentieth century between liberty and totalitarianism ended with a decisive victory for the forces of freedom—and a single sustainable model for national success: freedom, democracy, and free enterprise.... People everywhere want to be able to speak freely; choose who will govern them; worship as they please; educate their children—male and female; own property; and enjoy the benefits of their labor. These values of freedom are right and true for every person, in every society—and the duty of protecting these values against their enemies is the common calling of freedom-loving people across the globe and across the ages.[59]

It then states the basis and goals of the U.S. national security strategy:

> The U.S. national security strategy will be based on a distinctly American internationalism that reflects the union of our values and our national interests. The aim of the strategy is to help make the world not just safer but better. Our goals on the path to progress are clear: political and economic freedom, peaceful relations with other states, and respect for human dignity....
>
> In pursuit of our goals, our first imperative is to clarify what we stand for: the United States must defend liberty and justice because these principles are right and true for all people everywhere.[60]

As for threats to the United States, the *NSS* holds that the "gravest danger our nation faces lies at the crossroads of radicalism and technology"[61]—specifically, the acquisition of weapons of mass destruction by enemies of the United States. "Our enemies have openly declared that they are seeking weapons of mass destruction, and evidence indicates that they are doing so with determination. The United States will not allow these efforts to succeed."[62] Of particular concern is the possible acquisition of WMD by terrorist organizations via the assistance of so-called rogue states, which are defined as states that:

- brutalize their own people and squander their national resources for the personal gain of the rulers;
- display no regard for international law, threaten their neighbors, and callously violate international treaties to which they are party;
- are determined to acquire weapons of mass destruction, along with other advanced military technology, to be used as threats or offensively to achieve the aggressive designs of these regimes;
- sponsor terrorism around the globe; and
- reject basic human values and hate the United States and everything for which it stands.[63]

The *NSS* presumes that terrorist organizations are clients or allies of rogue states—with Iraq and North Korea mentioned by name—and that rogue states would be the most likely suppliers of WMD to terrorist organizations. Therefore, "we must be prepared to stop rogue states and their terrorist clients *before* they are able to threaten or use weapons of mass destruction against the United States and our allies and friends."[64] The *NSS* states preventive force is imperative because fanatical terrorist organizations and reckless dictators are undeterrable. It stipulates,

> Given the goals of rogue states and terrorists, the United States can no longer solely rely on a reactive posture as we have in the past. The inability to deter a potential attacker, the immediacy of today's threats, and the magnitude of potential harm that could be caused by our adversaries' choice of weapons do not permit that option. We cannot let our enemies strike first.

In the Cold War, especially following the Cuban missile crisis, we faced a generally status quo, risk-averse adversary. Deterrence was an effective defense. But deterrence based only upon a threat of retaliation is less likely to work against leaders of rogue states more willing to take risks, gambling with the lives of their people, and the wealth of their nations. . . .

Traditional concepts of deterrence will not work against a terrorist enemy whose avowed tactics are wanton destruction and targeting of innocents; whose so-called soldiers seek martyrdom in death and whose most potent protection is statelessness.[65]

To sustain a capacity for effective preventive military action, the *NSS* contends that the United States "must build and maintain our defenses beyond challenge,"[66] reflecting another central tenet of neoconservative ideology. This stipulation means that "our forces will be strong enough to dissuade potential adversaries from pursuing a military build-up in hopes of surpassing, or equaling, the power of the United States."[67] Indeed, countries like China should not even bother to try to compete militarily with the United States because it is not in their self-interest to do so: "In pursuing advanced military capabilities that can threaten its neighbors in the Pacific region, China is following an outdated path that, in the end, will hamper its own pursuit of national greatness. In time, China will find that social and political freedom is the only source of that greatness."[68]

The *NSS* provided the intellectual rationale and policy framework for a preventive war against Iraq as well as any other rogue state that had, or might someday have, the temerity to challenge America's post–Cold War global hegemony. The rogue state challenge was cast in terms of WMD acquisition, especially concerning nuclear weapons. In its essence, therefore, the Bush Doctrine was about forcible and preventive counter-proliferation to preserve America's military primacy and freedom of military action and to spread American political values abroad. As such, the doctrine was a dream come true for neoconservatives and nationalist hawks, both of whom were committed to permanent U.S. domination of the world.

THREE

BOGUS ASSUMPTIONS, WISHFUL THINKING

Saddam Hussein's regime has proven itself a grave and gathering danger. To suggest otherwise is to hope against the evidence.

—President George W. Bush,
radio address to the nation, September 13, 2002[1]

The Al Qaeda connection and nuclear weapons issue were the only two ways that you could link Iraq to an imminent security threat to the U.S. And the administration was grossly distorting the intelligence on both.

—Greg Theilmann,
State Department intelligence analyst[2]

By the time President George W. Bush ordered U.S. forces to invade Iraq, he and other top officials in his administration had painted a terrifying picture of Saddam Hussein. The dictator was, or soon to be, depicted as a Hitler with nuclear weapons—a mad, undeterrable despot on the verge of acquiring the ultimate weapon of mass destruction and hell-bent to use it against the United States. It was a picture that justified preventive war. But it would be a relative easy and cheap war. If the threat was dire, it was also readily disposable. The Bush administration and other war proponents conveyed no sense of risk of major blood and treasure sacrifice, to say nothing of a protracted war involving tens of thousands of American casualties and trillions of dollars. The war would be a "cakewalk," a larger-scale repeat of the unexpectedly swift and seemingly decisive victory in Afghanistan. Saddam Hussein's regime was militarily much weaker than it had been in 1991, and the oppressed Iraqi people, upon liberation, would naturally work to establish institutions of democratic governance.

The Iraqi threat was cast most starkly in two key speeches: Vice President Cheney's speech to the 103rd National Convention of the Veterans of Foreign Wars (VFW) on August 26, 2002, and President Bush's speech at the Cincinnati Museum Center on October 7, 2002. Cheney, in his speech, called Iraq "a mortal threat" to the United States: "The Iraqi regime has . . . been very busy enhancing its capabilities in the field of chemical and biological agents. And they continue to pursue the nuclear program they began so many years ago." Cheney added, "Many of us are convinced that Saddam will acquire nuclear weapons fairly soon." Once he acquired the full panoply of WMD, "Saddam Hussein could then be expected to seek domination of the entire Middle East, take control of a great portion of the world's energy supplies, directly threaten American friends throughout the region, and subject the United States or any other nation to nuclear blackmail." (Not even Hitler could have done all that.) Cheney was absolutely certain: "Simply stated, there is no doubt that Saddam Hussein now has weapons of mass destruction. There is no doubt that he is amassing them to use against our friends, against our allies, and against us."[3]

In Cincinnati, Bush said Iraq was "a grave threat to peace" because of its "history of aggression" and "drive toward an arsenal of terror." Iraq "possesses and produces chemical and biological weapons" and "is seeking nuclear weapons." Bush then went on to explain "why Iraq is different from other countries or regimes that also have terrible weapons":

> While there are many dangers in the world, the threat from Iraq stands alone—because it gathers the most serious dangers of our

age in one place. Iraq's weapons of mass destruction are controlled by a murderous tyrant who has already used chemical weapons to kill thousands of people. This same tyrant has tried to dominate the Middle East, has invaded and occupied a small neighbor, has struck other nations without warning, and holds an unrelenting hostility toward the United States. By its past and present actions, by its technological capabilities, by the merciless nature of the regime, Iraq is unique.

Bush went on to assert that Iraq possessed (1) a biological weapons arsenal "capable of killing millions"; (2) ballistic missiles with ranges "to strike Saudi Arabia, Israel, Turkey and other nations—in a region where more than 135,000 American civilians and service members live and work"; and (3) a "growing fleet of manned and unmanned aerial vehicles that could be used to disperse chemical or biological weapons across broad areas." Indeed, "we're concerned that Iraq is exploring ways of using these UAVs [unmanned aerial vehicles] for missions targeting the United States." The threat, moreover, was critical:

> Some ask how urgent this danger is to America and the world. The danger is already significant, and it only grows worse with time. If we know Saddam Hussein has dangerous weapons today—and we do—does it make any sense for the world to wait to confront him as he grows even stronger and develops even more dangerous weapons?

Bush then postulated an Iraqi alliance with al Qaeda and Iraq's possible transfer of WMDs to al Qaeda:

> We know that Iraq and the al Qaeda terrorist network share a common enemy—the United States. We know that Iraq and al Qaeda have had high-level contacts that go back more than a decade. . . . And we know that after September 11, Saddam Hussein's regime gleefully celebrated the terrorist attack on America.

Iraq could decide on any given day to provide a biological or chemical weapon to a terrorist group or individual terrorists. Alliance with terrorists could allow the Iraqi regime to attack America without leaving any fingerprints. . . . Saddam is harboring terrorists and the instrument of terror, the instruments of mass death and destruction. And he cannot be trusted. The risk is simply too great that he will use them, or provide them to a terrorist network.

Bush also did not see any meaningful difference between terrorist groups and rogue states: "Terror cells and outlaw regimes building weapons of mass destruction are different faces of the same evil. Our security requires that we confront both."

Bush then turned to the Iraqi nuclear threat. He claimed that the evidence, including Saddam Hussein's "numerous meetings with Iraqi nuclear scientists, a group he calls his 'nuclear mujahideen,'" supported the conclusion that "Iraq is reconstituting its nuclear weapons program." The threat was near and horrific:

If the Iraqi regime is able to produce, buy, or steal an amount of highly enriched uranium a little larger than a single softball, it could have a nuclear weapon in less than a year. And if we allow that to happen, a terrible line would be crossed. Saddam would be in a position to blackmail anyone who opposes his aggression. He would be in a position to dominate the Middle East. He would be in a position to threaten America. And Saddam Hussein would be in a position to pass nuclear technology to terrorists.

The president concluded his portrayal of the Iraqi threat by invoking the specter of a nuclear 9/11:

Some citizens wonder, after 11 years of living with this problem, why do we need to confront it now? And there's a reason. We've experienced the horrors of September the 11th. We have seen that those who hate America are willing to crash airplanes into buildings full of innocent people. Our enemies would be no less willing, in fact they would be eager, to use [a] biological or chemical, or nuclear weapon. Knowing these realities, America must not ignore the threat gathering against us. Facing clear evidence of peril, we cannot wait for the final proof—the smoking gun—that could come in the form of a mushroom cloud.[4]

Noah Feldman has observed that the American invasion of Iraq "was the product of several disparate, mutually conflicting strands of thought, some benightedly idealistic, others brutally realist, and almost all based on some misunderstanding of the likely consequences of the invasion in Iraq itself."[5] A review of prewar administration statements and of the neoconservatives' official and unofficial arguments certainly reveals no coherent U.S. grand strategy for Iraq. Such a strategy would have recognized the limits of U.S. military power as an instrument of foreign political change and paid at least some attention to how a successful and friendly post-Baathist political order would be established in Iraq. Rather, what we find is a mélange of declared and undeclared war aims with differing appeals to various policymakers who themselves were motivated by disparate and sometimes contradictory agendas—in short, "an 'overlapping agreement' about the wisdom of invasion among individuals who differed about the ends that an invasion promised to serve."[6] Those individuals included the president and vice president, Secretary of Defense Donald Rumsfeld, National Security Adviser Condoleezza Rice, and the influential neoconservative coterie of Scooter Libby, Paul Wolfowitz, Douglas Feith, and Richard Perle. The administration's war aims—the ends that an invasion promised to serve—comprised: preventing nuclear proliferation; exploiting Iraq's weakness; completing the "unfinished business" of the 1991 Gulf War; demonstrating a willingness to use American military power and use it unilaterally; asserting the principle of preventive military action; intimidating Iran, North Korea, and other rogue states; transforming the Middle East via establishing a model democracy in Iraq that other Arab states could emulate; creating an Arab client-state alternative to Saudi Arabia; eliminating an enemy of Israel; vindicating the Pentagon's "revolutionary" employment of force; expanding the executive branch's power; and last, but by no means least, ridding the world of evil.

The very number and diversity of aims, and the mutual antagonism of some, reflect a lack of consensus on what, exactly, the war was all about, as well as a lack of confidence in the persuasiveness of any single aim. Was the war about avenging 9/11, eliminating weapons of mass destruction, knocking off an ally of Osama bin Laden, punishing a dictator, freeing an oppressed people, flexing America's high-tech military muscle, helping Israel, democratizing the Middle East, intimidating other rogue states, suppressing global terrorism, reestablishing the imperial presidency, destroying evil, or all of the above? Did the multiplicity of war aims betray the war proponents' need to drape, for public consumption, the clothes of a war of necessity over what was in fact a war of choice? The failure to discover Iraq's much-hyped WMDs or an operational linkage between Saddam Hussein's regime and al Qaeda certainly produced an official shift of emphasis toward establishing freedom and democracy in the Middle East as the central justifications for the war.

The myriad motivations, hopes, and expectations that coalesced behind the Bush administration's 2003 decision for war against Iraq bring to mind the Johnson administration's 1965 decision to launch the Rolling Thunder bombing campaign against North Vietnam. As with the Bush administration and Iraq, there was no agreement within the Johnson administration on the bombing's purpose or its expected effects. Rolling Thunder was "a compromise means to secure a multitude of results," observes Mark Clodfelter. It was finally undertaken in March 1965 "because a majority [of Johnson's civilian advisers] perceived that bombing would help secure what each individually felt was the unique ingredient necessary for a stable, non-Communist South Vietnam."[7] Similarly, the invasion of Iraq was undertaken because key Bush administration policymakers believed that an invasion would help accomplish what each individually felt was the purpose of the invasion.

At least a dozen objectives for Rolling Thunder surfaced during the administration's pre-decision internal deliberations. President Johnson hoped the bombing would deter Hanoi from expanding the war in South Vietnam. Secretary of Defense McNamara believed the bombing would signal U.S. resolve to resist Communist aggression in the South. John McNaughton, McNamara's assistant secretary for international security affairs, also believed U.S. air operations would convey American resolve and patience (and, for good measure, contain Chinese Communist expansion in Southeast Asia). Gen. Maxwell Taylor, U.S. Army (Ret.), serving as U.S. ambassador to Saigon, along with presidential national security adviser McGeorge Bundy, believed that Rolling Thunder would serve primarily to boost the sagging morale of the U.S. client-regime in Saigon, which was losing the war to the Communists. For Secretary of State Dean Rusk and Assistant Secretary of State (for Far Eastern Affairs) William Bundy, the bombing campaign would enhance U.S. bargaining leverage with Hanoi should the Communists decide to stop fighting and negotiate. Still others believed that Rolling Thunder would destroy the Viet Cong's morale, reduce Communist infiltration down the Ho Chi Minh Trail, punish Hanoi for supporting the insurgency, and pave the way for the imminent introduction of U.S. ground troops into South Vietnam. Rolling Thunder was thus many things to many people and was driven by frustration over the Saigon regime's failing ground war in the south and the hope—vain, as it turned out—that the systematic bombing of North Vietnam might obviate the need to Americanize the ground war in the south.[8] In the end, the initiation of Rolling Thunder, which was quickly followed by the introduction of U.S. ground combat forces into South Vietnam, simply provoked Communist counter-escalation in the form of expanded infiltration down the Ho Chi Minh Trail. The bombing campaign neither halted that infiltration nor weakened Hanoi's will to win.

It remains unclear how seriously war proponents took the Iraqi threat that they so grossly inflated for political purposes. Four months after the

U.S. invasion of Iraq, Secretary of Defense Rumsfeld acknowledged that the administration "did not act in Iraq because we had discovered dramatic new evidence of Iraq's pursuit of weapons of mass murder. We acted because we saw the existing evidence in a new light, through the prism of our experience on September 11th."[9] In other words, the administration acted on the basis of an *imagined* threat. It *supposed* the *possibility* of a future similar attack, armed this time with Iraqi-supplied weapons of mass destruction, and acted to foreclose that theoretical possibility.

In his account of the Bush administration and the war on terror, Douglas Feith, a prominent neoconservative who served as undersecretary of defense for policy from 2001 to 2005, claims that "no one I know of believed Saddam was part of the 9/11 plot; we had no substantial reason to believe he was. Nor did we have any intelligence that Iraq was plotting specific operations with al Qaida or any other terrorist group."[10] Rather, the concern was Saddam Hussein's hatred of the United States and record of aggression combined with America's vulnerability to 9/11-like attacks. According to Feith, "The Administration's rationale [for war] did not depend solely on concern about weapons of mass destruction, *much less on whether Saddam had WMD stockpiles on hand.*"[11] Notwithstanding the stockpile threat (including the near-term threat of acquired nuclear weapons) portrayed by the White House, the real threat, according to Feith, was Hussein's retention of the personnel and facilities to produce chemical and biological weapons "and the intention to reinvigorate his programs," which could resume production "within a few weeks of a decision to go forward."[12] So armed, Hussein could then—maybe—transfer WMDs to anti-American terrorist organizations or perhaps could launch a new assault on Kuwait since "[p]ossession of WMD could put Saddam in a position to deter the United States from interfering."[13]

Richard Perle later echoed Feith's claim. The "salient issue was not whether Saddam had *stockpiles* of WMD but whether he could produce them and place them in the hands of terrorists," wrote Perle in January 2009. "The administration's appalling inability to explain that this is what it was thinking and doing allowed the unearthing of stockpiles to become the test of whether it had correctly assessed the risk that Saddam might provide WMD to terrorists."[14] (Neither Feith nor Perle explains how Saddam's possession in 1991 of a truly robust arsenal of deliverable chemical and biological munitions failed to deter the United States from interfering to reverse Iraq's conquest of Kuwait, which then was not the treaty ally it is today. They also fail to explain why Saddam did not restart WMD production as U.S. forces began massing against him.)

Thus, the United States went to war against Saddam Hussein's hostile *intentions* and the chance that he *might* resume production of chemical and biological weapons. As Richard Betts observes, "The intelligence community had almost no hard evidence that Iraq was retaining the chemical and biological weapons it had at the time of the 1991 Persian Gulf War, or had manufactured new ones, or was reassembling its nuclear weapons program." The community "failed to uncover much new information after UNSCOM [United Nations Special Commission on Iraq] inspectors left Iraq in 1998," and, worse still, "much of the information it did get came from defector reports that turned out to be fabricated or unreliable."[15] Iraq's hostility was considered a given, as was its retention of chemical and biological weapons that had gone unaccounted for in 1998. The intelligence community had been shocked by how much of Hussein's nuclear program had been successfully concealed before the Gulf War, and the Iraqi dictator, at least until November 2002 (when he agreed to permit the return of UN inspectors), was still acting as if he had something to hide.

That the administration deliberately deceived the American electorate (and perhaps itself) by postulating both an Iraqi WMD threat and an Iraqi–al Qaeda "alliance" far beyond the available evidence is no longer a matter of dispute.[16] In surveying the discrepancies between what Bush and other top administration officials were publicly claiming and what was actually known at the time, Joseph Pfiffner concluded in 2004:

> From the publicly available evidence, the president misled the
> country in implying that there was a connection between Saddam

and 9/11. The administration's claims about Iraq's nuclear capacity were based on dubious evidence that was presented in a misleading manner. Claims about chemical and biological weapons were based on legitimate evidence that was widely accepted internationally. . . . Claims of Saddam's ability to deliver these weapons, however, were exaggerated. Finally, there was circumstantial and inconclusive evidence that in 2002 the intelligence community may have been under unusual pressure to support the administration's goals.[17]

In his even more extensive survey of the evidence, Chaim Kaufmann believes that the administration was guilty of deliberate "threat inflation." He defines it as:

(1) claims that go beyond the range of ambiguity that disinterested experts would credit as plausible; (2) a consistent pattern of worst-case assertions over a range of factual issues that are logically unrelated or only weakly related—an unlikely output of disinterested analysis; (3) use of double standards in evaluating intelligence in a way that favors worst-case threat assessments; or (4) claims based on circular logic, such as Bush administration claims that [Saddam] Hussein's alleged hostile intentions were evidence of the existence of [WMD] whose supposed existence was used as evidence of his intentions.

Kaufmann concludes that "administration exaggerations of the Iraqi threat during 2002-03 qualify on all four grounds. The errors did not result from mistakes by U.S. intelligence agencies. Rather, top officials knew what policy they intended to pursue and selected intelligence assessments to promote that policy based on their political usefulness, not their credibility."[18] Wolfowitz virtually admitted as much when he told a *Vanity Fair* interviewer in May 2003, "We settled on the one issue that everyone could agree on, which was weapons of mass destruction, as the core reason."[19]

A 2004 study by the Carnegie Endowment for International Peace also detected a politically driven shift in intelligence assessments in 2002. It discovered a yawning gap between what was claimed and what was known, especially the "alliance" between Saddam Hussein and Osama bin Laden. The endowment reported:

> There was and is no solid evidence of a cooperative relationship between Saddam's government and al Qaeda. There was no evidence to support the claim that Iraq would have transferred WMD to al Qaeda and much evidence to counter it. The notion that any government would give its principal security assets to people it could not control in order to achieve its own political aims is highly dubious.[20]

In his exhaustive study of the administration's threat statements and the actual document-by-document intelligence available to the administration, John Prados, an analyst with the National Security Archive and long-standing observer of the CIA, concluded that the administration "consistently distorted, manipulated, and ignored [intelligence information], as the president, vice president, secretaries of defense and state, and others, sought to persuade the country that the facts about Iraq were other than what the intelligence indicated." It was "a case study in government dishonesty" in which "deception was systematic and carried out purposefully" to "create the conditions President Bush hoped would justify a war."[21]

Writing in 2006, CIA analyst Paul Pillar, who served as the national intelligence officer for the Near East and South Asia from 2000 to 2005, declared that the Bush administration "used intelligence not to inform decision-making, but to justify a decision already made. It went to war without requesting—and evidently without being influenced by—any strategic level intelligence assessments on any aspect of Iraq."[22] The intelligence community, on its own initiative, conducted an assessment of the problems the United States was likely to face in a post-invasion Iraq. The analysis presented a picture of a political culture that would not provide a fertile ground for democracy and foretold a long, difficult, and turbulent transition. It projected that a Marshall Plan-type effort would be required to restore the Iraqi economy, despite Iraq's abundant oil resources. It forecast that in a deeply divided Iraqi society, with Sunnis resentful over the loss of their dominant position and Shiites seeking power commensurate with their majority status, there was a significant chance that the groups would engage in violent conflict unless an occupying power prevented it. And it anticipated that a foreign occupying force would itself be the target of resentment and attacks—including by guerrilla warfare—unless it established security and put Iraq on the road to prosperity in the first few weeks or months after the fall of Saddam.[23]

The intelligence community also assessed the likely regional consequences of overthrowing Saddam Hussein and concluded that "any value Iraq might have as a democratic exemplar would be minimal" because of its being imposed by an outside power. It also determined that war and occupation more likely would "boost political Islam and increase sympathy for terrorists' objectives—and Iraq would become a magnet for extremists from elsewhere in the Middle East."[24] Pillar then went on to discuss the discrepancies "between the administration's public statements and the intelligence community's judgments," with the greatest being

> the relationship between Saddam and al Qaeda. The enormous attention devoted to this subject did not reflect any judgment by intelligence officials that there was or was likely to be anything like the "alliance" the administration said existed. The reason the connection got so much attention was that the administration wanted to hitch the Iraq expedition to the "war on terror" and the threat the American public feared most, thereby capitalizing on the country's militant post-9/11 mood.

The issue of possible ties between Saddam and al Qaeda was especially prone to selective use of raw intelligence to make a public case for war. In the shadowy world of international terrorism, almost anyone can be "linked" to almost anyone else if enough effort is made to find evidence of casual contacts, the mentioning of names in the same breath, or indications of common travels or experiences. Even the most minimal and circumstantial data can be adduced as evidence of a "relationship," ignoring the important question of whether a given regime actually supports a given terrorist group and the fact that relationships can be competitive or distrustful rather than cooperative.[25]

In a September 2006 interview with CBS News correspondent Katie Couric, President Bush himself confessed that "one of the hardest parts of my job is to connect Iraq to the war on terror."[26] To be fair, however, the Bush administration was hardly the first to exaggerate a foreign threat for the purpose of mobilizing public and congressional support for military action. (It was also not the first to downplay the potential risks and costs of contemplated armed intervention.) Presidents have regularly sold wars of choice as wars of necessity precisely because of the imperative of public support, especially in wars that could prove costly and prolonged. They have routinely proclaimed the presence of threatened vital interests and spoken of dire consequences given a failure to act. The Johnson administration, for example, warned that not fighting in Vietnam would jeopardize the credibility of U.S. alliances worldwide and encourage a Communist takeover of all Southeast Asia. Moreover, Bush and Cheney were certainly not alone in imagining the horror of 9/11-like attacks conducted with weapons of mass destruction; indeed, the specter of terrorists armed with destructive power heretofore monopolized by states was a legitimate fear long before 9/11. The 2002 *National Security Strategy* was quite right to define the marriage of radicalism and technology as a potentially grave security threat. And it was certainly reasonable, given Saddam Hussein's long-standing enmity toward the United States as well as his track record of reckless miscalculation, to imagine the possibility of his collaboration with anti-American terrorist organizations.

The Bush White House probably believed what it repeatedly said—namely, that a war with Iraq was necessary to prevent Saddam Hussein from acquiring nuclear weapons and possibly transferring them to al Qaeda. Calamity terrorizes the imagination. The shock of 9/11 frightened many Americans into believing all sorts of terrifying possibilities, and the White House, after all, had the responsibility for protecting the country from future attacks. A near-universal assumption within the national security community was that additional terrorist attacks were forthcoming, an assumption reinforced by the mysterious anthrax attacks of October 2001. Jacob Weisberg contends that the anthrax attacks had a much greater impact on White House thinking than is generally appreciated. As secretary of defense under the George H. W. Bush administration, Cheney had had to grapple with the real possibility that Saddam Hussein would use chemical and biological weapons against U.S. forces advancing into Kuwait. Weisberg reports that in 2001 Cheney became highly alarmed over the prospect of a bioterrorist attack in the form of smallpox virus supplied by Iraq. Against such an attack the United States was effectively defenseless absent a crash program to vaccinate all Americans (which itself would kill hundreds and sicken thousands), a program that Cheney favored but Bush vetoed.[27] Scott McClellan, who served as White House press secretary from 2003 to 2006, believes that the "influence of the anthrax attacks on policymaking within the White House shouldn't be underestimated. . . . I know President Bush's thinking was deeply affected by the anthrax attacks. He was determined not to let another terrorist attack happen on his watch and to challenge regimes believed to be seeking weapons of mass destruction."[28]

Yet it bears repeating that by March 2003, when Operation Iraqi Freedom (OIF) was launched, there was no evidence of Iraqi complicity in al Qaeda's 9/11 attacks on the World Trade Center and the Pentagon. Additionally, though the White House had sought to conflate al Qaeda and Saddam Hussein as a unitary threat, no hard evidence exists of any operational collaboration between the terrorist organization and Baghdad's Baathist regime. (Simple contact is not collaboration; indeed, the United States was in constant contact with the Soviet Union during the Cold War but was hardly Moscow's ally.) Notwithstanding official talk of smoking guns and mushroom clouds, no one found evidence of a functioning Iraqi nuclear weapons program, much less an imminent Iraqi bomb. As later recalled by Richard Haass, who in 2003 was director of the State Department's Policy Planning Staff, "When it came to nuclear weapons, the intelligence at the time did not support acting. Iraq did not possess nuclear weapons or even a nuclear weapons program worthy of the name. Nor was it inevitable that over time Iraq would have been able to develop nuclear weapons, given the international sanctions in place."[29] Saddam Hussein's purported nuclear intentions thus were simply *wished* into imminent capabilities very much as Soviet capabilities were wished into intentions during the Cold War.

It is instructive that the Bush administration proceeded with the invasion of Iraq only one month after Mohamed ElBaradei, the head of the International Atomic Energy Agency (IAEA), publicly declared that the IAEA inspectors who had been on the ground in Iraq during the months before the invasion had "found no evidence that Iraq has revived its nuclear weapons program since the elimination of the program in the 1990s. No prohibited nuclear activities have been identified during these inspections." ElBaradei went on to state, "We should be able within the next few months to provide credible assurance that Iraq has no nuclear weapons program."[30]

Haass might have added that in any event, there was no reason to believe that Saddam Hussein's potential use of WMDs—including nuclear weapons, had he possessed them—was exempt from the grim logic of nuclear deterrence. True, he had employed chemical weapons against Iranian infantry and Kurdish villagers in the 1980s, but his victims were incapable of effective retaliation in kind. More notable was his refusal during the Gulf War of 1991 to launch such weapons against Israel or Coalition forces, both of which were capable of devastating retaliation. Saddam Hussein, to be sure, was prone to miscalculation. Witness his disastrous invasions of Iran and Kuwait; his personality cult dictatorship, wherein his lieutenants eagerly told him what he wanted to hear; and his repeated misjudgments of America's willingness to use force. Hussein, however, was homicidal, never suicidal; he always loved himself more than he hated the United States. Unlike Hitler in his Berlin bunker, Hussein chose capture rather than suicide. As Steven Metz has observed,

> Hussein had a penchant for miscalculation, not for suicide. He was willing to use chemical weapons against the Iranians or his own people, but had not used them against coalition forces in 1991 specifically because he knew that to do so would risk his own grasp on power and survival. Despite the claim of the [Bush] administration, nothing, not even September 11, had changed Hussein's desire for survival and retention of power.[31]

The portrait of Saddam Hussein as undeterrable was of course a necessary ingredient in the case for preventive war. A deterrable Hussein (i.e., the real Hussein) would have been just that—deterrable—and therefore unworthy of a war. Just as other rogue dictators, none of whom had ever employed WMD against the United States, Israel, or a treaty ally of the United States, Saddam Hussein ruled a state consisting of vital assets—territory, population, economic and governmental infrastructure, and military forces—that could be held hostage to the threat of devastating U.S. retaliation. This largesse put Hussein in a strategically different category from bin Laden, who led an elusive, transnational terrorist organization with little in the way of a "return address" that could be held hostage.

The Bush administration's presumption of rogue state irrationality—to the point of being indifferent to self-preservation—was in fact a recipe for repeated strategic miscalculation, and it remains so today. The presumption assumes a generic irrationality irrespective of specific regimes' circumstances and regime leaders' personalities, and it does so even with few historical examples of genuinely insane state leaders. Political extremism and radicalism are not synonymous with irrationality. Bin Laden has demonstrated an impressive capacity to calculate ends and means relationships, to plan and execute successful terrorist operations, and to ensure his own self-preservation. And for all the neoconservative talk about "mad mullahs" in Tehran and the need to take military action against Iran before it acquires nuclear weapons (the neoconservatives apparently learned nothing from the American debacle in Iraq), there is no evidence that Iran's leadership is suicidal. On the contrary, Trita Parsi, in his masterful assessment of the history of relations among Israel, Iran, and the United States, believes that "Iran's rationality" is the probable

> reason why thus far it has not shared chemical or biological weapons with any of its Arab proxies such as Hezbollah, and why a nuclear Iran likely would not share weapons with terrorist groups. Israel has signaled Iran that it would retaliate against any nuclear attack on Israel by hitting Iran—regardless of who attacked Israel. Tehran has fully grasped the meaning of the signal—if any of Iran's proxies attacked Israel with a nuclear warhead, Israel would destroy Iran. But even without this stern warning, Iran would be unlikely to share the doomsday weapon with its proxies precisely because those groups would cease to be proxies if they acquired such a powerful weapon. Iran's ambition, after all, is to become the region's undisputed power; given its tendency to view all other actors as potential competitors, it's hardly likely Tehran would undermine its goal by sharing the sensitive technology. Judging from Tehran's past behavior, the Iranian leadership is too Machiavellian to commit such an irrevocable and devastating mistake.[32]

The White House's suggestion that Saddam Hussein might transfer nuclear munitions to al Qaeda was always far-fetched. First, the Iraqi dictator could never be sure that such a transfer could be made undetected. Further, just as all Stalinist-styled dictators, he was not in the habit of handing over power, to say nothing of the destructive power of nuclear weapons, to any organization outside his complete control, and he was certainly aware that bin Laden regarded the Baathist regime in Baghdad as an apostate government. As Adam Cobb has observed,

> No state has ever given terrorists more power than it, itself possesses. There is no incentive for rogue regimes to hand over their hard won nuclear capabilities, prestige and power to AQ [al Qaeda]. Regimes like Kim Jong Il's North Korea, [Mahmoud] Ahmadinejad's Iran, or Saddam's Iraq tend to be paranoid and obsessed with finding and eliminating alternative sources of power to their rule. The President and others have repeatedly said that Saddam "could" hand over WMD to AQ. It is certainly technically possible, but they have never provided more than vague innuendo to suggest what incentives Saddam might gain from doing so—this is because the proposition does not bear scrutiny.[33]

Robert Litwak concurs:

> [E]ven when a state-sponsorship exists, as between Iran and Hezbollah, major constraints exert a powerful effect. State sponsors employ terrorist groups as instruments of policy, and that implies a high degree of control. A WMD transfer would be an extraordinary act—both in its escalatory character and its consequent threat to regime survival. Crossing that Rubicon would mean relinquishing control of the most valuable military asset in a state's arsenal. The target state would be taking the risk that the unconventional weapon employed by the terrorist group might be traced back to it and thereby trigger a devastating U.S. retaliatory strike.[34]

The White House presumed an Iraqi willingness to transfer WMDs to al Qaeda on the basis of a shared hatred of the United States. This supposition ignored Saddam Hussein's regional focus, especially on Iran, an enemy he always regarded as more dangerous than the United States. It also ignored, as Litwak points out, his "paramount interest in maintaining and increasing his own power. Far from advancing [his regional and personal agendas], an Iraqi WMD attack on the American homeland (whether directed or assisted) would have guaranteed a regime-destroying U.S. retaliatory response."[35]

There were always powerful barriers to cooperation between al Qaeda and Baathist Iraq, as many experts, including Brent Scowcroft, George H. W. Bush's national security adviser, repeatedly pointed out before the Iraq War. "Saddam's goals have little in common with the terrorists who threaten us, and there is little incentive for him to make common cause with them," Scowcroft wrote in a *Wall Street Journal* op-ed urging the Bush administration not to attack Iraq. "He is unlikely to risk his investment in weapons of mass destruction, much less his country, by handing such weapons to terrorists who would use them for their own purposes and leave Baghdad as the return address." Even "[t]hreatening to use these weapons for blackmail—much less their actual use—would open him and his entire regime to a devastating response by the U.S."[36]

Al Qaeda regards nationalism as an apostate threat, a divider of Muslims from one another. Osama bin Laden's stated goal is the reestablishment of the caliphate—i.e., a politically indivisible Muslim community—and he saw Saddam Hussein and all other secular Arab leaders as infidels. For Hussein, whose role models were Saladin and Stalin, not Mohammed, and who spent eight years waging war against the existential threat to his regime posed by the Ayatollah Ruhollah Khomeini's Iranian theocracy, Osama bin Laden could never have been a trustworthy ally. It is noteworthy that bin Laden remained silent during the first three weeks of Operation Iraqi Freedom; only on April 18, 2003, as U.S. forces entered Baghdad, did he issue a taped message calling on Muslims to mount suicide attacks on Coalition forces.

In the context of the National Security Council's examination of who was behind the 9/11 attacks, two experts on Islamic terrorism observed of Saddam Hussein and Osama bin Laden that [bin Laden] was deeply contemptuous of Saddam Hussein. For believers like bin Laden, Saddam was the second coming of Gamal Abdel Nasser, a secular pharaonic ruler who destroyed the religion and oppressed the umma [the community of Muslim believers]. There is little evidence that Saddam viewed bin Laden and his ilk any differently than Egypt's secular ruler viewed [Islamist activists] Sayyid Qutb, Shuqri Mustafa, and their successors—as religious extremists who would enjoy nothing more than to see secular rule toppled. However attractive their anti-Americanism, they could only be handled with caution. There was nothing in the record to suggest that a central precept of the state sponsors [of terrorism] had changed: never get in bed with a group you cannot control. Both the Iranians and the Iraqis appeared to be reluctant to cooperate with an organization that might commit some enormity that could be traced back to them. The NSC analysts found it difficult to believe that al Qaeda had acted alone, but no other conclusion was warranted.[37]

No post-invasion evidence emerged to support the existence of an al Qaeda–Saddam Hussein alliance. The 9/11 Commission reported in 2005 that while there may have been contacts between al Qaeda and the Baathist regime, "we have seen no evidence that these . . . ever developed into a collaborative operational relationship. Nor have we seen evidence indicating that Iraq cooperated with al Qaeda in developing or carrying out attacks against the United States."[38] A more definitive 2007 Pentagon-sponsored study based on 600,000 documents seized in Iraq "found no 'smoking gun' (i.e., direct connection) between Saddam's Iraq and al Qaeda." The study also concluded that while Saddam's regime did provide some support to other terrorist groups in the Middle East, the "predominant targets of Iraqi state terror operations were Iraqi citizens, both inside and outside Iraq."[39]

There is no question that al Qaeda's leadership was, and remains, interested in acquiring nuclear weapons and fissile materials. Most nuclear proliferation experts have believed that since the end of the Cold War, the best places for terrorist organizations to find them are, in descending order of probability, in Russia, Pakistan, and the civilian nuclear stockpiles in more than forty other countries around the world.[40] In Russia, the threat is the possible theft or illicit transfer from one or more of its 200 to 260 storage sites for nuclear weapons and/or plutonium and highly enriched uranium. Many of these sites are poorly secured in terms of both their physical protection and the reliability of those who operate and guard the sites.[41] The year before the 9/11 attacks, a Department of Energy advisory group chaired by former Senate majority leader Howard Baker and former White House counsel Lloyd Cutler concluded that the "most urgent unmet national security threat to the United States today is the danger that weapons of mass destruction or weapons-usable material in Russia could be stolen and sold to terrorists or hostile nation states and used against American troops abroad or citizens at home."[42] In Pakistan, a U.S. ally whose top nuclear physicists have been involved in the global nuclear black market and whose primary security services have long-standing ties with al Qaeda, the Taliban, and other extremist groups, the threat is the possible loss of governmental control over its estimated fifty or more nuclear weapons and stocks of highly enriched uranium.[43] The axis of evil states are much less likely sources of materials for terrorists because "their stockpiles, if any, are small and exceedingly precious, and hence well-guarded. Iran does not, and Iraq did not, have nuclear weapons or significant quantities of fissile material." And while North Korea "probably does have weapons-grade material," it is not likely "to give away what its leadership almost certainly sees as the most precious jewel in its security crown."[44]

The Bush administration clearly understood the domestic political importance of publicly asserting a collaborative al Qaeda–Iraq relationship even if such a relationship did not exist: it suggested a connection between Iraq and 9/11 to the American electorate that was out for revenge. After the 9/11 attacks, Douglas Feith established a Policy Counter Terrorism Evaluation Group for the purpose of finding links between al Qaeda and Saddam Hussein's regime. The group provided an alternative intelligence assessment that differed from that of the CIA and other intelligence agencies, all of which had concluded that there was no convincing evidence of an operational relationship between Osama bin Laden and Baghdad. The group's assessment, entitled "Iraq and al-Qaida: Making the Case," was based on an examination of existing intelligence and claimed that the intelligence agencies were ignoring reports of collaboration. The group offered no new intelligence to support its conclusion that Iraq and al Qaeda had a "mature, symbiotic relationship." Subsequently, in March 2007, the Pentagon's acting inspector general rebuked Feith's effort to claim such a relationship as "inappropriate" because he failed to clarify why his conclusion diverged from those of the rest of the intelligence community.[45]

What of Iraq's nonnuclear weapons of mass destruction? As the invasion neared, the administration assumed that Iraq had some chemical munitions and biological agents—i.e., residual post–Gulf War stocks that remained unaccounted for by the UN inspection regime when it was ejected from Iraq in 1998. Yet even this claim was highly suspect by the time U.S. forces attacked Iraq on March 19, 2003. In August 1995, Gen. Hussein Kamel, who was Saddam Hussein's son-in-law and the former director of Iraq's Military Industrial Corporation (which was responsible for all of Iraq's weapons programs), defected to Jordan. Kamel told debriefers that all of Iraq's chemical and biological weapons had been destroyed on his orders back in 1991. (Even had the munitions not been destroyed, they would have deteriorated substantially by 2003, perhaps to the point where they would have been unusable.) More instructive, in November 2002, Saddam Hussein succumbed to the pressure of a huge U.S. military buildup in Kuwait and the Bush administration's increasingly strident rhetoric about the necessity of regime change in Baghdad. He permitted the UN inspectors to return and gave them more or less unfettered access to suspected weapons sites. Thus, coercive U.S. diplomacy had in effect forced Saddam to capitulate on the very issue that formed the primary public rationale for the coming war. If he had any WMDs, the inspectors, who then had access to previously off-limits presidential palaces and other government compounds, would eventually find them, and the inspectors' presence would forestall any attempted use of WMDs. The inspectors had four months to find any WMDs and examined 141 sites before they were pulled out because of the impending U.S. invasion. They reported that there was "no evidence or plausible indication of the revival of a nuclear weapons program in Iraq."[46]

How different the world might look now had Bush pocketed his enormous victory of coercing Saddam Hussein into accepting an inspection regime's "occupation" of his country, an occupation that would have precluded the necessity for a U.S. invasion and made a laughingstock of Hussein's pretensions on the world stage by exposing the emperor with no WMD clothes! At a minimum, the United States would have been spared a costly and unnecessary war, and Islamist terrorist organizations would have been denied another cause célèbre, to say nothing of a huge new recruiting and training ground. Additionally, the U.S. effort to establish the military and economic conditions for Afghanistan's political reconstruction would not have been starved of probable success by the massive diversion of American resources into Iraq. The resurrection of a neo-Taliban insurgency and Afghanistan's international reappearance as the world's leading opium exporter must be counted among the many opportunity costs of the decision to invade and occupy Iraq.

The White House's obsession with removing the Iraqi dictator, however, blocked any recognition of its stunning diplomatic triumph. The Bush administration wanted war, not inspections. As later recounted by Hans Blix, the director of the UN Monitoring, Verification, and Inspection Commission (UNMOVIC), "Although the inspection organization was now operating at full strength and Iraq seemed determined to give it prompt access everywhere, the United States appeared as determined to replace our inspection force with an invasion army."[47] The White House was completely indifferent to UNMOVIC's failure to discover any WMDs, even though the suspected sites that the United States and several other countries supplied to UNMOVIC "were supposedly the best that the various intelligence agencies could give." Blix was prompted to wonder, "Could there be 100-percent certainty about the existence of weapons of mass destruction but zero-percent knowledge about their location?"[48] Clearly, a disarmed Saddam Hussein was not enough for Bush; the dictator himself would have to go.

The conclusion that regime change always trumped finding WMDs as a war aim is reinforced by the Pentagon's invasion plan, which displayed a manifest indifference to seizing and securing suspected WMD sites. There was no directive from the Office of the Secretary of Defense to search for WMDs; incredibly, Rumsfeld believed that responsibility for the critical mission upon which the case for war had been made lay with presidential envoy L. Paul "Jerry" Bremer III and not the Defense Department![49] Only on the eve of the invasion did the U.S. Army's chief intelligence officer for the invasion take it upon himself to throw together a scratch force, but these personnel were untrained in the challenges of finding and securing WMDs, especially given the vague or outdated information on the master list of 946 locations the Defense Intelligence Agency had identified as possible WMD storage sites or production facilities.[50]

Did administration policymakers take the Iraqi WMD threat seriously? If not, why not? And if so, why wasn't capturing the sites assigned top operational priority? Indeed, if the administration's primary concern was the possibility of WMDs, especially fissile material and even finished weapons, falling into al Qaeda's hands, why didn't it focus on the most likely potential source of proliferation, namely, the poorly guarded Soviet weapons and highly enriched uranium storage facilities in Russia?

To seize and secure Iraq's suspected WMDs would have required a sufficiently large and dedicated invasion force to capture the hundreds of suspected sites quickly (before terrorists and profiteers got to them) and to seal Iraq's long borders to prevent any munitions and chemical and biological warfare substances from being spirited out of the country. For example, U.S. forces failed to secure the 120-acre Tuwaitha Nuclear Research Center (believed to have contained almost two tons of partially enriched uranium) before unknown people ransacked it.[51] (In July 2003, an IAEA inspection team reported that at least ten kilograms of uranium compounds, suitable for use in a radiological device, or a so-called dirty bomb, were missing from Tuwaitha.)[52] If, in fact, the main purpose of the invasion was to disarm Iraq—to remove the putative threat Saddam Hussein's possession of WMDs posed—then the invasion plan should have reflected that objective. But it did not.

In *COBRA II: The Inside Story of the Invasion and Occupation of Iraq,* an incisive assessment of the invasion plan and its implementation, Michael Gordon and Bernard Trainor discovered "a surprising contradiction":

> The United States did not have nearly enough troops to secure the hundreds of suspected WMD sites that had supposedly been identified in Iraq or to secure the nation's long, porous borders. Had the Iraqis possessed WMD and terrorist groups been prevalent in Iraq as the administration so loudly asserted, U.S. forces might well have failed to prevent WMD from being spirited out of the country and falling into the hands of the dark forces the administration had declared war against.[53]

Those who planned Operation Iraqi Freedom, chief among them Secretary of Defense Rumsfeld and U.S. Central Command (CENTCOM) commander Gen. Tommy Franks, either did not take the proliferation threat seriously or were dangerously derelict in their duty. Rumsfeld and Franks happily dived into the minutiae of planning the invasion, but they apparently paid little if any attention to the requirement of seizing control of Iraq's much-touted WMD. During the invasion, however, Rumsfeld declared, "We know where they are."[54]

Iraq's conventional military forces were certainly no threat by 2003, and the Bush administration was quite right to convey the impression that the regime's conventional forces could and would be quickly destroyed. The Iraqi air force and navy had virtually disappeared in the 1990s, and the Iraqi army had been reduced to a paper force. Crippled in 1991, further gutted by twelve years of military sanctions, commanded by professionally inferior regime loyalists, and badly positioned and trained to repel or punish a foreign invader, the army was incapable of defending Iraq, much less invading U.S. client-states in the Middle East. It imploded upon contact with U.S. forces. Indeed, until the very end, Saddam Hussein continued to regard an internal coup as the greatest danger his regime faced. Notwithstanding the 1991 Gulf War and the more recent U.S. destruction of the Taliban regime in Afghanistan, he still viewed the United States as a weak-willed superpower incapable of forcing him from power.[55]

Thus, on the eve of the U.S. invasion, Saddam Hussein was contained and deterred. He posed no significant threat to the United States and no unmanageable threat to regional U.S. security interests. Iraq was a nuisance and an irritant but not a deadly menace. As Colin Powell told an interviewer a week after the 9/11 attacks, "Iraq isn't going anywhere. It's in a fairly weakened state. It's doing some things we don't like. We will continue to contain it."[56] Gen. Anthony Zinni, who was Gen. Tommy Franks's predecessor as commander of U.S. CENTCOM, believes that Saddam posed little threat. "We bombed him almost at will," he said in a 2004 speech to the Center for Defense Information. "No one in the region felt threatened by Saddam. . . . So to say that containment didn't work, I think is not only wrong . . . but the proof is in the pudding, in what kind of [Iraqi] military our troops faced when we went in there. It disintegrated in front of us."[57]

Iraq's fellow states in the axis of evil, Iran and North Korea, posed far more serious threats to U.S. security interests in the Persian Gulf and Northeast Asia, respectively. Indeed, Baathist Iraq served as a barrier to the expansion of Iranian power and influence in the Gulf, which is why the Reagan administration backed Saddam Hussein in his war against the Ayatollah Khomeini's Iran. Whatever else the secular Iraqi dictator may have been, he was an enemy of both the mullahs in Tehran and Islamist extremism in his own country. Saddam Hussein's Iraq had not experienced any suicide bombings;[58] indeed, he had effectively thwarted the establishment of an Islamist terrorist organizational presence in Iraq. The al Qaeda in Iraq organization emerged only in post-Baathist Iraq.

Iraq's weakness relative to Iran and North Korea figured prominently among the myriad motivations that plunged the Bush administration into the present war. Clearly, by the fall of 2002 at the very latest, the White House was determined to launch a preventive war against Iraq regardless of its objectively meager case that Iraq posed a grave and gathering danger to the United States. It wanted war no matter what. Equally clearly, the administration was captivated by its speedy and easy destruction of the Taliban regime in Afghanistan and believed it could gain a quick and decisive victory in Iraq. (The U.S. win in Afghanistan appears far less decisive today than it did in 2001, given the survival of Osama bin Laden and the Taliban leader Mullah Omar and the reappearance of an increasingly sophisticated neo-Taliban insurgency that by 2008 had gained control of much of southern and eastern Afghanistan. Indeed, the war in Afghanistan never really ended, and the writ of Hamid Karzai's central government does not extend much beyond Kabul. The U.S.-led NATO counterinsurgency campaign in Afghanistan suffers from insufficient force, inconsistent strategy, excessive reliance on airpower, and conflicting rules of engagement. Making matters worse has been, as noted, Afghanistan's reemergence as the world's leading supplier of opium. The Iraq War essentially starved Afghanistan of U.S. military and other resources that might have converted the country from a failed state into a functioning one.)[59]

Decisions for wars of choice rest on a reasonable assumption of success; absent military feasibility, otherwise convincing arguments for war are moot. Iraq was clearly the lowest hanging fruit among the three states the president had publicly named as candidates for forcible regime change. It could be crushed with relatively little collateral damage and with virtually no risk of effective Iraqi retaliation. Though Iran and North Korea were more dangerous, they were also much tougher regimes to defeat militarily than the relatively feeble regime in Iraq was. Unlike Baghdad, which had virtually no means of striking back against a U.S. attack, Tehran had regional terrorist options and could disrupt the flow of oil out of the Persian Gulf. The subsequent U.S. military occupation of Iraq also provided Iran an abundance of targets for retaliation. Finally, Iran had powerful friends in Russia and China and had secretly buried much of its nuclear activities in subterranean sites in populated areas, posing intelligence challenges and, in the event of U.S. air strikes, virtually guaranteeing high levels of collateral damage. Pyongyang was believed to have nuclear weapons. It was also in a position, via its massed artillery just north of the demilitarized zone, to rain destruction on the greater Seoul area. War with North Korea would have threatened catastrophic damage to South Korea, because the "North Koreans would perceive and respond to a U.S. attack on their nuclear infrastructure not as a limited counterproliferation action but as the beginning of a general war on the Korean peninsula meant to bring down the [Pyongyang] regime."[60] Such a war, according to Gen. Gary Luck, then former commander of U.S. forces in South Korea, would entail economic costs of $1 trillion and result in 1 million casualties.[61] Beyond the probable horrific levels of collateral damage, additional factors restraining the United States were the lack of a reliable intelligence picture of North Korea's vast, underground nuclear weapons program and South Korea's staunch opposition to any U.S. attack on North Korea.

Iraq, in short, was helpless, whereas Iran and North Korea were not. Andrew Bacevich has observed that, in 2003, "neither the Baath Party regime nor the Iraqi army, crippled by defeat and well over a decade of punishing sanctions, threatened anyone except the Iraqi people." Because the "hawks within the Bush administration understood this quite well," Bacevich believes, "[t]hey hankered to invade Iraq not because Saddam was strong and dangerous but because he was weak and vulnerable, not because he was implicated in 9/11 but because he looked like an easy mark."[62] Bush chose war with Iraq because it was feeble; he grudgingly chose diplomacy with Iran and North Korea because war with either would have involved substantial military risks.

Mobilizing American public opinion for war with Iraq required presenting a worst-case depiction of its threat while putting the costs and consequences of overthrowing Saddam Hussein in the best possible light.

Yes, a war was necessary, but it was going to be quick and cheap. The administration correctly judged the destruction of the dictator's regime to be a relatively easy military task, but it profoundly misjudged its potential political and strategic results. War planning focused almost exclusively on dispatching the old regime as rapidly and cheaply as possible and at the expense of thinking about what would replace it and how. In some cases, the administration's war aims amounted to little more than expectations based on wishful thinking and reinforced by a self-serving embrace of faulty historical analogies.[63] For example, the administration assumed that some form of democratic governance would naturally arise from the ashes of Baathist rule. After all, had not democracy emerged in Japan during America's postwar occupation? The administration further assumed that America's manifestly good intentions in Iraq and the Iraqi people's gratitude for being liberated from tyranny would foreclose the possibility of postwar armed resistance to U.S. forces. Again, was this not the case when the Allies liberated France?

"We have great information," Cheney assured skeptical House Majority Leader Dick Armey in the summer of 2002. "They're going to welcome us. It will be like the American army going through the streets of Paris. They're sitting there ready to form a new government. The people will be so happy with their freedoms that we'll probably back ourselves out of there within a month or two."[64]

Indeed, the White House felt the war in Iraq was going to be easier than what transpired in Afghanistan. "It is important for the world to see that first of all, Iraq is a sophisticated society with about $16 billion [in annual oil] income," President Bush declared to a group of American conservative thinkers in the Oval Office just before the invasion. "The degree of difficulty compared to Afghanistan in terms of the reconstruction effort, or from emerging from dictatorship, is, like, infinitesimal. I mean Afghanistan has *zero*." By contrast, "Iraq is a sophisticated society. And it's a society that can emerge and show the Muslim world that it's possible to have peace on its borders without rallying the extremists. And the other thing that will happen will be, there will be less exportation of terror out of Iraq."[65]

Confidence that a quick and easy victory lay ahead in Iraq begs the question of "how to assess the guileless optimism of the war's architects," observes Stephen Holmes, "especially when professed by men who vaunt their lack of illusions. Had they never heard of worst-case scenarios? What sort of foreign policy assumes that democracy has no historical, cultural, economic, and psychological preconditions?"[66] The apparent assumption was that democracy is society's natural state and that it automatically resurfaces once "unnatural" tyranny is removed. "There was a tendency among promoters of the war to believe that democracy was a default condition to which societies would revert once liberated from dictators," recounts Francis Fukuyama, a neoconservative who once supported the war but now believes it was a mistake.[67] There seemed to be no recognition, much less an understanding, either of the often long and violent history characterizing the transition from autocracy to democracy or of the possibility that antidemocratic organizations, such as Hamas and Hezbollah, would exploit elections, free speech, and other democratic institutions to expand their political power.

Danielle Pletka, the American Enterprise Institute's vice president for foreign and defense policy studies, confesses that before the invasion,

> I felt secure in the knowledge that all who yearn for freedom, once free, would use it well. I was wrong. There is no freedom gene, no inner guide that understands the virtues of civil society, of secret ballots, of political parties. And it turns out that living under Saddam Hussein's tyranny for decades conditioned Iraqis to accept unearned leadership, to embrace sect and tribe over ideas, and to tolerate unbridled corruption.[68]

The administration's other apparent assumption was that the instrument of tyranny's removal in Iraq—U.S. military power—was irresistible. There was no expectation of an insurgent response, much less an appreciation of the limits of American conventional military supremacy as an instrument for effecting fundamental political change in foreign lands and for dealing with the challenges of irregular warfare. Perhaps this arrogance was not surprising for a White House and neoconservative community mesmerized by America's military power and committed to a "war on terror" that from the beginning inflated the importance of military solutions to what at bottom are political problems. The U.S. military experience in Vietnam, Lebanon, and Somalia—indeed, the larger history of Western military performance against determined irregular foes—ought to have alerted policymakers to the risks inherent in a Western military invasion of a non-Western country. But it did not. Beyond the realm of operational planning, the war's potential costs and risks were essentially ignored.

It was apparently unimaginable to the administration's principal war proponents that some Iraqis, especially those of the politically dominant minority Sunni Arab community who were about to be forcibly dispossessed of their power, might regard an American invasion and occupation of Iraq as acts of conquest to be resisted by all available means, including the tried and tested methods of insurgent guerrilla warfare. The possibility that an invasion might also provoke the administrative collapse of the Iraqi state, leaving U.S. forces adrift in a sea of anarchy, evidently escaped the administration's imagination as well even though, for all practical purposes, Saddam Hussein *was* the Iraqi state.

The combination of self-serving, bogus assumptions about the danger and urgency of the Iraqi threat to America's security and of the equally self-serving, wishful thinking about the costs and consequences of removing that threat by force condemned Operation Iraqi Freedom to strategic failure.

The Bush administration wanted war with Iraq because it wanted to destroy Saddam Hussein's regime; moreover, it wanted to destroy that regime so badly that it conjured up the specter of a grave and gathering mortal threat to the United States that did not in fact exist. President Bush and Vice President Cheney may indeed have believed, or convinced themselves, that Saddam Hussein posed such a danger. But it is also true that selling the war as one of necessity, rather than as the war of choice it actually was, was essential to mobilizing the necessary public and congressional support for launching it. Pitching Saddam as a "mad" and "unbalanced" leader who was prepared to attack the United States, armed with weapons of mass destruction, and allied to al Qaeda proved a powerful and terrifying image to an American electorate still reeling from the shocks of 9/11. Any American president who failed to annihilate such a despot and his regime would have been guilty of criminal dereliction of duty. But the Iraq that the Bush administration invaded posed no significant, much less mortal, threat to the United States.

Why, then, the invasion?

— FOUR —

THE REASONS WHY

There is still—and I say this with a heart of sorrow—no Iraqi people but [rather] unimaginable masses of human beings, devoid of any patriotic idea, imbued with religious traditions and absurdities, connected by no common tie, giving ear to evil, prone to anarchy and perpetually ready to rise against any government whatsoever.

—King Faisal of Iraq,
March 1933[1]

A friendly, free, and oil-producing Iraq would leave Iran isolated and Syria cowed; the Palestinians more willing to negotiate seriously with Israel; and Saudi Arabia with less leverage over policymakers here and in Europe. Removing Saddam Hussein and his henchmen from power presents a genuine opportunity—one President Bush sees clearly—to transform the political landscape of the Middle East.

—William Kristol,
testimony before the Senate Foreign Relations
Committee, February 7, 2002[2]

The "whys" of the Iraq War are multiple and varied. Some overlap; others contradict; still others have been discredited by events in Iraq since the U.S. invasion. The case for war rested on what amounted to a loose coalition of arguments, motives, hopes, and expectations. The Bush administration could publicly coalesce around the specter it exploited to mobilize public opinion—a nuclear-armed Saddam Hussein allied to al Qaeda—but beyond that there were other agendas at play.

In identifying and examining these agendas, it is useful to distinguish between those war proponents who were motivated mainly or even solely by perpetuating America's global military hegemony and those who, while supportive of hegemony, were inspired primarily by the vision of a global democratic peace and, more specifically, the vision of a democratic Iraq that would serve as a model for the rest of the Middle East. The first group has been labeled "primacists" and "nationalist hawks" and the second as "neo-Wilsonians" and "democratic imperialists." The distinction is important because the groups' corresponding belief systems contributed to the disastrous lack of preparation for events in post-Baathist Iraq. The primacists' focus is on preventing or defeating challenges to U.S. hegemony and not on remaking the world in America's image. Primacists are more or less indifferent to the goal of spreading democracy overseas except insofar as it advances U.S. strategic dominance. For primacists, the main job in Iraq was to destroy the Baathist regime and its potential to threaten future U.S. military freedom of action in the Persian Gulf. This job encompassed neither a prolonged occupation nor nation building. The administration's primacists, among them Secretary Rumsfeld and Vice President Cheney, believed that the armed forces' purpose was to fight and win wars and not police foreign civil unrest or run civic action programs to win hearts and minds. Thus, the Defense Department, at Rumsfeld's request and backed by Cheney, was granted responsibility for handling post-Baathist Iraq. For Rumsfeld, Operation Iraqi Freedom was the opportunity

> to prove that the Afghan success story was a model for future operations. His scheme for the Iraq campaign seemed designed to be a lightning raid, at the conclusion of which the raiders would return to base. He showed little interest in what would happen to the

country once the regime had been destroyed. His main concern was that American forces should not remain to put down roots as part of some Clinton-style nation-building exercise, as had happened in the Balkans.[3]

For democratic imperialists, military hegemony is not an end but a means to an end: the whole point of having military hegemony is to use it to advance American political values around the world. Getting rid of Saddam's regime was simply the precondition for Iraq's political reconstruction. Though democratic imperialists failed to envisage the difficulties in transforming Iraq into a democracy—some believed democracy would naturally arise following the country's liberation by the United States—they nonetheless understood that regime change involved more than simply overthrowing the old regime. For democratic imperialists, the great historical referent experience was the U.S. transformation of defeated Nazi Germany and imperial Japan, and they cited both examples as proof of what could be done in Iraq.

Unfortunately, the democratic imperialists, who included Wolfowitz, Feith, and the later converts Bush and Rice, never crafted a plan to introduce democratic governance in Iraq. They failed to marshal any experts on Iraq or on democratic institution building, to create an organization to integrate the various tasks of Iraq's political reconstruction, and to establish firm political control over U.S. military operations in Iraq. They apparently believed that the political situation in post-invasion Iraq would somehow take care of itself. Some had faith that returning Iraqi exiles, notably Ahmed Chalabi and his Iraqi National Congress, would establish a popular and stable post-Baathist government in Baghdad. Yet by turning both the war and the postwar over to the Defense Department, the White House guaranteed what in effect became the primacists' hostile takeover of the democratic imperialists' agenda in Iraq.

What follows is an identification and critical discussion of the various objectives war proponents sought or hoped to accomplish by invading Iraq and overthrowing Saddam Hussein. To repeat, different war hawks had different motives and expectations. For example, whereas Rumsfeld saw in Iraq an opportunity to vindicate his conception of modern warfare in the face of widespread U.S. Army skepticism and even opposition, Wolfowitz, an intellectual and true believer in the possibility and imperative of ridding the Middle East of tyranny, saw in Iraq the opportunity to establish a democracy that others in the region would be compelled by popular pressure to emulate. The reasonableness of the proponents' objectives also varied widely. Some, like overthrowing Saddam Hussein's regime, were quite feasible; others, such as establishing democracy in Iraq, were very problematic; and still others, such as expunging terrorism, were fantastic. Simply identifying the various motives and expectations of those who wanted war is not enough, however; those motives and explanations beg for critical assessment, especially given the Iraq War's largely disastrous consequences for the United States. As was the case with the Truman administration's decision to cross the 38th Parallel in Korea in 1950 and the Johnson administration's decision to commit U.S. ground combat forces to South Vietnam's defense in 1965, the Bush administration's decision to invade Iraq was anchored in a swamp of false assumptions, wishful thinking, poor reasoning, and cultural and historical ignorance.

Eliminating Iraq as a post-9/11 security threat (however inflated) served as the primary official rationale for the war, and the Bush White House undoubtedly believed, or at least wanted to believe, that Iraq posed a "grave and gathering" danger to the United States. The administration certainly sold the war to the American electorate on that basis. Although there were other motives for going to war that were unrelated to U.S. security, they were, even collectively, insufficient to persuade most Americans that a war with Iraq was necessary.

One of the administration's major motives was *to redeem the false victory of 1991*. A remarkable aspect of America's two wars against Iraq is the continuity of the key decision makers involved. Saddam Hussein and Tariq Aziz provided the critical continuity on Iraq's side, whereas George H.

W. Bush, Cheney, Powell, Rice, and Wolfowitz provided it for the American side. By the late 1990s on the American side (except for Powell, who opposed both wars with Iraq), there was a growing feeling that the 1991 Gulf War had been a hollow victory. This view was especially strong among leading neoconservatives, including those who had moved into the George W. Bush administration. Many had believed Operation Desert Storm's stunning military victory would provoke Saddam Hussein's overthrow, but the Iraqi dictator remained in power, defying the United States and the international community. He became a standing embarrassment to American foreign policy, a symbol of the limits of U.S. conventional military supremacy, and even proof that Americans lacked the political will to vanquish their adversaries.

Saddam Hussein's survival, especially after his implication in an alleged plot to assassinate George H. W. Bush during the former president's 1993 visit to Kuwait, meant that not marching on to Baghdad in 1991 had been a mistake. Hussein's destruction became a family matter. In 1998 the younger Bush told a friend, "Dad made a mistake in not going into Iraq when he had an approval rating in the nineties. If I'm ever in that situation, I'll use it—I'll spend my political capital." During the 2000 presidential election campaign, the younger Bush told PBS's Jim Lehrer, "I'm just as frustrated as many Americans are that Saddam still lives. I will tell you this: If we catch him developing weapons of mass destruction in any way, shape, or form, I'll deal with him in a way he won't like."[4] And, of course, there was the very personal aspect: "There's no doubt that [Saddam's] hatred is mainly directed at us," said Bush in a September 28, 2002, radio address. "There's no doubt he can't stand us. After all, this is a guy that tried to kill my dad at one time."[5] (Understandably, Bush did not mention that during the Gulf War of 1991, the Coalition's air forces under the authority of his dad tried to kill Saddam Hussein by targeting all of the dictator's known residences and suspected road convoys.)[6]

Neoconservative opinion unanimously condemned the unfinished war of 1991 as well as the Clinton administration's refusal to take Saddam

Hussein down. In *The War over Iraq*, Lawrence Kaplan and William Kristol predictably condemned the George H. W. Bush and Clinton administrations' policies toward Iraq:

> [The] first Bush and Clinton administrations opted for a combination of incomplete military operations and diplomatic accommodation. Rather than press hard for a change of regime, President Bush halted the U.S. war against Iraq prematurely and turned a blind eye as Saddam slaughtered the insurgents whom the United States had encouraged to revolt. For its part, the Clinton administration avoided confronting the moral and strategic challenge presented by Saddam, hoping instead that an increasingly weak policy of containment, punctuated by the occasional fusillade of cruise missiles, would suffice to keep Saddam in his box.[7]

Indeed, many neoconservatives, seeing in George W. Bush the foreign policy son of the father, supported Senator John McCain in the 2000 Republican presidential primaries and then did not hesitate, at least before 9/11, to lambaste the new president Bush for being soft on Saddam. On July 30, 2001, former CIA officer and neoconservative author Reuel Marc Gerecht denounced the Bush administration's Iraq policy in the influential neoconservative journal the *Weekly Standard*. In an essay entitled "The Cowering Superpower," Gerecht declared,

> From the spring of 1996, the Clinton Administration's Iraq policy was in meltdown; under the Bush administration, it has completely liquefied. . . . It would be better to see the Administration start explaining how we will live with Saddam and his nuclear weapons than to see senior Bush officials, in the manner of the Clintonites, fib to themselves and the public.[8]

Would there have been a second U.S. war against Iraq had there not been a first? Had Saddam not invaded Kuwait in 1991, or had the George

H. W. Bush administration decided not to reverse the invasion of Kuwait by force, what would the level of enmity have been between the United States and Iraq and between the Bush family and Saddam Hussein? Would the 9/11 attacks have been sufficient to trigger an American invasion in 2003? Christian Alfonsi believes that

> what made the invasion of Iraq inevitable was Saddam Hussein's triumph over the Bush national security team in 1992 [by surviving the 1991 war while Bush suffered political defeat in the United States], and the fear that he would repeat the triumph in 2004. This fixation on Saddam ran through the Bush dynasty like a malignant strain of DNA, a pathogen always a threat to appear under the right conditions of crisis. . . . Once this pathogen had been released into the American body politic [following the 9/11 attacks], the views of the neoconservatives about regime change in Iraq provided a foreign policy rationale for the war, and faulty intelligence about weapons of mass destruction provided a political rationale that resonated with the American people.[9]

Alfonsi's judgment suggests that there would have been no second war against Iraq had George W. Bush not been elected in 2000 and had Vice President Al Gore assumed the presidency instead. This question, of course, can never be answered, but it is worthy of speculation given the consequences of the Bush decision for war.

A centrist Democratic president certainly would not have brought into office the foreign policy team that Bush did, including a reactionary and unilateralist vice president who exerted unparalleled influence on policy and a secretary of defense who, in alliance with the vice president, effectively marginalized the State Department and the president's national security adviser in foreign policy decision making. Furthermore, it is most unlikely that neoconservatives would have exerted the kind of influence on a Gore administration that they did on the Bush White House. The neoconservatives despised the Clinton administration, which Gore served, for its embrace of multilateralism, lack of resolve in using force, and toleration of Saddam Hussein's continuance in power. These circumstances, in turn, suggest that a Gore White House would not have used the 9/11 attacks as justification for an invasion of Iraq. Vice President Gore was much more knowledgeable and experienced in foreign policy than George W. Bush was, and he had worked in an administration that was a great deal more alert to the al Qaeda threat than was the pre-9/11 Bush White House. It is thus reasonable to argue that a Gore administration would not have expanded a necessary war against al Qaeda into an unnecessary war against Iraq. Indeed, it is hard to see how the United States would have waged a war with Iraq in 2003 absent the confluence of George W. Bush, neoconservative influence, and 9/11.

———————

Another objective of the Iraq War was *to demonstrate a new willingness to use force*. During the 1990s, the neoconservatives, many of whom would enter the upper tiers of the George W. Bush administration in 2001 and push for war against Iraq, were openly contemptuous of the disparity between U.S. conventional military supremacy and any presidential unwillingness to use it aggressively on behalf American interests and values. They worried that

> the United States, the world's dominant power on whom the maintenance of international peace and the support of liberal democratic principles depends, will shrink from its responsibilities and—in a fit of absent-mindedness, or parsimony, or indifference— allow the international order that it created and sustained to collapse. Our present danger is one of declining military strength, flagging will and confusion about our world.[10]

They deplored post–Cold War cuts in defense spending and the Vietnam War's chilling effects on America's willingness to use force and use it decisively. Especially galling was the persistence of those effects long after the

Soviet Union's demise, which in their view removed the principal check on the expansion of U.S. power and influence in the world. The United States was mired in strategic bewilderment at a time when it ought to have been using its global hegemony to topple tyrannies worldwide. Thus, "the idea of regime change [in Iraq] gripped neoconservative intellectuals as an unambiguous, principled blueprint for action backed by overwhelming military force that would reassert the moral primacy and unchallenged political power of the United States as the world's lone superpower."[11]

Neoconservatives were particularly dismissive of the Weinberger-Powell Doctrine, which they (rightly) believed proscribed the use of force in all but the most exceptionally favorable military and political circumstances. In their view, the doctrine was a recipe for inaction or, worse, appeasement. They were highly critical of the manner in which the Gulf War was terminated because it left Saddam Hussein in power. As David Frum and Richard Perle succinctly put it, "Saddam had survived; therefore, we had lost."[12] The neoconservatives also deplored the Clinton administration's hesitant and half-hearted uses of force in Somalia, Haiti, and the Balkans—all examples, they believed, of the Vietnam syndrome's persistent crippling of American statecraft.[13] They favored forcible regime change in Baghdad long before 9/11 and condemned the Clinton White House for its lack of decisiveness in dealing with Saddam Hussein.

The neoconservatives believed that the Vietnam War and America's subsequent hesitant uses (and nonuses) of force adversely affected America's strategic reputation and encouraged its enemies, including Saddam Hussein and Osama bin Laden, to believe that the United States had become a gutless superpower (or, in Richard Nixon's famous characterization, "a pitiful, helpless giant") and a state whose military might vastly exceeded its will to use it. The United States was defeated in Vietnam, run out of Lebanon and Somalia, and had become so casualty phobic by the time of its Balkan interventions that it placed the safety of its military forces above the missions they were designed to accomplish. The neoconservatives felt Iraq offered a seemingly low-cost opportunity to demonstrate the credibility of American power and to strengthen deterrence by putting other actual and aspiring rogue states on notice that defying the United States invited military destruction. Michael Ledeen, a leading neoconservative proponent of preventive war against Iraq and Iran, summed up the neoconservative mood long before the Iraq War. "Every ten years of so," he said in a speech to the American Enterprise Institute, "the US needs to take some crappy little country and throw it against the wall, just to show we mean business."[14] Richard Clarke believes that "Bush personally went to war [against Iraq] chiefly to prove that the United States was undeterred by 9/11, that we could take combat casualties without running away, and that we could beat up the region's biggest bully."[15] Richard Haass belies that Bush "and those around him wanted to send a message to the world that the United States was willing and able to act decisively. Liberating Afghanistan was a start, but in the end it didn't scratch the itch. . . . He may have also sought to accomplish what his father did not."[16]

Bush, Cheney, and Rumsfeld also thought that America's reputation encouraged America's enemies to be aggressive. As Rumsfeld informed reporters shortly after the 9/11 attacks, "A lot of people in the world had come to conclude that the United States was gun-shy, that we were risk-averse. The President and I concluded that whenever it occurred down the road that the United States was under some sort of threat of attack, the United States would be leaning forward, not back."[17] Bush believed that the 9/11 attacks were the product of terrorists "who saw our response to the hostage crisis in Iran, the bombings [of] the Marine barracks in Lebanon, the first World Trade Center attack, the killing of American soldiers in Somalia, the destruction of the two embassies in Africa, and the attack on the USS *Cole*. The terrorists concluded that we lacked the courage and character to defend ourselves, and so they attacked us."[18] Cheney claimed that "the terrorists came to believe that they could strike America without paying any price. And so they continued to wage those attacks, making the world less safe and eventually striking the United States on 9/11 . . . time and time again the terrorists hit America and America did not hit back hard enough."[19] One of Rumsfeld's favorite pronouncements was that "weakness is provocative."

In his last speech as secretary of defense, Rumsfeld warned, "It should be clear not only that weakness is provocative, but the perception of weakness on our part can be provocative as well."[20]

Interestingly, neither the Clinton nor the Bush administrations retaliated against the al Qaeda suicide bombing attack against the USS *Cole* on October 12, 2000, which killed seventeen U.S. naval personnel and nearly sank the warship. The attack occurred three weeks before the 2000 presidential election and three months before Clinton left office. Did the Bush administration's subsequent inaction reflect a failure to take the al Qaeda threat seriously until the 9/11 attacks? John Lehman, a member of the 9/11 Commission and the former secretary of the navy during the Reagan administration, told investigative reporter Philip Shenon that the Bush administration's failure to retaliate for the *Cole* was "astounding. Nobody doubted it was al-Qaeda." But the administration's neoconservatives were "just besotted" with such other issues as missile defense, Iraq, North Korea, and China. "They were living in another world; they had their own construction of the world, and the *Cole* was not part of that world. Al-Qaeda was just not part of their threat scenario." Lehman believes that a retaliatory response to the *Cole* "could well have avoided 9/11. I totally believe that. It would have changed the calculations for Osama."[21]

In fairness it must be said that perceptions of weakness—real or imagined—have repeatedly prompted enemies, from imperial Japan and Nazi Germany to bin Laden, to question America's willingness and ability to fight effectively, especially in protracted, high-casualty wars. Saddam Hussein had low regard for America's fighting power in 1991 and in 2003 because of what he perceived as America's unwillingness to suffer casualties and track record of weak-willed interventions. His outlook on the eve of the Gulf War was that the United States was bluffing and that if it came to war, his forces could inflict politically unacceptable levels of casualties on American forces.[22] Even in 2003, as in 1991, thanks to

the distortions of his ideological perceptions, Saddam simply could not take the Americans seriously. After all, had they not run away from Vietnam after suffering what to him was a "mere" 58,000 dead? Iraq had suffered 51,000 dead in just one battle on the Fao Peninsula against the Iranians. In the 1991 Gulf War, the Americans had appeared to be on the brink of destroying much of the Iraqi military, including the Republican Guard, but then inexplicably stopped—for fear of casualties, in Saddam's view. Somalia, Bosnia, and Kosovo all added to Saddam's belief that the Americans could not possibly launch a ground invasion that would seriously threaten his regime. At best they might be willing to launch an air campaign similar to OPERATION DESERT FOX in 1998 with a few small ground attacks around Iraq's periphery. But from Saddam's point of view, the idea that the Americans would attack all the way to Baghdad appeared ludicrous.[23]

No less a target of the neoconservatives' ire was the Clinton administration's embrace of multilateralism. Neoconservatives viewed allies, alliances, and especially the United Nations as encumbrances on America's use of force. Their exhibit A was the 1999 NATO war with Serbia over Kosovo, in which potentially swift and decisive military action was sacrificed on the altar of preserving the lowest common denominator of political consensus within the alliance. Neoconservatives also believed the Soviet Union's disappearance reduced the strategic value of allies, whose potential military contributions to collective action were in any event declining as the U.S. lead in advanced military technologies widened. They felt the United States then could and therefore should act alone unless its allies were available free of political charge. An attendant belief was that American power, by virtue of its service on behalf of such universal values as freedom and democracy, was inherently legitimate. In *The War over Iraq*, Kaplan and Kristol condemned former vice president Gore for characterizing the Bush Doctrine's commitment to American preeminence as glorifying the notion of dominance. "Well," they asked, "what's wrong with dominance in the service of sound principles and high ideals?"[24] Neoconservatives are true believers in

American exceptionalism and the universality of American values. For them, U.S. military action against Iraq required no international legitimization in the form of a UN or NATO mandate.

Thus, in addition to demonstrating the credibility of U.S. military power to America's enemies, an invasion of Iraq would also show America's friends and allies, many of whom opposed the war, that the United States would no longer permit its freedom of military action to be constrained by allied opinion or the perceived need for prior international legitimization. The United States was prepared to act unilaterally even in defiance of world opinion. From the start of its confrontation with Iraq, the Bush administration made it clear that it would take military action against Baghdad with or without UN, NATO, or other international approval. Vice President Cheney opposed the very idea of soliciting a UN mandate. As far as the Bush White House was concerned, America's allies could either follow or get out of the way.

The issue of political will gained ever greater prominence as OIF descended into a protracted war. Along with promoting democracy, the "will to victory" replaced the war aim of eliminating Iraq's nonexistent WMD threat. As the war dragged on and became increasingly unpopular and as the White House searched in vain for a winning strategy, "staying the course"— i.e., avoiding defeat—became the administration's mantra. President Bush repeatedly declared that Iraq was a test of American will, that the insurgents' strategy targeted America's political stamina, and that if the United States abandoned its commitment to Iraq, horrible things would follow, including the expansion of Iran's power and influence in the Middle East. "There would be nothing worse for world peace," he told a Pennsylvania audience in October 2007, "[than] if the Iranians believed that the United States didn't have the will and commitment to help young democracies survive. If we left before the job was done, there would be chaos. Chaos would embolden not only the extremists and radicals who would like to do us harm, but it would also embolden Iran."[25]

A major White House objective behind OIF was *to assert the principle of preventive military action*, which is not to be confused with preemption. Though the Bush administration used the term "preemption" in referring to the need for preventive war, there are key legal and policy differences between preemptive military action and preventive war. Preemption is an attack initiated on the basis of incontrovertible evidence that an enemy attack is imminent. As such, it is an extension of the right of self-defense and therefore permissible under international law. Actual cases of preemption are rare. Prior to the Iraq War, the most oft-cited modern example was Israel's preemption of what appeared to be an impending Egyptian attack in June 1967.

Preventive war, in contrast, is war initiated in the belief that military conflict, while not imminent, is inevitable and that to delay action would involve greater risk. The logic of preventive war runs something like this: you and I are going to wage war sooner or later. Currently I'm stronger than you are, but knowing I won't be as time passes, I start the war with you right now. Preventive war is launched to forestall the consequences of unfavorable trends in the military balance between the attacker and the attacker's enemy. It is thus indistinguishable from outright aggression, and, indeed, most wars, including the Iraq War, are initiated for preventive reasons. Saddam Hussein posed no imminent threat to the United States in 2003 for he was certainly not preparing to attack the United States (or any U.S. allies). But the Bush administration believed that war with Saddam Hussein was inevitable (a self-fulfilling prophecy if there ever was one), and that it was better to have that war before Iraq acquired nuclear weapons. From the late 1940s through the early 1960s, significant pressures in the United States pushed for preventive war against the Soviet Union and Communist China before they acquired nuclear weapons or nuclear arsenals capable of deterring the United States; however, the Truman, Eisenhower, and Kennedy administrations all rejected preventive war in favor of containment and deterrence.[26]

For the Bush administration, after 9/11, it was imperative not only to demonstrate a new willingness to use force but also to demonstrate that the United States was prepared to strike first. The administration's loud, post-9/11 embrace of preventive war as a matter of declared doctrine was the most significant American foreign policy departure since the Truman administration's adoption of containment in the late 1940s. Its preventive war strategy presupposed the inadequacy of such reliable Cold War policies of deterrence and containment, a conclusion President Bush drew months before ordering the invasion of Iraq. "In the Cold War," stated the White House's 2002 *National Security Strategy*, "we faced a generally status-quo, risk-averse adversary. . . . But deterrence based on a threat of retaliation is less likely to work against states more willing to take risks, gambling with the lives of their people, and the wealth of their nation. . . . Traditional concepts of deterrence will not work against a terrorist enemy."[27] In an earlier speech at West Point, Bush declared, "Deterrence, the promise of massive retaliation against nations, means nothing to shadowy terrorist networks with no nation or citizens to defend." He added, "Containment is not possible when unbalanced dictators with weapons of mass destruction can deliver those weapons or secretly provide them to terrorist allies."[28]

In the run-up to the Iraq War, President Bush made repeated statements to the effect that a nuclear-armed Saddam Hussein would be undeterrable and therefore the United States had to remove him from power before he acquired nuclear weapons.[29] He made the classic argument for preventive war: since war with Iraq was inevitable, the United States should initiate it before the relative military balance became adversely affected by Hussein's possession of deliverable nuclear weapons. Launching a preventive war against Iraq would not only thwart nuclear proliferation in Iraq, it would also embody America's willingness to strike first against perceived emerging threats before they fully matured. "If we wait for security threats to materialize, we will have waited too long," said Bush at West Point. "We cannot let our enemies strike first."[30]

The conflation of al Qaeda and Baathist Iraq, and more generally "shadowy terrorist networks" and rogue states, however, obscured critical differences between non-state actors' and states' vulnerability to deterrence. The assumption, against all logic and the available evidence, that Saddam

Hussein was as undeterrable as Osama bin Laden constituted a strategic error of the first order because it propelled the United States into an unnecessary and strategically disastrous war as well as into endorsing a form of war that violated the central norm of the international political order the United States had established after World War II.[31] President Truman, in rejecting calls for preventive war against the Soviet Union in the late 1940s, declared in a 1950 radio address to his fellow Americans, "We do not believe in aggression or preventive war. Such a war is the weapon of dictators, not [of] free democratic countries like the United States."[32]

The Bush administration's embrace of preventive war also promoted the centerpiece of the neoconservative agenda—preserving America's global military hegemony against any and all comers. As the 2002 *National Security Strategy* declared, "Our forces will be strong enough to dissuade potential adversaries from pursuing a military build-up in hopes of surpassing, or equaling the power of the United States." It went on to lecture China: in "pursuing advanced military capabilities that can threaten its neighbors in the Asia-Pacific region, China is following an outdated path that, in the end, will hamper its own pursuit of national greatness."[33] Regional challengers who refused to be dissuaded thus would face the prospect of credibly demonstrated preventive military action.

———————

Another administration war aim was *to intimidate Iran, North Korea, and other rogue states.* Administration war proponents believed, or at least hoped, that knocking off one axis of evil regime would cow the other two into abandoning their programs to acquire nuclear weapons. OIF would provide a credible demonstration to Tehran and Pyongyang of what could happen to them if they persisted in their attempts to obtain nuclear weapons. Implicit in this belief was the administration's confidence that the United States could achieve a swift and decisive victory in Iraq followed by minimal U.S. force deployments in that country. Writing just after Saddam Hussein had been driven from power but before the emergence of a protracted insurgency in

Iraq, Frum and Perle triumphantly declared that by overthrowing Saddam, "we gave other potential enemies a vivid and compelling demonstration of America's ability to win a swift and total victory over significant enemy forces with minimal U.S. casualties. The overwhelming American victory in the battle of Baghdad surely stamped a powerful impression upon the minds of the rulers of Teheran and Pyongyang."[34]

The administration also apparently assumed that Tehran and Pyongyang *could* be intimidated, even though both had established reputations of stern defiance in response to attempted external coercion. War proponents seemingly dismissed the possibility that OIF might scare Iran and North Korea into accelerating their drive for nuclear weapons capacity. Indeed, the fact that America's conventional military supremacy encouraged rogue states' interest in neutralizing that supremacy via possession of a nuclear deterrent seemed to escape those who believed the road to a nuclear-disarmed Iran and North Korea ran through Baghdad. It can be assumed that neither Pyongyang nor Tehran were discouraged by America's descent into a protracted war in Iraq that sapped U.S. military power and promised to exert as chilling an effect—an Iraq syndrome—on America's subsequent use of force as had the Vietnam syndrome before it.[35] Indeed, the Bush administration's very selection of Iraq over Iran and North Korea as the demonstration target of its policy of counterproliferation via forcible regime change probably hardened Tehran's and Pyongyang's determination to acquire nuclear weapons. As former national security adviser Zbigniew Brzezinski observes, "America's ability to cope with nuclear nonproliferation has . . . suffered [as a result of the U.S. invasion of Iraq]. The contrast between the attack on the militarily weak Iraq and America's forbearance of the nuclear-armed North Korea has strengthened the convictions of the Iranians that their security can only be enhanced by nuclear weapons."[36] Thus, threatening a government with regime change *increases* its desire for nuclear weapons. "Consider what the world looks like to Iran," urges Fareed Zakaria:

It is surrounded by nuclear powers (Russia, India, Pakistan, Israel), and across two of its borders sit tens of thousands of U.S. troops (in Iraq and Afghanistan). The president of the United States has repeatedly made clear that he regards the regime in Tehran as illegitimate, wishes to overthrow it, and funds various groups whose aims are similar. If you were Tehran, would this make you feel like giving up your nuclear program?[37]

Indeed, it is reasonable to argue that the American invasion and occupation of Iraq, far from intimidating Iran, has actually advanced Iran's strategic interests. In Saddam Hussein's Iraq, Iran faced a hostile, highly centralized, Sunni-dominated regime with pan-Arab pretensions. The Iraqi regime posed both a military and ideological threat to Tehran and had already waged a bloody eight-year war with Iran. "As Iran's rulers look next door [today], there is a new Iraq," notes Ray Takeyh. "The once docile and repressed Shi'ite forces have been empowered, and the once imperious Sunni Arabs stand isolated and marginalized." Though the future of Iraq remains uncertain, "one thing that appears definite is that the ideological antagonisms that once led to tension, conflict, and ultimately war between the two states have all but evaporated."[38] Undoubtedly, Takeyh says, "post-Saddam Iraq with its empowered Shi'ite majority is likely to emerge as a close ally, if not actual subsidiary, of the Islamic Republic," which "now stands as one of the principal beneficiaries of America's regime change policy."[39]

Trita Parsi believes the "Bush administration has expedited Iran's emergence as a key power in the Middle East by swiping its immediate rivals—Afghanistan's Taliban and Iraq's Saddam Hussein—off the geopolitical chessboard."[40] Christopher Fettweis goes further:

> For the hard-liners in Tehran, the war in Iraq has been a godsend. Over and over again, one hears that the victor of this war will be Iran, and with good reason: Its regional clout has risen, nascent democratic movements [in Iran] have been silenced, and Iranian credibility in the broader Islamic world [has] received a boost as the United States has floundered.[41]

Indeed, with "so much of the U.S. military tied up in Iraq, the Iranians do not believe the U.S. has the resources to attack them and then deal with the consequences," contends Peter Galbraith. "They know that a U.S. attack on Iran would have little support in the U.S. and none internationally. . . . President Bush's warnings count for little with Teheran because he now has a long record of tough language unmatched by action."[42]

The Bush administration certainly displayed no real understanding of why Iran has long sought to become a nuclear weapons state, a desire situated in the realms of deterrence and prestige rather than in aggressive war. The claim that its possession of even a small number of deliverable nuclear weapons would permit Iran to dominate the Persian Gulf is preposterous. Nuclear weapons are practically worthless as instruments of coercive diplomacy, and under any set of circumstances the United States has the secure retaliatory capacity sufficient to destroy Iran as a state and society. As Thomas Powers has observed,

> The world's experience with nuclear weapons to date has shown that nuclear powers do not use them, and they seriously threaten to use them only to deter attack. Britain, France, Russia, China, Israel, South Africa, India, Pakistan, and North Korea have all acquired nuclear weapons in spite of international opposition. None has behaved recklessly with its new power. What changes is that nuclear powers have to be treated differently; in particular they cannot be casually threatened.[43]

Robert Kagan, a neoconservative historian who avidly supported the decision to invade Iraq, points out that Iran, like China and India, is a proud and ancient civilization that once dominated its region only to be subsequently "plundered, colonized, and humiliated by the European empires."[44] Iran sees itself as the Persian Gulf's natural and rightful hegemon and regards the United States, which for almost two centuries has asserted hegemony in the Western Hemisphere, as the primary obstacle to Iran's regional dominance. Kagan maintains,

Iran defines and ennobles itself by its willingness to stand up to the United States, the predominant and overbearing superpower, which also happens to be the Great Satan. These passions and ambitions long preceded the Bush administration, as did Iran's conviction that only as a nuclear weapons state could it fend off pressures from the American superpower and its allies. It learned this lesson not from the Iraq War of 2003 but from the Iraq War of 1991, when the United States demonstrated how easily it could brush aside the massive Iraqi conventional army that Iran itself had been unable to defeat. But Iran's nuclear program is not only about security. Like India, Iran pursues nuclear weapons to establish itself as a great power in its region and beyond. Because the western liberal world insists on denying Iran its "right" to nuclear power, the question has also become a matter of honor.[45]

Kagan concludes that the "notion that the present Iranian regime would trade away its honor and self-respect, indeed its very sense of itself, in return for material goods such as money or unreliable security guarantees from the Great Satan seems fanciful."[46]

Former Bush administration officials, Israel, and a chorus of neoconservative commentators continue to insist that Iran's possession of nuclear weapons is not acceptable. The argument for possible preventive military action against Iran is familiar: the target regime is a spiteful, undeterrable enemy. Much of the argument rests on the frightening personality of Iranian president Ahmadinejad. Neoconservatives have painted him, just as they did Saddam Hussein, as a madman itching to acquire nuclear weapons, which he would happily transfer to terrorist organizations, and as a modern-day Persian Hitler who has to be stopped before it is too late. A Holocaust denier who has publicly called for Israel's extermination, Ahmadinejad's rantings are scary indeed, as were Hitler's in *Mein Kampf*. While Ahmadinejad is president of a state that has sponsored far more international terrorism than Saddam Hussein ever did, in terms of power wielded he is hardly the führer of Iran.

By 1939, Hitler *was* the Nazi state, having eliminated all potential political rivals and cowed all military dissent. In contrast, the Iranian presidency is relatively weak. Iran is a theocracy in which power is wielded in the first instance by those possessing religious authority, which Ahmadinejad does not. The governing authority in Iran is not the president but the chief of state, or the Supreme Leader Ali Hoseini-Khamenei. The supreme leader, who is appointed for life by an Assembly of Experts consisting of eighty-six religious scholars elected by popular vote for an eight-year term, has the final say over Iran's domestic and foreign policies and can reverse or overrule presidential initiatives. Any decision for war, including the disposition and possible use of weapons of mass destruction, would certainly not be Ahmadinejad's to make.[47]

Ironically, the Bush administration's elimination of Iraq's Baathist regime profited the extremists in Iran far more than it did the United States. Saddam Hussein's Iraq in 2003, though weakened by war and more than a decade's worth of sanctions, nevertheless remained a barrier to Iranian ambitions in the Persian Gulf. Even as U.S. forces were massing for an invasion, the Iraqi dictator continued to regard Iran as the greater external threat to his regime. His regime's collapse not only eliminated a regional rival, but it also opened Iraq to a degree of Iranian political and military penetration that was never possible under Saddam Hussein. Partially offsetting this strategic gain is of course the presence of U.S. military forces in Iraq; however, those forces provide targets for Iranian retaliation, at least until the end of 2011, when the last American troops are scheduled to depart Iraq. Moreover, there is every reason to believe, barring Iraq's disintegration, that any Iraqi government based on the country's Shiite majority will be friendly to Iran. Expelling Saddam Hussein's minority Sunni Arab–based secular regime removed the primary source of Iraqi-Iranian antagonism.

———

One of the Bush White House's most ambitious war aims was *to provoke the political transformation the Middle East*. This goal reflected the neoconservatives' story line on the Middle East, which George Packer captured succinctly before the invasion.

> The Arab world is hopelessly sunk in corruption and popular discontent. Misrule and a culture of victimhood have left Arabs economically stagnant and prone to seeing their problems in delusional terms. The United States has contributed to that pathology by cynically shoring up dictatorships; Sept. 11 was one result. Both the Arab world and official American attitudes toward it need to be jolted out of their rut. An invasion of Iraq would provide the necessary shock, and a democratic Iraq would become an example of change for the rest of the region. Political Islam would lose its hold upon the imagination of young Arabs as they watched a more successful model arise in their midst. The Middle East's center of gravity would shift from the region's theocracies and autocracies to its new, oil-rich democracy. And finally, the deadlock in which Israel and Palestine are trapped would end as Palestinians, realizing that their own backers were now tending their own gardens, would accept compromise. By this way of thinking, the road to Damascus, Teheran, Riyadh and Jerusalem goes through Baghdad.[48]

White House speechwriter Frum has recounted how, as war with Iraq approached, George W. Bush came to see regime change in Baghdad:

> If the United States overthrew Saddam next [after overthrowing the Taliban in Afghanistan, Bush reasoned], it could create a reliable American ally in the potential superpower of the Arab world. With American troops so close, the Iranian people would be emboldened to rise against the mullahs. And as Iran and Iraq built moderate, representative, pro-Western regimes, the pressure on the Saudis and the other Arab states to liberalize and modernize would intensify. It was a great gamble—but also quite a prize.[49]

To be sure, not all of the Bush administration's national security decision makers believed in initiating the transformation of the Middle East via establishing democracy in Iraq. For Wolfowitz and other democratic imperialists, the forceful promotion of democracy in the region was a matter of profound conviction long before the 9/11 attacks. George W. Bush and Condoleezza Rice, who before 9/11 embraced the realist approach to foreign policy and its attendant elevation of stability over democracy, became committed converts to the messianic "freedom" mission only after 9/11. Indeed, Rice, following the president's lead, had surprised her realist colleagues on the National Security Council staff by becoming a "fervent believer" in peace through democratization.[50] In an August 2003 editorial for the *Washington* Post, she said, "Much as a new democratic Germany became a linchpin of a new Europe, so a transformed Iraq can become a key element of a very different Middle East in which the ideologies of hate will not flourish."[51] She later declared to students at the American University in Cairo: "For sixty years, my country . . . pursued stability at the expense of democracy in this region here in the Middle East—and we achieved neither. Now, we are taking a different course. We are supporting the democratic aspirations of all people."[52] Rice, who viewed herself as the president's confidante, friend, tutor, protector, and enabler, apparently supported invading Iraq from the get-go. "There is no evidence that Rice raised major objections to the war or serious questions about the false intelligence that justified it."[53] On the contrary, according to Scott McClellan, "in private, she complemented and reinforced Bush's instincts rather than challenging them or questioning them. As far as I could tell from internal meetings and discussions, Condi invariably fell in line with Bush's thinking. If she wasn't actually shaping his thinking, she knew how to read him and how to translate his ideas, feelings, and proclivities into concrete policies."[54] Rice, like most of Bush's other foreign policy advisers, "played right into his thinking, doing little to question it or to cause him to pause long enough to fully consider the consequences before moving forward."[55] She "was more interested in figuring out where the president stood and just carrying out his wishes while expending only cursory effort on helping him understand all the considerations and potential consequences."[56]

In contrast, primacists Dick Cheney and Donald Rumsfeld never displayed any convincing concern over Iraq's democratic prospects. They were always much more focused on getting rid of Saddam Hussein than on nation building, including bringing democratic governance to Iraq. They preferred, if confronted with the choice, a strategically friendly authoritarian Iraq to an unfriendly democratic Iraq. They did not believe in using U.S. military power to remake the world in America's image.[57] They nonetheless publicly echoed the White House's line on the desirability of transforming the Middle East via regime change in Iraq. For example, in his VFW speech of August 2002, Cheney declared:

> Regime change in Iraq would bring about a number of benefits to the region. When the gravest of threats are eliminated, the freedom-loving peoples of the region will have a chance to promote the values that can bring lasting peace. As for the reaction of the Arab "street," the Middle Eastern expert Fouad Ajami predicts that after liberation, the streets in Basra and Baghdad are "sure to erupt in joy the same way the throngs in Kabul greeted the Americans." Extremists in the region would have to rethink their strategy of jihad. Moderates throughout the region would take heart. And our ability to advance the Israeli-Palestinian peace process would be enhanced, just as it was following the liberation of Kuwait in 1991.[58]

Douglas Feith believes that the aim of democratization was always secondary to removing both Saddam Hussein from power and his threatening WMD "programs," and he chides President Bush for dropping the threat rationale for the war once it became clear that no claimed stockpiles of Iraqi WMD existed. Bush "effectively set aside the rationale for the war. Beginning in the fall of 2003, his public remarks on Iraq changed drastically. By and large, he stopped talking about Saddam's brutal record and the threat posed by the

Iraqi regime." Instead, "he stressed that in Iraq we now have an opportunity to bring *democracy* to the Arab and Muslim worlds." According to Feith, Bush and his key political advisers "apparently decided that the failure to find WMD stockpiles was such an embarrassment that the President should not even try to explain it or put it into context. Rather, the Administration tried to change the subject."[59] Feith believes that by switching from WMD to democratization as the rationale for the war, Bush "changed the definition of success," which in turn "causes many Americans to question why we should be investing so much blood and treasure for Iraqis." Incredibly, Feith still thinks President Bush "had solid grounds for worrying about the dangers of leaving Saddam in power," the most important of which was, in Feith's view, "to end the danger that Saddam might provide biological or [other] weapons of mass destruction to terrorists to use against us."[60]

Scott McClellan contends that "the dream of a democratic Middle East was actually the most powerful force behind President Bush's drive to war." Furthermore, "the decision to downplay the democratic vision as a motive for war was basically a marketing choice" because "Bush and his advisers knew that the American people would almost certainly not support a war launched primarily for the ambitious purpose of transforming the Middle East." The result was "a disconnect between the president's most heartfelt objective in going to war and the publicly stated rationale for that war"—i.e., Iraq's alleged WMD threat.[61] According to McClellan, Bush had a core belief that people everywhere have a right to live in freedom, and

what drove Bush toward military confrontation [with Iraq] more than anything else was an ambitious and idealistic post-9/11 vision of transforming the Middle East through the spread of freedom. This view was grounded in a philosophy of coercive democracy, a belief that Iraq was ripe for conversion from a dictatorship into a beacon of liberty through the use of force, and a conviction that all this could be accomplished at nominal cost. The Iraqis were understood to be a modern, forward-looking people who yearned for liberty but couldn't achieve it under the brutal, tyrannical regime of Saddam Hussein. The president and his leadership team believed victory in Iraq could be achieved swiftly and decisively, and that the Iraqi people would then welcome and embrace freedom.[62]

President Bush actually first publicly endorsed democratic transformation as a war aim in his prewar February 2003 American Enterprise Institute speech and in his March 17 speech in which he gave Saddam Hussein forty-eight hours to leave the country. "Unlike Saddam Hussein," he said, "we believe the Iraqi people are deserving and capable of human liberty. And when the dictator has departed, they can set an example to all of the Middle East of a vital and peaceful and self-governing nation."[63] Replacing dictatorship with democracy, even a democracy imposed by a foreign power (beginning with his American Enterprise Institute speech, Bush repeatedly referenced America's success in transforming imperial Japan into a democracy), would change Iraq from an aggressor into a peaceful state; therefore, it would no longer be considered a threat to global security. Indeed, Bush and the neoconservatives believed that Islamist terrorism was rooted in the prevalence of autocratic rule and economic stagnation in the Arab world; thus, democratization would cure the disease of terrorism.

In a televised address to the nation on September 7, 2003, Bush declared:

> In Iraq, we are helping ... to build a decent and democratic society at the center of the Middle East. ... The Middle East will become a place of progress and peace or it will be an exporter of violence and terror that takes more lives in America and other free nations. The triumph of democracy and tolerance in Iraq, in Afghanistan and beyond would be a grave setback for international terrorism. The terrorists thrive on the support of tyrants and the resentments of oppressed peoples. When tyrants fall, and resentment gives way to hope, men and women in every culture reject the ideologies of terror

and turn to the pursuits of peace. Everywhere that freedom takes hold, terror will retreat.[64]

During the remainder of his presidency, Bush became a vocal exponent of the "democratic peace" theory, which holds that democracies are inherently peaceful toward one another, and of America's mission to promote democracy around the world. In his 2006 edition of *The National Security Strategy of the United States of America,* he declared in Trumanesque fashion, "It is the policy of the United States to seek and support democratic movements and institutions in every nation and culture, with the aim of ending tyranny in our world. In the world today, the fundamental character of regimes matters as much as the distribution of power among them."[65]

The combination of the 9/11 attacks and the influence of neoconservative thinking prompted both Bush and Rice, once self-avowed realists, to embrace the democratic peace theory and the view that America's (and the world's) long-term security is therefore best served by promoting the spread of democracy worldwide. For the Bush White House, this idea meant that the United States should use its strength to change the global status quo, including employing military force to overthrow tyrannical regimes. In selecting Iraq as the place to start, the White House hoped to ignite a political chain reaction in the Middle East. For the Bush administration, as for Osama bin Laden, the political status quo in the Middle East was unacceptable.

It is of course far too early to reach any conclusions about the ultimate regional consequences of America's attempted political experiment in Iraq. Will Iraq survive as a unitary state? Will it become a liberal democracy? An illiberal democracy? Or will it revert to an autocracy? Would a (best-case) liberal democracy in Iraq undermine autocracies elsewhere in the region, and if so, how? Do the Arab masses of the Middle East really yearn for secular democratic governance? Are America's fundamental political values really universal?

Only time will tell. That said, three points are in order. First, transitions to democracy, particularly liberal democracy, have historically been prolonged and often violent. Seven hundred years separate the Magna Carta and universal suffrage in Great Britain. France's road to democracy was punctuated by revolution and civil war. Even in the case of the United States a bloody civil war determined the political status of African Americans and the relationship of states to the central government. American women were denied the vote until 1920, and it was not until the 1960s that African Americans achieved full legal equality throughout the United States. This historical lag does not mean that democracy is doomed in Iraq, but its prospects in Iraq are at best problematic, especially given Iraq's lack of any democratic experience before 2003, the country's profound and violent ethno-sectarian divisions, the presence of warring militias, a (so far) weak and corrupt central government, massive unemployment, and the persistence of Islamist terrorism.

Second, elections, written constitutions, and other democratic institutions can and have been exploited by antidemocratic parties to achieve power. Hitler used elections and the provisions of the Weimar Constitution to establish a dictatorship in Germany. Likewise, Hamas in the West Bank and Gaza and Hezbollah in Lebanon have used electoral processes to advance their political clout. Democracy may not turn out to be the cure for the political ills of the Middle East but rather the vehicle on which political extremism rides to power. Democracy is certainly no cure for terrorism. Witness the terrorism in Western Europe during the 1970s and 1980s, the Oklahoma City bombing of 1995, and the persistent indigenous Muslim terrorism in Great Britain and Spain. Fred Kaplan observes,

> Democracy and terrorism are not opposites. They can, and sometimes do, coexist in the same country. One is not a cure for the other. The emergence of democracy marks the starting point of politics, not its end. Politics by nature involves conflicts. A democracy thrives or crumbles on how well it deals with those conflicts, on whether the resulting government can mediate conflicting claims without violent rancor. There is nothing inherently civilizing about holding elections—nothing unusual, much less contradictory, about a putatively democratic government embroiled in war or chaos.[66]

Third, the claim by President Bush and the neoconservatives that America's success in fostering democracy in postwar Japan demonstrates the possibility of doing the same in Iraq is yet another example of abusing a historical analogy to promote policy. Having established democracy in Japan was indeed a great American success story, but it rested on circumstances that are not present in Iraq. If democracy comes to Iraq, it will be for current reasons pertaining to Iraq and not to Japan sixty years ago.

In his March 6, 2003, speech at the American Enterprise Institute, President Bush declared:

> We will remain in Iraq as long as necessary and not a day more. America has made and kept this kind of commitment before in the peace that followed a world war. After defeating enemies, we did not leave behind occupying armies, we left behind constitutions and parliaments. We established an atmosphere of safety in which responsible, reform-minded local leaders could build lasting institutions of freedom. In societies that once bred fascism and militarism, liberty found a permanent home.
>
> There was a time when many said that the cultures of Japan and Germany were incapable of sustaining democratic values. Well, they were wrong. Some say the same of Iraq today. They are mistaken. The nation of Iraq, with its proud heritage, abundant resources and skilled and educated people, is fully capable of moving toward democracy and living in freedom.[67]

The postwar German and Japan analogies do not hold, however. Of the two, Japan is key. In Germany, the United States shared occupation responsibilities with three other powers, while in Japan, like Iraq, the United States wielded near-absolute authority. The Japan analogy is, if anything, still discouraging because the United States enjoyed key advantages in Japan that it does not have in Iraq. A brief review of those advantages underscores the potentially intractable challenges the United States confronts today in attempting to establish a stable and enduring democracy in Iraq.

The first advantage the United States had in Japan (compared to Iraq) was the nature of Japan and Japanese society. Japan in 1945 was an ancient state populated almost entirely by ethnic Japanese. Its society was not only homogenous but also conformist and obedient to its emperor, whom the Truman administration wisely decided to retain as head of state. General MacArthur, America's proconsul in Japan, could take Japan's social and political cohesion for granted. Iraq, in contrast, is a relatively new state that was cobbled together after World War I from the Ottoman Empire's ashes and is profoundly divided along ethno-sectarian divisions, which exploded into violence during the American occupation. Japan, even in defeat, was a resilient nation, whereas Iraq is an Arab Yugoslavia that may not survive as a unitary state.

A second advantage was Japan's insular geography. As an island state whose maritime approaches were completely controlled by U.S. naval and air power, Japan could be sealed off from externally sponsored and armed subversive groups seeking to infiltrate the country. In contrast, Iraq is nearly landlocked, has easily penetrated borders, and is surrounded by neighbors who have their own agendas in the country. Ever since the U.S. occupation began, Iran has both sponsored militias operating inside Iraq and provided technical assistance to insurgent groups, and Saudi and other jihadis have been infiltrating into Iraq through Syria.

A third advantage was competence. U.S. planning for the occupation of Japan began six months after the Japanese attack on Pearl Harbor, and by the time Japan surrendered, MacArthur had at his disposal an interagency occupation staff comprising hundreds of experts on Japan and on virtually all aspects of governance related to Japan's political reconstruction. Then there was MacArthur himself, a man uniquely suited to become "a stock figure in the political pageantry of Japan: the new sovereign, the blue-eyed shogun, the paternalistic military dictator, the grandiloquent but excruciatingly sincere Kabuki hero."[68] MacArthur played his role with consummate skill and with a completely free hand from Washington. By the time he departed Japan in 1951, he was revered as a godlike figure.[69] MacArthur enacted a political and social revolution in Japan: he destroyed the institutions of militarism, restarted the Japanese economy, wrote a democratic constitution, granted women suffrage, established a free press, fostered the formation of political parties and labor unions, and enacted land and educational reform. In Japan, the United States, in short, converted a decisive military victory into a stunning political success that endures until this day. The contrast with its approach to Iraq could not be greater. The Bush administration had no plan for Iraq's political reconstruction, did not integrate U.S. civil and military authority in the country, and installed an occupation agency—the Coalition Provisional Authority (CPA)—led by Bremer and staffed largely by amateurs, ideologues, and political hacks, most of them on ninety-day contracts and self-isolated in the 3,600-acre Green Zone. These blunders led to monumental waste and mismanaged resources that were allocated to rebuild Iraq's infrastructure. Bremer, MacArthur's rigid and arrogant analog in Iraq during the occupation's first year, was responsible for the disastrous decisions to dissolve Iraq's regular army and to ban virtually all Baathist members from future government employment. He had little education or experience relevant to his job. He had never managed a large organization or budget, had never worked in the Middle East or on Persian Gulf issues, had no experience in any postwar occupation or reconstruction effort, and knew little about the oil industry. And, of course, just as almost every other American CPA employee, he spoke no Arabic and knew virtually nothing about Iraqi society and history.

The fourth, and perhaps most important, comparative advantage the United States had in postwar Japan was the absence of any armed resistance to the American occupation. There was not a single act of politically motivated violence against U.S. occupation forces during the more than six years that MacArthur ruled supreme in Japan. Quite the opposite has been the case in Iraq, where insurgent and other violence against U.S. forces, though declining, has entered its eighth year. Several factors discouraged resistance in Japan: first, when MacArthur entered Japan, a country slightly smaller than Iraq, his overwhelming force (500,000 troops and twenty-three divisions) permitted him to seize complete control of the country.[70] In contrast, the United States invaded Iraq with a notoriously insufficient force (total Coalition forces numbered less than 200,000). Second, the Japanese accepted the U.S. occupation as legitimate, admitting they had been utterly defeated and formally and unconditionally surrendering before the U.S. occupation began, whereas Iraq's Baathist regime never surrendered formally or informally. Indeed, the emperor himself had legitimized the surrender by breaking precedent when he directly addressed the Japanese people over the radio and called on all Japanese to accept the war's termination. He went on to legitimize the American occupation by permitting MacArthur to rule through him (the emperor). In Iraq, of course, there was no analog for the emperor or, for that matter, MacArthur.

In September 2002, five months before the U.S. invasion of Iraq, novelist and former secretary of the navy (and now U.S. senator from Virginia) James Webb summarized the dangers of the Bush administration's faulty reasoning implicit in the Japan analogy:

> The connotations of "a MacArthurian regency in Baghdad" show how inapt the comparison [with the situation in Iraq] is. Our occupation forces never set foot inside Japan until the Emperor had formally surrendered and prepared Japanese citizens for our arrival. Nor did MacArthur destroy the Japanese government when he took over as proconsul after World War II. Instead, he was careful to work his changes through it, and took pains to preserve the integrity of the imperial family. Nor is Japanese culture in any way similar to Iraq's. The Japanese are a homogeneous people who place a high premium on respect and they fully cooperated with MacArthur's forces after having been ordered to so by the Emperor. The Iraqis are a multiethnic people filled with competing factions who in many cases would view a U.S. occupation as infidels invading the cradle of Islam. Indeed, this very bitterness provided Osama bin Laden the grist for his recruitment efforts in Saudi Arabia when the United States retained bases on Saudi soil after the Gulf War.[71]

Webb could have mentioned another difference: the international community also regarded the U.S. occupation of Japan as legitimate. Japan had been a brutal aggressor state in the 1930s and 1940s, and its victims rejoiced in America's defeat of Japan. The United States liberated East Asia from Japanese rape, pillage, and slaughter, and victims of Japanese aggression regarded the U.S. occupation of Japan as an indispensable guarantee against a resurgence of Japanese militarism.

The contrast with the U.S. occupation of Iraq could not have been greater. The Bush administration's preventive war against Iraq aroused a firestorm of international political opposition, which was underscored by America's failure to secure even a simple majority among UN Security Council members for use of force against Iraq. In fact, only two of the council's five permanent members, the United States and Great Britain, favored such action. This outcome was a far cry from the solid UN mandate President George H. W. Bush sought and received for the war against Iraq in 1991. All major Arab states opposed the 2003 war, as did France, Germany, Russia, China, and—unexpectedly—Canada, Mexico, and Turkey. Indeed, democratic Turkey's refusal to permit U.S. ground forces to launch operations from its territory was a major political embarrassment for the Bush administration and significantly weakened the initial U.S. attack on Iraq by precluding a second, "northern front" led by the U.S. Army's 4th Infantry Division. Even among old NATO allies, public opinion was profoundly averse toward the Bush administration's foreign policy. A Pew Research Center poll taken on the eve of the U.S. invasion revealed the following rates of disapproval of Bush's foreign policy: Britain, 65 percent; France, 87 percent; Germany, 85 percent; Italy, 76 percent; Spain, 79 percent; and Turkey, 85 percent.[72]

Neoconservatives also saw regime change in Iraq as an opportunity *to create a regional alternative to Saudi Arabia.* Before the Iranian revolution of 1979, the United States had relied on the twin pillars of Iran and Saudi Arabia to secure its oil interests in the Persian Gulf. The fall of the shah of

Iran made oil-bloated but militarily weak Saudi Arabia the centerpiece of that effort, and it was Iraq's implicit threat to Saudi Arabia that prompted President George H. W. Bush's decision for war in 1991.

Twelve years later, neoconservatives hoped to transform Iraq into both a democracy and a surrogate for U.S. security interests in the Persian Gulf. Fouad Ajami has described Iraq's allure for those who wanted to reduce America's strategic dependence on not just Saudi Arabia but also Egypt, another autocracy that has produced a disproportionate share of Islamist terrorist leaders, most notably al Qaeda's organizational genius and second in command, Ayman al-Zawahiri.

> Over the horizon loomed the prospect of Iraq as a new, favored base of the Pax Americana in the Arab world. More secular and emancipated than Saudi Arabia, much closer to the sea lanes of the [Persian] Gulf and to the vast oil reserves of the region than Egypt, a new Iraq held out great attraction to the American imperium and its architects. The promise of Iraq was that of a new beginning—a base of American influence free of the toxic anti-Americanism at play in both Saudi Arabia and Egypt, and of the social and religious mores that weighed so heavily on the Saudi realm. In Iraq, American war planners and a powerful coalition of defense and policy thinkers saw an opportunity to end the American dependence on the old pillars of the American presence [in the Middle East], and to construct a new imperium in Araby.[73]

Wolfowitz, Perle, and other neoconservatives regarded Saudi Arabia as a major ideological, financial, and recruiting source for terrorism by virtue of its massive private financing of al Qaeda and other terrorist groups and the Saudi monarchy's official promotion, throughout the Muslim world, of its own extreme Wahhabist version of Islam.[74] Though there is little evidence that Bush or Cheney shared this view, the 9/11 attacks threatened to undermine the half-century-old security bargain between the United States and Saudi

Arabia—i.e., U.S. military protection in exchange for U.S. access to Persian Gulf oil at acceptable prices. If Islamist terrorism was rooted in Arab autocracy, as Bush and Rice argued, then Saudi Arabia was part of the problem. It certainly became more difficult to remain silent on the Saudi monarchy's corruption, bigotry, and propagation of the very kind of Islamist extremism that had produced the 9/11 attacks. Besides Pakistan and the United Arab Emirates, Saudi Arabia had diplomatically recognized the Taliban regime of Afghanistan in the 1990s. But even if Saudi Arabia had had no connection with terrorism, prewar concerns arose about the Saudi regime's longevity. The combination of its country's explosive population growth, its drastic decline in per capita income (during the 1990s), and the staggering profligacy of the 30,000-member House of Saud all pointed toward an inevitable collapse of the Saudi state absent fundamental reforms.[75]

According to Kaplan and Kristol,

> Iraq's experience of liberal democratic rule . . . could increase the pressure already being felt by Teheran's mullahs to open that society. Iraq's model will be eyed warily by Saudi Arabia's theocrats to the south, where male unemployment stands at 30 percent, population growth is rapid, and the populace is restive for change. Meanwhile, Iraq could even replace Saudi Arabia as the key American ally and source of oil in the region. A democratic Iraq would also encourage the region's already liberalizing regimes—such as those in Qatar, Morocco and Jordan—to continue on their paths toward democracy. Then too, a Baghdad *under American supervision* would surely improve its relations with the region's other democracies, Turkey and Israel.[76]

For neoconservatives, Operation Iraqi Freedom offered an opportunity to groom a new, Persian Gulf–based, heavyweight strategic partner as an insurance policy against the political uncertainties surrounding the future U.S.-Saudi relationship while freeing the United States to take a less tolerant and more demanding attitude toward the House of Saud. The underlying assumption was, of course, that the Iraqis would be so grateful for their liberation from Saddam Hussein that they would happily allow the United States to use their country as a regional surrogate for U.S. strategic interests. Such a client-state might even be persuaded to recognize Israel, to withdraw from the Organization of Petroleum Exporting Countries (OPEC), and to permit the United States to establish U.S. military bases on its soil as a means of containing the expansion of Iranian power and influence in the region. To the neoconservatives, a

> "friendly" Iraq would reduce the need to cater to Saudi Arabia, whose friendship was looking increasingly problematic given the fact that fifteen of the nineteen 9/11 hijackers had been Saudis. In the longer term, Iraq could serve as a secure operating base or jumping off point for subsequent U.S. efforts to extend Pax Americana across the broader Middle East. Here lay the ultimate strategic rationale for the war: invading Iraq would set the stage for the further employment of U.S. power aimed at eradicating the conditions breeding violent Islamic radicalism. As applied to Iraq, "liberation" was a code word: the real aim was more akin to pacification and control.[77]

The depth of the neoconservatives' animosity toward Saudi Arabia was evident in a briefing to the Defense Policy Board that Perle orchestrated in July 2002. Perle invited Laurent Murawiec, a Rand Corporation analyst and French national, to address the DPB on the general topic of fighting the war on terrorism. Murawiec's PowerPoint presentation, which was quickly leaked to the press, portrayed Saudi Arabia as a far more important enemy than Iraq was and concluded that the United States should, if necessary, drive the kingdom's Wahhabite royal family from power by sanctioning the Saudi economy. The briefing caused a furor and compelled Secretary of State Powell to reassure the Saudi ambassador that the Muraweic presentation was more or less a prank and did not represent the administration's position.[78] In his later book with David Frum, however, Perle and his coauthor went so far as to suggest a U.S. invasion to seize Saudi Arabia's oil-rich Eastern Province.

Neoconservative hopes for a democratic, Israel-friendly Iraq were fanned by Ahmad Chalabi, an Iraqi exile, confidence man, and possible Iranian agent of influence who played upon the neoconservatives' ignorance of Iraq (and Arab culture in general) to convince them that Iraq could be easily liberated and that he was the man to lead Iraq into its democratic and pro-American future.[79] Chalabi not only fed Cheney, Bush administration neoconservatives, and others bogus information regarding the state of Iraq's WMDs and Baghdad's ties to al Qaeda but also promised them an Iraq that would serve as a surrogate for U.S. and Israeli interests in the region. Specifically, he pledged to end Iraq's trade boycott with Israel, to permit Israeli companies to do business in Iraq, and to rebuild the old oil pipeline connecting Iraq's northern oilfields to the Israeli port of Haifa (the pipeline had been shut down since 1948). He also assured the Americans and Israelis he would build a secular Shiite democracy in Iraq. Chalabi, who with some of his fellow exiles in the United States had founded the Iraqi National Congress in 1992, clearly manipulated the neoconservatives for his own purposes; indeed, he wanted to lead a government in exile that would return to Iraq and saw U.S. military power as his ticket back. He deliberately pitched his message to the neoconservatives because he recognized they had become influential in the George W. Bush administration, and he knew that the way to get their attention was to hold out the vision of an Israel-friendly Iraq.

The neoconservatives proved easy marks. First, they overlooked two obvious facts: Chalabi had a clear interest both in inflating the WMD threat Saddam Hussein posed and in pandering to Wolfowitz, Perle, Ledeen, and other neoconservatives, and a Jordanian court had convicted and sentenced Chalabi to twenty years in prison for bank fraud (and ordered him to repay $230 million in embezzled funds). Then the neoconservatives bought Chalabi and his promises. "Chalabi was the crutch the neocons leaned on to justify their intervention," observed former CENTCOM commander Anthony Zinni. "He twisted the intelligence that they based it on, and provided a picture so rosy and unrealistic they thought it would be easy."[80] Why were the neoconservatives so taken with an exile who had not set foot on Iraqi soil in forty-five years, had no political following in the country, and did have a criminal record?

> One word: Israel. They saw the invasion of Iraq as the precondition for a reorganization of the Middle East that would solve Israel's strategic problems, without the need for an accommodation with either the Palestinians of the existing Arab states. Chalabi assured them that the Iraqi democracy he would build would develop diplomatic and trade ties with Israel, and eschew Arab nationalism. . . . Had the neocons not been deluded by gross ignorance of the Arab world and blinded by wishful thinking, they would have realized that the chances of Chalabi or any other Iraqi leader could deliver on such promises were always remote.[81]

The dream of Iraq as an American strategic outpost in the Middle East, complete with the U.S. military basing rights necessary to intimidate Iran, died on November 17, 2008, when the United States signed an agreement with the government of Nouri al-Maliki that, at Iraqi insistence, mandated the departure of all U.S. forces from all Iraqi territory by the end of 2011.

———————

Besides creating a regional substitute for Saudi Arabia, another of the Bush White House's war aims was to *eliminate an enemy of Israel*. The personal and ideological ties of prominent neoconservatives to the state of Israel and particularly the Likud Party are matters of fact and have been much discussed.[82] Jacob Heilbrunn has sensibly observed, "It is quite true that while not all neoconservatives are Jews, the majority of neoconservatives were, and are, Jewish; it is also true that they tend to propose foreign policy goals that support and favor Israel."[83] It is also true that President George W. Bush arguably has been the most pro-Israel American president since the Israeli state was founded in 1948. This observation does not suggest that the Bush White House went to war for the sake of Israel's security interests. It does mean, however, that administration war proponents, especially the president and the neoconservatives, believed OIF offered the major benefit of removing a declared enemy of Israel. "The neocons were American nationalists who believed it was always in America's interest to help Israel succeed over its enemies," observes Gary Dorrien. "They never claimed that the United States needed to sacrifice some interest of its own for the sake of Israel's well-being. To them, the assertion of closely related interests and identical values was an article of faith that secured Israel's protection and provided the United States with its only democratic ally in the Middle East."[84]

The neoconservatives believed the United States and Israel had profound shared interests in the Middle East, especially when it came to the war on terrorism. As defined by the Bush White House, the war on terrorism made little practical or strategic distinction among al Qaeda, Hamas, and Hezbollah or, for that matter, between the U.S. campaign against al Qaeda and the Israelis' counterterrorist operations in the West Bank, Gaza, and southern Lebanon. In the wake of the 9/11 attacks, Israeli prime minister Ariel Sharon and other Israeli leaders certainly wasted no time in contending that Israel's war against Hamas and Hezbollah was the same as America's war against those who perpetrated the 9/11 attacks. Sharon placed Israel in the vanguard of the Bush administration's declared war on terrorism, and there is no evidence that the White House made any more of a distinction between Palestinian and al Qaeda terrorism than it did between Osama bin Laden and Saddam Hussein.

Ironically, the initial Israeli response to the Bush administration's evident push for a military showdown with Iraq was opposition. The Israelis viewed Iran as the primary enemy and Iraq, though hostile, as a check on Iranian power. Many also questioned the neoconservatives' argument that establishing democracy in Iraq would provoke a democratic revolution in Iran. Once it became clear that Bush was going to war no matter what, however, Israel became supportive, asserting that Iraq should be the first step toward a follow-up war with Iran.[85]

Has Israel benefited strategically from Operation Iraqi Freedom? Clearly, the United States has removed one of its enemies, though not a particularly dangerous one given Saddam Hussein's lack of WMDs and given his impotent conventional military forces. Yet in destroying the Baathist regime in Baghdad, the United States indeed removed a major check on Iranian power in the Gulf and set the stage for an amicable Iraqi-Iranian relationship based on the new political power of the enfranchised Shiite majority in Iraq. Iranian influence in Iraq is greater now than at any time since Iraq was founded as in independent state in 1932. Moreover, as noted, far from scaring Iran into dropping its program to acquire nuclear weapons, the U.S. invasion of Iraq seems to have accelerated that program. Further, Iran's support and encouragement of Hezbollah in southern Lebanon has certainly not diminished, and Israel's security and military prestige clearly suffered from its strategically ineffectual performance against Hezbollah in the Second Lebanon War of July–August 2006. Finally, the continuing costly and unpopular war in Iraq probably renders possible U.S. military action against Iran to disrupt Tehran's nuclear program less likely than would otherwise be the case. As Robert Gates, Rumsfeld's successor as secretary of defense, warned a West Point audience in April 2008, "Another war in the Middle East is the last thing we need and, in fact, I believe it would be disastrous on a number of levels."[86] In short, a strong case can be made that OIF, far from improving Israel's security, has further endangered it.

A major war aim, at least for Secretary of Defense Rumsfeld, was *to vindicate the Pentagon's "defense transformation."* Rumsfeld came into office persuaded that new advances in reconnaissance, precision strike, command and control, and other technologies afforded the United States the opportunity to substitute speed for mass—i.e., to win future wars quickly with far less force and logistical support. Specifically, he believed the combination of standoff precision air strikes and relatively small special operations forces on the ground could replace large and logistically ponderous regular ground forces. Army leaders resisted. They believed that war could not be fought on the cheap and that this assessment was especially true of so-called stability operations, including counterinsurgency, which required large numbers of "boots on the ground" for years and even decades. For Rumsfeld, however,

> the future belonged not to the GI slogging it out in a foxhole, but weapons from space and more use of air power. The army did not figure high in his plans. In fact, Rumsfeld wanted to save money by cutting army programs so he would have more funds to devote to space and air power. In Rumsfeld's mind, close combat, the army's raison d'etre, was a thing of the past. Future wars would be conducted by missiles and other technological tools—areas where the United States had a clear advantage.[87]

Meanwhile, the army's leadership remained wedded to the Weinberger-Powell Doctrine of overwhelming force, which Rumsfeld and his neoconservative and "transformationist" allies regarded as obsolete "legacy" thinking. According to Dale Herspring,

> Powell's approach was anathema to Rumsfeld. He was not interested in a war involving large numbers of troops. Instead, Iraq presented an opportunity for him to prove his military transformation theory by defeating and subduing Iraq with as few troops as possible. The United States certainly did not have the overwhelming force that Powell recommended. To Rumsfeld, the Powell Doctrine was out of date. Besides, [Richard] Perle considered Powell to be a "soft liner," not the kind of individual who should be in a top-level position. As a result, Rumsfeld and his colleagues would do everything possible to marginalize Powell to steal the action from him at every opportunity. There was too much at stake with the impending war in Iraq to allow someone like a former four-star general to mess things up.[88]

Iraq offered Rumsfeld an opportunity to discredit the Weinberger-Powell Doctrine and, with it, the requirement for a large (ten-division) and heavy army of six armored and mechanized infantry divisions.[89] "Heartened by the small-force stunning victory in Afghanistan, the rapid defeat of Iraq on his [Rumsfeld's] terms would break the spine of Army resistance to his transformation goal once and for all."[90] Thus, Rumsfeld insisted on an invasion force far smaller (145,000 troops) than that deemed prudent by experienced Army planners (258,000 based on experience in Bosnia and 520,000 based on the Kosovo model).[91] The difference was that Rumsfeld did not want U.S. forces engaged in stability operations in post-Baathist Iraq, whereas such operations were part of army doctrine. "Rumsfeld wanted to get into Iraq, crush Saddam's army, overthrow his regime, then get out," observes Fred Kaplan.

> The whole point of military transformation, as he saw it, was to demonstrate that America could project power and topple rogue regimes with a small, light force and that, therefore, it could do so repeatedly, anytime, anywhere, at low cost and little effort. To get involved in a serious postwar occupation—stabilization, security, nation-building, and all the rest—would nullify the concept; it would bog down lots of troops for a long time.
>
> In short, Rumsfeld did not miscalculate how many troops would be needed to stabilize Iraq after the war, as some critics later charged; he understood the calculations all too well. Rather than ratchet up the troop levels to meet that mission, he simply sidestepped the mission. He wasn't interested in it, didn't think postwar stabilization was what a modern military—especially a transformational one—ought to be doing.[92]

Rumsfeld didn't want *any* plan for post-Baathist Iraq, and because President Bush had granted Rumsfeld complete authority over the entire American enterprise in Iraq, there was no plan. Rumsfeld wanted "a hit-

and-run invasion," and he got it.[93] His simple dismissal of the massive post-invasion looting of Baghdad and other Iraqi cities—"Stuff happens" and "Freedom's untidy"[94]— and his refusal to order the looting halted, observes George Packer, reflected "the sense that Rumsfeld communicated to his commanders—and his commanders communicated down the chain to the platoon level—that we were not there to run Iraq. We were there to get rid of the regime, and get out. Which meant that no one was going to run Iraq, and there would be a void in which chaos was bound to explode." It was "a tremendous self-inflicted wound."[95]

Lt. Gen. Ricardo Sanchez, who commanded Coalition forces in Iraq during the critical first year of the U.S. occupation, has stated flatly that "there was no plan for Phase IV [postwar stability] operations in Iraq."[96] Indeed, in his memoir he cites an April 16, 2003, order by CENTCOM commander Gen. Tommy Franks to withdraw American combat units from Iraq within 120 days, an order that Franks would not have issued on his own authority.[97] (The order was reversed in July by Gen. John Abizaid, Franks's successor, when an incipient Iraqi insurgency became apparent.) Sanchez further recalls a memorandum from Rumsfeld, also issued in April 2003, "directing the Defense Department to proceed with his ongoing military transformation guidance." Sanchez noted that Rumsfeld's directive "was issued *during* the invasion of Iraq and *before* Franks' redeployment order. It was as if both the war and the postwar operations were secondary. But Rumsfeld was deadly serious about his transformation order, and he put tremendous pressure on the services to comply."[98]

By going in fast, relatively light, and blind to possible post-invasion military requirements, Rumsfeld created a fundamental contradiction between the war plan and the critical objectives of quickly securing Iraq's suspected WMD sites and the provision of security necessary for Iraq's political reconstruction. "The administration convinced itself that it could dislodge the [Saddam Hussein] regime without doing the hard work of rebuilding a new Iraq or without committing itself to troop levels that were needed in most other postwar conflicts."[99] Though the White House repeatedly cited the analogy of America's success in rebuilding postwar Japan as proof that the United States could also reconstruct Iraq as a new democracy and ally, as we have seen, postwar Japan's circumstances, not the least of which was the presence of overwhelming U.S. military force in Japan after Japan's formal surrender, bear no comparison with the situation in post-Saddam Iraq.[100]

Rumsfeld believed that the Weinberger-Powell Doctrine was obsolete because he felt that new technology was dissolving traditional Clausewitzian concerns about fog, friction, and chance. Future wars would not be big, costly, and uncertain, requiring overwhelming force to ensure victory; rather, they would be short and cheap—"shock and awe" wars—and therefore relatively free of political risk. Thus, for "Rumsfeld and his coterie, here lay the appeal of having a go at Iraq. Operation Enduring Freedom in Afghanistan had proved something of a test drive for their ideas. The secretary of defense was counting on a swift victory over Saddam to fully validate his vision and to discredit once and for all the generals who were obstructing his reforms."[101] His determination to discredit the Weinberger-Powell Doctrine made him a natural ally of the neoconservatives, who regarded the doctrine as a recipe for realist military timidity unbecoming of the world's sole remaining superpower.

An arrogant disregard for professional military, especially U.S. army, opinion was a hallmark of Rumsfeld's tenure as secretary of defense. But Rumsfeld's worst offense was his evident failure to understand that war is, as Carl von Clausewitz declared, a continuation of policy by other means. He mistook military operations for strategy, forgetting that wars are waged not for their own sake or to demonstrate military prowess but rather to achieve political objectives. In the case of the Iraq War, that goal meant more—much more—than simply destroying Saddam's regime. It meant establishing the security necessary for Iraq's political reconstruction and, in turn, invading in sufficient force and sticking around in post–Saddam Hussein Iraq for years if necessary. In fact, the United States has since done so in spite of Rumsfeld.

In fairness to Rumsfeld, however, it must be observed that America's traditional approach to war emphasizes war as a *substitute* for policy—i.e., as a military contest to be waged and won for its own sake. "Americans are wont to regard war and peace as two sharply distinctive conditions," observes British strategist Colin Gray. "The U.S. military has a long history of waging war for the goal of victory, paying scant regard to the consequences of the course of its operations for the character of the peace that will follow."[102] Americans have also approached modern war as primarily a scientific and technological challenge rather than a human one, and this position has bred a tendency to underrate materially inferior enemies and their superior intangibles, such as strategy, organizational quality, and a willingness to fight and die. Americans have won their major wars largely through amassing overwhelming firepower at the right time and place, and every one of those victories has been against conventional (regular) enemies. As Gray notes,

Few, if any, armies have been equally competent in the conduct of regular and irregular warfare. As institutions, however, the U.S. armed forces have not been friendly either to irregular warfare or to those in its ranks who were would-be practitioners and advocates of what was regarded as the sideshow of insurgency. American soldiers . . . have always been prepared nearly exclusively for "real war," which is to say combat against a tolerably symmetrical, regular enemy.[10]

Rumsfeld's obsession with the technological transformation of the U.S. military into a lighter and more agile instrument that could quickly win wars and do so on the human cheap, irrespective of political policy and context, was thus symptomatic of the American tradition of war. But that tradition was exceptionally antithetical to success in Iraq because the object of Operation Iraqi Freedom was nothing less than Iraq's total political transformation. Rumsfeld either did not understand the disconnect between his invasion plan and the war's political objective, or he did understand it but simply chose to ignore it because he had no intention of prolonging the U.S. military's stay in Iraq beyond the destruction of Saddam Hussein's regime. In either case, he subverted President Bush's purpose in Iraq.

The American experience in Iraq has discredited Rumsfeld's move to divorce military operations from political purpose—indeed, perhaps the legacy of America's very approach to war, especially in a world where irregular warfare within states has largely displaced regular warfare among states. Antulio Echevarria, director of research at the U.S. Army War College's Strategic Studies Institute, believes the United States "is geared to fight wars as if they were battles, and thus confuses the winning of campaigns . . . with the winning of wars." He further contends that "the characteristics of the U.S. style of warfare—speed, jointness, knowledge, and precision—are better suited for strike operations than for translating such operations into strategic successes."[104] Former West Point history professor Frederick W. Kagan also believes the primary culprit in delivering politically sterile victories is the Pentagon's conception of war. The reason why "the United States [has] been so successful in recent wars [but has] encountered so much difficulty in securing its political aims after the shooting stopped," he argues, "lies partly in a 'vision of war' that see[s] the enemy as a target set and believe[s] that when all or most targets have been hit, he will inevitably surrender and American goals will be achieved." Unfortunately, this vision ignores the importance of "how, exactly, one defeats the enemy and what the enemy's country looks like at the moment the bullets stop flying."[105]

Rumsfeld's conception of what the Iraq War was all about—i.e., demonstrating transformed U.S. military power by knocking off a long-standing irritant regime in the Persian Gulf—underscored the differences between the Bush administration's nationalist hawks and democratic imperialists. Idealistic neoconservatives like Paul Wolfowitz certainly embraced demonstrations of American military primacy, but they also believed that primacy was meant to serve the higher end of global democratization. There is no evidence that Rumsfeld believed in the democratic peace theory or that he cared about post-Baathist Iraq's political future except insofar as the new regime in Baghdad remained strategically friendly to the United States. Unlike the neoconservatives, neither he nor Cheney ever felt the urge to publicly criticize the tyrannical and bigoted Saudi monarchy, America's oldest ally in the region. In "Defending Ourselves: Why Should We Attack Iraq?"—his comprehensive statement to the Senate Armed Services Committee on September 19, 2002, on why war with Iraq might be necessary—Rumsfeld made not a single reference to freedom or democracy, which by then had become staples of the White House's rhetoric.[106]

A supreme irony of Rumsfeld's fixation on military transformation, which he and his spokesmen credited for delivering the swift and cheap overthrow of Saddam Hussein, is that Iraq's debilitated, demoralized, and poorly trained conventional forces hardly constituted a meaningful test of the transformation hallmarks of speed and precision. The United States enjoyed literally overwhelming advantages in technology and operational competence. OIF essentially pitted the New England Patriots against a bad high school football team. With the outcome never in doubt, it would have made no difference how many mistakes the Patriots made. "It is difficult, in reality, to say whether or not Operation Iraqi Freedom 'validated' any particular concept," observes Kagan. "The Iraqi military was so weak that just about any American plan would have succeeded in driving Saddam from power, so success in the war can hardly be said to have proved that one approach was better than any other."[107]

A team study conducted by the U.S. Army's Strategic Studies Institute in 2004 warned against treating OIF as the basis for drawing lessons about future conflicts. *Toppling Saddam: Iraq and American Military Transformation* concluded that the 2003 outcome was the "product of a powerful interaction between coalition strengths and Iraqi weaknesses. Our strengths were indeed essential for the outcome, but so were Iraqi shortcomings: both advanced technology *and* a major skill imbalance were required." The study went on to observe:

> This explanation holds some very different implications for trans-formation than the "speed, precision, and situation awareness" view now commonplace in accounts of the war. In particular, we see the nature of the opponent as being at least as important for the outcome

as our own strengths: both were necessary but neither was sufficient. Without the skill imbalance afforded by Iraqi shortcomings, we cannot safely assume that our technology would produce the same results. But if so, then we cannot safely assume that speed, precision, or situation awareness will yield 2003-like effects against more skilled opponents elsewhere. To extrapolate from a case where technology could exploit a massive skill imbalance into future conflicts where our enemies might be better skilled would be a dangerous stretch. And this in turn suggests that a transformation agenda that would trade speed for mass and standoff precision for close combat could be a risky choice.[108]

As a deliberate expansion of the global war on terrorism, the Iraq War also served a major domestic political objective of the Bush White House— the *reestablishment of an "imperial" presidency.* If, in Iraq, Rumsfeld saw an opportunity to vindicate his transformationist military agenda and vanquish the U.S. Army's naysayers, Cheney saw an opportunity to cement the restoration of pre–Vietnam War/Watergate era presidential power on matters of national security. That power was essentially unchecked by Congress or the Supreme Court from the onset of World War II until the early 1970s, when the White House was besieged by Congress's reassertion of its constitutional prerogatives in foreign policy, including using its appropriations power to restrict the executive branch's direction of military activity in Indochina, and in domestic policy with its impeachment of President Nixon for abusing the Constitution.

The argument here is not that the White House went to war to strengthen the executive branch but rather that by deliberately linking Iraq to the war on terrorism proclaimed after the 9/11 attacks, the Bush administration reinforced a pursuit of another agenda that had been on the table from the day Bush and Cheney were sworn into office. Put simply, the Bush administration successfully sought to convert the 9/11 attacks into a rationale for not only a preventive war against Iraq but also an assertion of extraordinary presidential wartime prerogatives vis-à-vis the legislative and judicial branches of government. The Iraq War served simply to enlarge and extend the war on terrorism. The White House claimed extraordinary prerogatives, including the power to authorize torture (and to hand over detainees to foreign governments known to employ torture), to conduct warrantless surveillance (including wiretaps, mail openings, and burglaries), to arrest and detain suspected "enemy combatants" without trial and deny them the protections of the Geneva Convention, to ignore congressional statutes and international treaties that restrict the behavior of U.S. military and other security forces, and to interpret and enforce (or not enforce) all congressional statutes as the executive saw fit. In essence, the Bush White House believed it was above the law on matters of national security, including the definition and prosecution of the war on terrorism.[109]

Cheney was the key Bush administration player on this issue for two reasons. First, he believed that the executive branch's prerogatives on matters of war and peace were virtually unlimited. He felt neither Congress nor the Supreme Court should have any real say in framing issues of national security or in executing national security decisions, including those related to going to war, withholding information, conducting domestic surveillance, and choosing interrogation techniques of suspected enemies in the war on terrorism. Cheney essentially subscribed to Nixon's expressed view (to interviewer David Frost in 1977): "When the President does it, that means it's not illegal."[110]

According to an extensive assessment of the Bush administration's views on presidential power:

> Cheney was determined to expand the power of the presidency. He wanted to reduce the authority of Congress and the courts and to expand the ability of the commander in chief and his top advisers to govern with maximum flexibility and minimum oversight. He hoped to enlarge the zone of secrecy around the executive branch, to reduce

the power of Congress to restrict presidential action, to undermine the limits imposed by international treaties, to nominate judges who favored a stronger presidency, and to impose greater White House control over the permanent workings of government. And Cheney's vision of expanded executive power was not limited to his and Bush's tenure in office. Rather, Cheney wanted to permanently alter the constitutional balance of American government, establishing powers that future presidents would be able to wield as well.[111]

Cheney had served as President Gerald Ford's chief of staff after the Watergate crisis over Richard Nixon's impeachable abuses of presidential power and during the height of both the congressional investigations into CIA abuses and the congressionally imposed restrictions on the president's use of force in Southeast Asia. Cheney subsequently embraced the "unitary executive" theory, which interprets article 2 of the U.S. Constitution and vesting of executive power in the president as granting the president complete control of the executive branch and its declared functions, including the use of force as commander in chief. The theory regards virtually any congressional attempt to limit the president's control of the executive branch or to alter executive branch policies in the national security arena as unconstitutional interference.[112]

In 1987 Congressman Dick Cheney was the ranking Republican on the congressional committee that investigated the Iran-contra scandal that engulfed the Reagan administration. Cheney filed a dissent from the final committee report in which he argued that the Reagan White House's misdeeds were constitutionally protected exercises of inherent presidential powers and that Congress had no right to employ its power of the purse to interfere with the president's exercise of those powers.[113] In December 1990 as secretary of defense, Cheney declared that the George H. W. Bush administration required no congressional authorization for the war it launched one month later against Iraq. And in December 2005, in defense of the National Security Agency's warrantless wiretapping program, then–Vice President Cheney declared:

Watergate and a lot of things around Watergate and Vietnam during the 1970s, served, I think, to erode the authority I think the president needs to be effective, especially in the national security area. . . . Especially in the day and age we live in . . . the president of the United States needs to have his constitutional powers unimpaired, if you will, in terms of the conduct of national security policy.[114]

Second, Cheney exercised unprecedented power as vice president.[115] In no other preceding American presidential administration has a vice president had so much policy influence, especially on national security issues; thus, with good reason many commentators referred to the White House as the Bush-Cheney administration. His influence was a function both of his own bureaucratic assertiveness—he circumvented the National Security Council staff by creating a counterpart in the Office of the Vice President and recruited his former mentor and longtime ally, Rumsfeld, as secretary of defense—and of President Bush's relative ignorance of foreign affairs and unfamiliarity with the ways of political Washington.[116] It was Cheney and his staff and allies, not Secretary of State Powell, who framed U.S. policy responses to the terrorist attacks of 9/11. Indeed, Cheney succeeded in isolating Powell and marginalizing National Security Adviser Condoleezza Rice, who always seemed "[p]reoccupied with her own private role as Bush's friend and personal foreign policy tutor."[117] And it was Cheney, more than anyone else, who publicly asserted the White House's sole right to decide national security policy. For Cheney, the war on terrorism, which the administration expanded to include the invasion and occupation of Iraq, created a perpetual emergency that both invited and mandated an expansion of presidential authority that even Nixon would have envied. Though other wartime presidents, including Abraham Lincoln and Franklin Roosevelt, laid claim to exceptional authority, they did so as pragmatists and politicians who were sensitive to public opinion. Further, they always regarded the prerogatives they asserted as conditional to the emergency of war.[118] They claimed exceptional authority as a means to an end, not as an end itself. In contrast, argues Jack Goldsmith, who served as assistant attorney general in the Office of Legal Counsel during 2003–2004, the Bush White House often asserted presidential power "in ways that seemed unnecessary and politically self-defeating" because "the administration's conception of presidential power had a kind of theological significance that often trumped political consequences." The Bush White House clearly failed to understand, as did Lincoln and Roosevelt, that "presidential power is primarily about persuasion and consent rather than unilateral executive action."[119]

The late Arthur M. Schlesinger, Jr., once observed that Lincoln and Roosevelt used emergency power, on the whole, with restraint because both men understood that the "truly strong President is not one who relies on his power to command but one who recognizes his responsibility, and opportunity, to enlighten and persuade."[120] As Goldsmith notes, however:

> We are unlikely to come to think of President Bush in this way, for he has not embraced Lincoln's and Roosevelt's tenets of democratic leadership in crisis. He has been almost entirely inattentive to the soft factors of legitimization—consultation, deliberation, the appearance of deference, and credible expressions of public concern for constitutional and international values—in his dealings with Congress, the courts, and allies. He has instead relied on the hard power of prerogatives. And he has seen his hard power diminished in many ways because he has failed to take the softer aspects of power seriously. This irony will likely be the Bush presidency's legacy for executive power.[121]

———

As preposterous as the objective may appear to some, *ridding the world of evil* was, at least for George W. Bush personally, a powerful motivator for a preventive war against Iraq. Bush was, if anything, more Wilsonian than Woodrow Wilson himself in the way he conceptualized the forces at play in the world. Although he entered the White House as a self-proclaimed realist, he was also a born-again Christian and leader of a party whose core base consists of fundamentalist evangelicals. Given the shock of the 9/11 attacks and the influential presence of neoconservatives who believed that it was America's mission to fight evil in the world, it is no wonder that Bush, who regarded terrorism as evil and Saddam Hussein as a terrorist, saw the war against Iraq as a war against evil.

"No other president in living memory has spoken so often about good and evil, right and wrong,"[122] so writes ethicist Peter Singer in his *The President of Good and Evil: The Ethics of George W. Bush*. He goes on to warn that

> it is a mistake to divide the world neatly into good and evil, black and white without shades of gray, in a manner that eliminates the need to learn more about those with whom one is dealing. For an unreflective person, having a sense of "moral clarity" that disregards the shadings in human motivation and conduct can be a vice, not a virtue. When it is coupled with a firm belief that the nation you lead is on the right side of history, pursuing "God's justice," and even that there is some divine plan that has put you in the position of leader of that nation, what you see as moral clarity, others will see as self-righteousness. When that self-proclaimed moral clarity is coupled with actions that fail to live up to the rhetoric, others will see it as hypocrisy. In the president of the most powerful nation on earth, self-righteousness and hypocrisy are dangerous vices.[123]

No explanation of the Bush administration's march to war in Iraq can ignore President Bush's Manichaean view of the world, especially his interpretation of the 9/11 attacks and America's role in responding to them. His reduction of the war on terrorism to a simple contest between good and evil and his own apparent self-regard as a divine agent of good inhibited sound strategic thinking and policy flexibility and blinded him to, among other things, the profound differences between the nature of al Qaeda and

Saddam Hussein's Iraq. Glenn Greenwald, in his 2007 study of the Bush presidency, concluded that

> what lies at [its heart] is an absolutist worldview capable of understanding all issues and challenges only in the moralistic, overly simplistic, and often inapplicable terms of "Good vs. Evil." The president is driven by his core conviction that he has found the Good, that he is a crusader for it, that anything is justified in pursuit of it, and that anything which impedes his decision-making is, by definition, a deliberate or unwitting ally of Evil. This mentality has single-handedly prevented him from governing, changing course, and even engaging realities that deviate from those convictions. The president's description of himself as "the Decider" is accurate. His mind-set has dominated the American political landscape throughout his presidency, and virtually all significant events of the Bush Era are a by-product of his core Manichaean mentality.[124]

Bush's Manichaeanism (a trait shared, ironically, with Osama bin Laden) is a function primarily of his profound religious convictions. He is a once dissolute, now born-again Christian who apparently believed he was doing God's will as president. Shortly after his reelection as governor of Texas in 1998, Bush attended a Methodist church service in Dallas in which the pastor indirectly urged him to run for president in 2000. Afterward Bush telephoned the Southern Baptist evangelist James Robinson and told him, "I've heard the call. I believe God wants me to run for president."[125] Bush later told Bob Woodward that as he approached the decision to order the invasion of Iraq, "I was praying for strength to do the Lord's will. . . . I pray[ed] that I be as good a messenger of His will as possible."[126] After the invasion he reportedly told Prime Minister Mahmoud Abbas of the Palestinian National Authority, "God told me to strike at al Qaeda and I struck them, and then he instructed me to strike at Saddam, which I did, and now I am determined to solve the problem in [sic] the Middle East."[127]

Bush's self-regard as an agency of divine will was certainly consistent with his belief in America's moral exceptionalism and its mission to bring freedom and democracy to the rest of the world. In this aspect, he was the presidential soul mate of Woodrow Wilson, a righteous Presbyterian for whom international politics was a struggle between good and evil. Bush's public statements in the days, weeks, and months following the 9/11 attacks are filled with references to evil. Consider the following examples:

But our responsibility to history is clear: To answer these [9/11] attacks and rid the world of evil. (September 14, 2001)[128]

We are planning a broad and sustained campaign to secure our country and eradicate the evil of terrorism. (September 15, 2001)[129]

These terrorists . . . represent evil and war. (September 17, 2001)[130]

I see things this way: The people who did this act on America . . . are evil people. They don't represent an ideology, they don't represent a legitimate political group of people. They're flat evil. That's all they can think about, is evil. (September 25, 2001)[131]

We are on a mission to say to the rest of the world, come with us—come with us, stand by our side to defeat the evil-doers who would like to rid the world of freedom as we know it. (September 26, 2001)[132]

The evildoers struck. . . . But they will not touch the soul of America. They cannot dim our spirit. . . . Now is the time to root out evil so that our children and grandchildren can live with freedom as the beacon all around the world. (October 4, 2001)[133]

Our war is against evil. (October 10, 2001)[134]

The hijackers were instruments of evil. . . . Behind them is a cult of evil. (October 11, 2001)[135]

America's new war [is] against terrorism and against evil. . . . The evil ones have tried to hijack a religion to justify their murder . . . we fight against evil people. (October 17, 2001)[136]

So we're determined to fight this evil [al Qaeda terrorist groups], and fight until we're rid of it. (November 6, 2001)[137]

[T]he great purpose of our great land . . . is to rid this world of evil and
   terror. (November 11, 2001)[138]

I believe good triumphs over evil. . . . Across the world and across the
   years, we will fight these evil ones, and we will win. (November 21,
   2001)[139]

It is the calling of our time, to rid the world of terror. (November 29,
   2001)[140]

Terrorism is a movement, an ideology that respects no boundary of
   nationality or decency. The terrorists despise creative societies and
   individual choice—and thus they bear a special hatred for America.
   (December 7, 2001)[141]

[T]his is a struggle between evil and good. (February 6, 2002)[142]

I view this current conflict as . . . us versus them, and evil versus good. And
   there's no in between. (February 16, 2002)[143]

Moral truth is the same in every culture, in every time, in every place. . . .
   We are in a conflict between good and evil, and America will call
   evil by its name. (June 1, 2002)[144]

Clearly, President Bush viewed the war on terrorism as a Manichaean
contest between light and darkness, equated terrorism with evil, and believed
that America's mission, "the calling of our time," was to rid the world of evil.
He also repeatedly declared that the war in Iraq was the "central front" in the
war on terrorism. Though past presidents have often cast America's enemies
as morally malevolent (it helps to rally public support for war), none—not
even Wilson—did so as repeatedly, and with such apparent fervor, as George
W. Bush did after the 9/11 attacks. For Bush, the war on terrorism was a
moral crusade and he was its divinely designated leader. What counted was
not strategic clarity but rather moral clarity, which clears away all ambiguity,
uncertainty, complexity, perplexity, and doubt. Bush is a true believer in the
goodness of God, the United States, democracy, and freedom and in the evil
of terrorism and tyranny. He saw every terrorist killed or captured, every
terrorist plot thwarted, and every rogue regime overthrown as victories in a

zero-sum game between good and evil and without a morally tenable ground between the two. He believes that moral truth is universal across time and all cultures, that the United States was rightfully out to rid the world of evil, and, apparently, that the United States *could* do it.

Such moral simplicity and certainty, while perhaps admirable in a preacher, are not enough to craft an effective national security strategy. "Great leadership often involves putting aside self-doubt, bucking conventional wisdom, and listening to an inner voice that tells you the right thing to do. That is the essence of strong character," observes Frances Fukuyama. "The problem is that bad leadership can also flow from these same characteristics: steely determination can become stubbornness; the willingness to flout conventional wisdom can amount to lack of common sense; the inner voice can become delusional."[145]

Strategy must deal first and foremost with the realities of power (including, for the United States, the limits of its own power), the political roots of most wars (including al Qaeda's war against the United States and its allies), and the fact that political and military considerations usually trump moral ones in the predominately amoral world of international politics (e.g., the reliance on dictatorships as allies in the war on terrorism). Morally black-and-white choices are scarce in a gray world, and to believe otherwise is to invite policy failure, even disaster. Idealism untempered by a healthy realism—a sound sense of what is possible, an understanding of how the world works, knowledge of other peoples and cultures, respect for the law of unintended consequences, and so forth—led Bush into failure in Iraq just as it led Wilson into failure at Versailles. Doubt can cripple, but it can also lead to caution, which was not a hallmark of George W. Bush's foreign policy. Singer and Greenwald both have pointed to the debilitating effects of Bush's Manichaean worldview on sound strategic reasoning. Adds Jacob Weisberg, referring to Bush's famous remark to Senator Joe Biden that "I don't do nuance":

That line was probably spoken with self-deprecating irony, but it captures the truth about the intellectually constricting lens of his faith. Bush rejects nuance not because he's mentally incapable of engaging with it, but because he has chosen to disavow it. Applying a crude religious lens that clarifies all decisions as moral choices rather than complicated trade-offs helps him fend off . . . deliberation and uncertainty.

But closing one's mind to complexity isn't mere intellectual laziness; it's a fundamental evasion of freedom, God-given or otherwise. . . . A simple faith frees George W. Bush from the kind of agonizing and struggle his father went through in handling the largest questions of his presidency, and helps him cope with the heavy burden of the job. But it comes at a tragic cost. A too crude religious understanding has limited Bush's ability to comprehend the world. The habit of pious simplification has undermined the Decider's decision-making.[146]

An excellent example of pious simplification was Bush's reduction of terrorism to "evil" and terrorists to "evildoers." Such characterizations strip terrorism in general, and al Qaeda in particular, of any political context. It is as if terrorists commit terrorism for its own sake—for the sheer joy of being evil—or as if they were incomprehensible aliens from another planet. Are terrorists really nothing more than members of a "cult of evil"? Do not terrorist organizations have agendas beyond exercising the means of terrorism? Is not terrorism a means to political or other ends? Is not terrorism, like guerrilla warfare or strategic bombing (which, by the way, was a weapon of mass terrorism as the United States and Great Britain conducted it during World War II), simply a means or method of violence employed to achieve objectives external to terrorism itself? Has not Islamic terrorism arisen within a specific Middle Eastern political context, including centuries of hostile Western intrusion? Was there no connection between the 9/11 attacks and the U.S. presence and policies in the Arab world?

However morally reprehensible terrorism may be (and there is no agreed definition of terrorism), most terrorist organizations are seeking to change the political status quo, and their reliance on terrorism testifies to their *political desperation* and *military weakness*, not to their love of evil. Indeed, like guerrilla warfare, terrorism is a form of irregular warfare, or as so defined by C. E. Callwell in his classic 1896 work, *Small Wars: Their Principles and Practice*, it is a "small war" of "all campaigns other than those where both sides consist of regular troops."[147] As such, terrorism, like guerrilla warfare, is a weapon of the weak against a regular (i.e., conventional) enemy that cannot be defeated on his own terms or quickly. Absent any prospect of a political solution, what options other than irregular warfare are available to the militarily helpless? Does George W. Bush know that Israel's creation as an independent state in 1948 in no small measure stemmed from the bombings and assassinations conducted by self-avowed Jewish terrorists, two of whom—Menachem Begin and Yitzhak Shamir—later became prime ministers and one of whom (Begin) was awarded the Nobel Peace Prize?[148]

"Terrorism may be the only feasible means of overthrowing a cruel dictatorship, the last resort of free men and women facing intolerable persecution," argues Walter Laqueur. "In such conditions, terrorism could be a moral imperative rather than a crime—the killing of Hitler or Stalin early on in his career would have saved the lives of millions of people."[149] Suppose, for the sake of illustration, that the only opportunity to kill Hitler before 1939 was to detonate a large bomb in an orphanage during his visit. Would not the slaughter of scores of innocent children be a small price to pay to forestall the slaughter of millions later? In short, in circumstances where the choice is between one of two evils, might selecting the lesser evil be justified? The United States chose to fight alongside Stalin to defeat Hitler and effectively became a cobelligerent with Saddam Hussein in Iraq's war with Ayatollah Khomeini's Iran. In both cases, Franklin Roosevelt and Ronald Reagan, respectively, allied themselves with two of the twentieth century's greatest practitioners of state terrorism for the purpose of defeating what they regarded at the time as the greater evil.

Bush's very choice of the term "war on terrorism" is further testimony to the pitfalls of simplification, pious or not. First of all, the term "war," as

British military historian Michael Howard has pointed out, "arouses an expectation and a demand for military action against some easily identifiable adversary leading to decisive results."[150] But where are the historical examples of decisive military action against terrorism? The global incidence of Islamic terrorism has mushroomed since U.S. military forces were unleashed in Afghanistan and Iraq. While conventional military power has marginal utility against such a fanatical, elusive, and decentralized terrorist organization as today's al Qaeda and its affiliates, this military power is also an instrument of brute force that can and has generated streams of recruits for Islamic terrorist organizations.

James Sheehan has described the differences in the way Americans and Europeans have viewed terrorism and how to combat it:

> Americans tended to see terrorism as a global movement that directly threatened their national security. To defeat it would require a war like the one that had destroyed the Axis powers in the Second World War—a comparison underscored by the constant association of September 11 with the Japanese bombing of Pearl Harbor. Europeans, who had been fighting their own forms of local terrorism for several decades, were inclined to see it as a persistent challenge to domestic order rather than an immediate international threat. The proper remedy was more effective policing, stricter laws, better surveillance. They wanted to extradite terrorists and try them as criminals, not wage war against states that were suspected of supporting them. . . . Few Europeans doubted that terrorism was a serious issue, but most did not accept the official American position that a global struggle for national survival had begun on September 11.[151]

Second, by labeling the effort to stop the terrorists as a "war on terrorism," Bush committed the United States to making war against a method of violence and presumably against all those who employ it regardless of whether their terrorism is directed against American interests. Do Basque or Sri Lankan terrorists threaten the United States? What U.S. state interests do Chechen terrorists threaten? What about terrorism directed against enemies of the United States? Has the United States not backed such terrorism—e.g., against the Sandinista regime in Nicaragua and the Soviet occupation of Afghanistan—in the past? Because eradicating a form of irregular warfare that has appealed to the politically desperate and militarily weak across the millennia is impossible, the war against terrorism encourages an endless and less than sufficiently discriminating struggle that could entangle the United States with unnecessary enemies.

––––––––––

Steven Metz has observed that the

rationale for military intervention against Iraq . . . was always a polyglot of ideas and themes, none of them entirely persuasive in isolation but together making a convincing case. The problem was that such a complex rationale was difficult to sell to the American public. Hence the administration elected to emphasize the theme likely to find the most receptive audience in the post-September 11 political environment: weapons of mass destruction.

Moreover it sought to conflate the various types of WMD, suggesting that "[p]ossession of *any* WMD by Saddam Hussein . . . equated to possession of the *worst* type of WMD—deliverable nuclear weapons."[152]

The Bush White House deliberately invoked the specter of a soon-to-be nuclear-armed Saddam Hussein allied with al Qaeda to mobilize public and congressional support for a war of regime change against Iraq. No persuasive evidence accompanied the invocation because there wasn't any. But there were *no other politically convincing reasons to go to war*. Only a clear and present—a grave and gathering—danger would do.

Chaim Kaufmann points out,

[The Bush administration] made four main arguments to persuade the public of [its] case against Saddam Hussein: (1) he was an almost uniquely undeterrable aggressor who would seek any opportunity to kill Americans virtually regardless of risk to himself or his country; (2) he was cooperating with al-Qaeda and had even assisted in the September 11, 2001, terrorist attacks against the United States; (3) he was close to acquiring nuclear weapons; and (4) he possessed chemical and biological weapons that could be used to devastating effect against American civilians at home or U.S. troops in the Middle East. Virtually none of the administration claims held up, and the information needed to debunk nearly all of them was available both inside and outside the U.S. government before the war. Nevertheless, administration officials persistently repeated only the most extreme threat claims and suppressed contrary evidence.[153]

Bush and Cheney seem to have believed in the Iraqi menace they postulated; perhaps it was a case of a wish being the father to the thought. But the White House also understood that the war it wanted could be sold only on the basis of Iraq as a direct national security threat.

To be sure, there were always plenty of reasons to despise Saddam Hussein and support his removal from power. But were they reasons for war, especially preventive war? A U.S. invasion of Iraq could not be sold on purely moral, political, or reputational grounds. Singly or together, liberating Iraq from tyranny, establishing a democracy there, redeeming the botched war termination of 1991, doing Israel a strategic favor, scaring Iran and North Korea, and showing off transformed U.S. military power were not compelling reasons for war in the marketplace of domestic public opinion. Americans were certainly not going to be led into a war solely to demonstrate a will to go to war.

Yet among war proponents, especially the neoconservatives and their key White House and Defense Department allies, considerations of power and reputation seemed paramount. To them, the war was less about Iraq than it was about the United States in the post-Soviet world. Saddam Hussein "was simply a demonstration model to show the new resolve of the United States and its postmodern rules of international behavior."[154] The war was about perpetuating America's global military supremacy and mustering the commensurate political will to employ that supremacy on behalf of universal American values. It was about casting off, once and for all, the Vietnam syndrome and the crippling constraints of the Weinberger-Powell Doctrine. It was about showing the world, friend and foe alike, who was boss. It was about supplanting realism and multilateralism with value exportation and unilateralism. It was about ditching deterrence and containment in favor of military prevention.

The war was, in short, about the arrogance of power, an interpretation perfectly consistent with the realist theory of international politics, which holds, among other things, that power unbalanced is power inevitably asserted. Free of the restraining influence of the Soviet Union, the United States, after some residual Vietnam syndrome fits and starts in the 1990s and traumatized by the 9/11 attacks, finally moved to assert the full measure of its sudden global military hegemony. Reinforcing that assertion of power, John Darwin has astutely observed, were two deep-rooted American attitudes toward the rest of the world:

> The first was unilateralism: the reluctance to be bound by the rules of others . . . [which] sprang from beliefs about America's "exceptional" origins as a democratic society in a world ruled by despots or the feudal detritus of the European nobility. The second was universalism: what was good for America was good for the world. Democratic institutions on the American model, America's version of the market economy, and a commercial culture for mass consumption were the best guarantees of wealth and stability. To refuse to adopt them was a hostile act against progress and peace. Unilateralism and universalism were harmless foibles in an isolationist power. In the world's only superpower they became the chief elements of an imperial outlook.[155]

The marriage of universalism, unilateralism, and unchecked military power—the neoconservatives' dream come true—turned out to be a recipe for disastrous strategic overreach, of which there are many historical instances. Indeed, the history of the rise, and especially the fall, of great powers has been the history of what historian Paul Kennedy famously called "imperial overstretch," and the U.S. experience has been no exception. In Iraq in 2003, as in Korea in 1950 and Vietnam in 1965, its excessive confidence in its own military power propelled the United States into a situation in which that power came up short of achieving the political purpose for which it was employed. The supreme irony, of course, is that in Iraq a military action that was in part consciously designed to awe the world—to establish the image of America's military irresistibility—degenerated quickly into an embarrassing advertisement of the limits of U.S. conventional military supremacy and of the persistence of the American public's intolerance of protracted warfare against irregular enemies. Those who wanted to rid American statecraft of the curse of the first Vietnam War succeeded only in serving up a second. (And some still salivate for a third—i.e., a war against Iran.)

Fukuyama, in *America at the Crossroads*, his 2006 critique of the neoconservative thinking that led to the fiasco in Iraq, noted the structural flaws and contradictions underlying the concept of America's "benevolent hegemony" vis-à-vis the rest of the world. First, "benevolent hegemony rests on a belief in American exceptionalism that most non-Americans simply find not credible."[156] Few people in the rest of the world believe the United States acts disinterestedly in international politics. America has interests as well as values, and when it has to choose between the two, it will usually choose the former. Thus, while attempting to establish democracy in Iraq, it allies itself with dictatorships in Egypt and Pakistan and with a theocracy in Saudi Arabia because the governments in Cairo, Islamabad, and Riyadh are more important to the United States as partners in the war on terrorism than they would be as democracies, especially democracies open to subversion by Islamist extremist parties. Second, "benevolent hegemony . . . presupposes an extremely high level of competence on the part of the hegemonic power."[157]

Clearly, American competence has not been on display in Iraq; on the contrary, the U.S. performance in Iraq has been a monument to the toxic combination of arrogance, ignorance, poor planning, worse execution, and a willful refusal to acknowledge, much less correct, mistake after mistake after mistake. The Bush administration knew little about Iraq and never really understood the difficulties and complexities of converting Saddam Hussein's Iraq into a democratic beacon for the Middle East. Third, proponents of benevolent hegemony refuse to recognize that "[t]here are sharp limits to the American people's attention to foreign affairs and willingness to fund projects overseas that do not have clear benefits to U.S. interests."[158] Most Americans do not believe that it is their country's mission to convert the rest of the world into like democracies, and they have limited tolerance for costly crusades overseas that have little or no foundation in promoting concrete national security interests. More to the point, "Americans are not, at heart, an imperial people. Even benevolent hegemons sometimes have to act ruthlessly, and they need a staying power that does not come easily to a people who are reasonably content with their own lives and society."[159]

The decision to invade Iraq may turn out to be the most adversely consequential foreign war in American history. To be sure, the invasion removed Saddam Hussein and his regime from power and permitted the installation of a nominally democratic political system in Baghdad. Iraqis also enjoy unprecedented freedom of speech and communication. However, to repeat, the Iraq War also has alienated U.S. friends and allies around the world; exposed the limits of American military power for all to see and exploit; soured civil-military relations to the point where retired generals are publicly indicting their former civilian superiors for mismanagement and incompetence; depleted U.S. land power and retarded the recapitalization of U.S. air and naval power; weakened the dollar; encouraged Russian and Chinese strategic hostility; vindicated, to millions of Muslims, al Qaeda's story line about American imperial ambitions in the Middle East; aided and abetted the electoral victories of Hamas and Hezbollah; transformed Iraq into a recruiting and training ground for Islamist terrorism; promoted the expansion of Iranian power and influence in the region; encouraged Iran to accelerate its quest for nuclear weapons; and enabled the probable establishment of a Shiite regime in Baghdad aligned with Tehran that could undermine Saudi Arabia and other Sunni Arab states with significant Shiite minorities or even provoke a regional civil war along sectarian lines. As for the situation inside Iraq, the war has generated more than 4 million refugees and internally displaced persons, with most members of Iraq's middle class, including doctors, lawyers, engineers, teachers, and other professionals, having fled the country. It has also fractured the country

> into a quasi-warlord society ruled by multiple, competing armed groups that often engage in criminal behavior and in armed combat with each other. For everyone except the Kurds in the north and political dissidents, Iraq is now far more dangerous than it was under Saddam Hussein as a result of terrorism, insurgency, crime, political assassination, and sectarian conflict, as well as the deterioration of public health.[160]

Given these consequences, an autopsy of the invasion decision is imperative. On December 18, 1941, just eleven days after the Japanese attack on Pearl Harbor, President Roosevelt issued an executive order directing the establishment of a commission, headed by Supreme Court Justice Owen Roberts, to "ascertain and report the facts relating to the attack." Its purpose was to "provid[e] for sound decisions whether any derelictions of duty or errors of judgment on the part of the United States Army or Navy personnel contributed to [Japanese success]; and if so, what these derelictions or errors were, and who were responsible therefore."[161] Though the attack occurred on his watch, Roosevelt did not hesitate to order an investigation that had the potential for greatly embarrassing his administration. Almost four years later, on November 15, 1945, a Democratic-controlled Congress established a bipartisan Joint Committee on the Investigation of the Pearl Harbor Attack consisting of five members of the Senate and five members of the House of Representatives. The committee was tasked to make "a full and complete investigation of the facts relating to the events and circumstances leading up to or following the attack made by Japanese armed forces upon Pearl Harbor." In its report, delivered on July 20, 1946, the committee declared that "we seek to find lessons to avoid pitfalls in the future to evolve constructive suggestions for the protection of our national security, and to determine whether there were failures in our own military and naval establishment which in any measure may have contributed to the extent and intensity of the disaster."[162]

Such an inquiry into the decision to launch the Iraq War should now be convened. (A separate inquiry into the decisions about the post-invasion occupation should also be established.) The aims should be (1) to establish how the United States came to launch a war against an enemy that had nothing to do with the 9/11 attacks and posed no unmanageable threat to the United States and (2) to identify the organizational, policy, and other changes necessary to ensure that such a war is never repeated. This inquiry could be politically explosive, given likely continuing hostilities in Iraq and the culpability in the decision to invade Iraq of virtually the entire American foreign policy establishment, including its congressional and media components, which could have exerted restraint on the rush to war. But the gravity and the consequences of the decision to invade Iraq demand no less than a thorough and, as far as possible, impartial investigation.

The model for this inquiry would be the bipartisan 9/11 Commission, which Congress established and which achieved a remarkable consensus in both its assessment and recommendations. The Bush White House initially opposed the 9/11 Commission's creation but later relented to public and congressional pressure; and even the Obama administration might oppose formation of an Iraq War Commission for fear that such an inquiry might interfere with or divert attention from its own Iraq policy. But that is all the more reason for an Iraq War Commission. Unless led by an extraordinary statesman like Roosevelt, the executive branch will resist formal inquiries into its own misjudgments and mistakes. Partisan considerations, however, should not be permitted to override the profound national interest in avoiding future Iraq wars. Disastrous foreign policy mistakes, like fatal accidents, mandate investigation.

— FIVE —

CONSEQUENCES:
AN IRAQ SYNDROME?

Never fight unless you have to. Never fight alone. And never fight for long.

> —Secretary of Defense Robert Gates,
> speech to the Corps of Cadets at West Point, April 21, 2008[1]

The only thing remarkable about the current war in Iraq is how precipitously American public support has dropped off. Casualty for casualty, support has declined far more quickly than it did during either the Korean War or the Vietnam War. . . . More important, the impact of deteriorating support will not end when the war does. In the wake of the wars in Korea and Vietnam, the American public developed a strong aversion to embarking on such ventures again. A similar sentiment—an "Iraq syndrome"—seems to be developing now, and it will have important consequences for U.S. foreign policy for years after the last American battalion leaves Iraq.

> —John Mueller,
> "The Iraq Syndrome"[2]

The preceding analysis has argued that the Iraq War was, at bottom, about the exercise of American power in the post-Soviet and post-9/11 era. As we have seen, there were many other motivations for war with Iraq as well as expectations of what the war would accomplish. But central to the entire enterprise was a confidence in American military power; a commitment to sustaining and, if possible, strengthening America's global military primacy; and above all, a yearning to demonstrate, to friend and foe alike, that the United States was not afraid to use its military power when and where it saw fit, including the initiation of preventive war.

Underlying this yearning, however, was a blindness to the limits of U.S. military power. Conventional military supremacy effectively deters a conventional military attack on the United States and its overseas interests— no mean accomplishment given the sorry record of nonnuclear deterrence among states during the three centuries separating the Peace of Westphalia and the conclusion of World War II. The Department of Defense deserves great credit for creating military forces that no sane enemy would challenge in traditional regular combat. Waging conventional warfare against the United States is a recipe for certain defeat. Saddam Hussein made that mistake in 1991 and survived only because the George H. W. Bush administration wisely rejected a march on Baghdad and a subsequent assumption of responsibility for Iraq.

It is worth recalling then–Secretary of Defense Dick Cheney's views on why the United States settled for the ejection of Iraqi forces from Kuwait instead of the forcible overthrow of Saddam Hussein. In an interview with *New York Times* columnist Patrick Tyler published on April 13, 1991, Cheney declared:

> If you're going to go in and try to topple Saddam Hussein, you have to go to Baghdad. Once you've got Baghdad, it's not clear what you do with it. It's not clear what kind of government you would put in place of the one that's currently there now. Is it going to be a Shia regime, a Sunni regime or a Kurdish regime? Or one that tilts toward the Baathists, or one that tilts toward the Islamic fundamentalists? How much credibility is that government going to have if it's set up by the United States military when it's there? How long does the

United States military have to stay to protect the people that sign on for that government, and what happens to it once we leave?[3]

Five years later, in a 1996 interview with PBS's *Frontline*, Cheney again stated that

the idea of going into Baghdad . . . or trying to topple the regime wasn't anything I was enthusiastic about. I felt there was a real danger here that you would get bogged down in a long drawn-out conflict, that this was a dangerous, difficult part of the world. If you recall we were all worried about the possibility of Iraq coming apart, the Iranians restarting the conflict that they'd had . . . with the Iraqis over eastern Iraq. We had concerns about the Kurds in the north, the Turks get very nervous every time we start to talk about an independent Kurdistan. . . . Now you can say, well, you should have gone to Baghdad and gotten Saddam. I don't think so. I think if we'd done that we would have been bogged down there for a very long period of time with the real possibility we might not have succeeded.[4]

George W. Bush's father, the forty-first president, also foresaw the unacceptable risks that his son and then–Vice President Cheney later ignored. In his 1998 co-memoir with Brent Scowcroft, George H. W. Bush recounted:

I firmly believed that we should not march into Baghdad. Our stated mission . . . was a simple one—end the aggression, knock Iraq's forces out of Kuwait, and restore Kuwait's leaders. To occupy Iraq would instantly shatter our coalition, turning the whole Arab world against us, and make a broken tyrant into a latter-day Arab hero. It would have taken us way beyond the imprimatur of international law bestowed by the resolutions of the Security Council, assigning young soldiers to a fruitless hunt for a securely entrenched dictator and condemning them to fight in what would be an unwinnable urban guerrilla war. It could only plunge that part of the world into even greater instability and destroy the credibility we were working so hard to establish. . . .

Going in and occupying Iraq, thus unilaterally exceeding the United Nations' mandate, would have destroyed the precedent of international response to aggression that we hoped to establish. Had we gone the invasion route, the United States could conceivably still be *an occupying power in a bitterly hostile land. It would have been a dramatically different—and perhaps barren—outcome.*[5]

Force is a poor vehicle for effecting fundamental political change overseas without similar, exceptional conditions of the kind the United States enjoyed in postwar Germany and Japan. Foreign military occupation provokes resistance unless the alternative to occupation is something worse, which is rarely the case. Only in situations in which a third-party external threat to the occupied territory is present and seen as such by the occupied population—e.g., the Soviet threat to U.S.-occupied Germany and Japan— is an occupation likely to succeed.[6] Moreover, resistance to occupation is likely to be indirect and irregular—e.g., guerrilla warfare or terrorism—for two reasons. Because the occupied are militarily weak compared to the occupier, and because of the historically demonstrated vulnerability of states practicing conventional (i.e., direct) warfare, especially democracies, to defeat by non-state enemies practicing irregular warfare.[7] There is a reason why the Vietnamese Communists, Lebanese terrorists, Somali warlords, al Qaeda's leaders, and Iraqi insurgents all opted for irregular warfare against the United States: it was, and remains, the only *politically* effective way of war available to them. U.S. conventional military supremacy drives our intelligent adversaries into the practice of irregular warfare, the object of which is not military victory—an impossibility—but rather the erosion of America's political will to continue fighting. Irregular warfare poses tremendous challenges to regular (conventional) military establishments, which are, structurally and doctrinally, oriented toward open, force-on-force combat with like enemies in circumstances free of operational and tactical restraints relative to the requirements of successful counterinsurgency.

Given that the decision to invade Iraq was motivated substantially by a perceived need to demonstrate America's capacity and will to use force, and given that the result was to advertise the limits of American power, it makes sense to conclude this work by examining the Iraq War's likely impact on future American attitudes toward the use of force. It remains a little discussed subject in the avalanche of literature on the consequences of the Iraq War.

As we have seen, central to the Bush Doctrine and the neoconservative critique of post–Cold War U.S. foreign policy is a celebration of American global military primacy, a confidence that U.S. military power can be employed to promote the spread of American political values abroad, and an embrace of preventive war to eliminate rising threats before they mature. Prime targets of the neoconservatives' ire before 9/11 were the George H. W. Bush administration's "premature" termination of the 1991 Gulf War, the Clinton administration's aversion to using force unilaterally, and—above all—the Weinberger-Powell Doctrine, which called for using force only in circumstances involving threatened vital interests and when public support and military success were assured. It would be a great irony if a preventive war launched in response to the Bush Doctrine's declared imperatives ended up sparking a return to some form of the Weinberger-Powell Doctrine.

The American debacle in Iraq, however, seemingly vindicates the restrictive use-of-force doctrine propounded by Secretary of Defense Caspar Weinberger and Joint Chiefs of Staff chairman Gen. Colin Powell in the 1980s and early 1990s. That doctrine expressed the Pentagon's take on the lessons of the Vietnam War. It called for the last-resort application of overwhelming force on behalf of vital interests and of clearly defined and achievable political-military objectives, and it insisted on reasonable assurance of enduring public and congressional support.

In the case of Iraq, insufficient force was employed on behalf of exceptionally ambitious objectives resulting in an unexpectedly bloody protraction of hostilities and an attendant loss of domestic political support. Indeed, the rationales upon which public support was mobilized for war—e.g., White House claims (widely questioned by experts at the time) that Iraq was an ally of al Qaeda and on the verge of acquiring nuclear weapons—were discredited by the U.S. occupation of Iraq. War was, moreover, hardly the option of last resort. Deterrence and containment had worked effectively against Saddam Hussein since the 1991 Gulf War; indeed, sanctions and the threat of war kept him from acquiring nuclear weapons and from invading his neighbors. In late 2002, the Bush administration successfully coerced Hussein into permitting the unfettered return of UN weapons inspections, which eventually would have confirmed the absence of an Iraqi WMD threat without a war, and showed how really weak Baathist Iraq had become.

Does the Iraq War portend abandonment of America's promiscuous, post–Cold War overseas interventionism and a return to the cautious Weinberger-Powell Doctrine? Will the Iraq War, as the Vietnam War did before it, exert a chilling effect on American statecraft, especially regarding the use of force? Is the war laying the foundations for an Iraq syndrome analogous to the Vietnam syndrome? Does the Iraq War vindicate the realist foreign policy advocates' rejection of using force to promote expanding American values overseas? Should the use of force be confined to protecting concrete strategic interests? Is strategic retrenchment the best insurance policy against another quagmire like that in Iraq?

This chapter attempts to shed light on and answer these questions. The Iraq War almost certainly will prompt a major debate over the circumstances justifying future threatened or actual uses of U.S. force, and many will argue strongly in favor of greater caution and restraint. "No more Iraqs" could become as popular a policy prescription inside the Pentagon in the coming decades as were the refrains "No more Vietnams" in the 1970s, 1980s, and 1990s and "Never Again" (the Korean War) in the 1950s and early 1960s. Yet the unpopular Korean War was followed by the unpopular Vietnam War, which was followed by the unpopular Iraq War. The chilling effects of Korea and Vietnam proved transitory, and those of Iraq may as well. Activist presidents are not bound by the Pentagon's conservative use-of-force doctrines. Such doctrines moreover may inhibit American statecraft, especially a threatened use of force on behalf of diplomacy. The Weinberger-Powell Doctrine is a case in point. A doctrine designed to prohibit a repetition of the casual and ultimately disastrous intervention in Vietnam swung the pendulum to the opposite extreme—i.e., paralysis in the form of military inaction or, when action was required, the elevation of force protection above the mission the force was designed to accomplish. Those who would return the United States to that doctrine should remember its consequences as well its origins and its weaknesses as well as its strengths. The Iraq War experience likely will encourage future administrations to pay far more attention to the potential unintended consequences of using major force than the George W. Bush administration paid to those resulting from its decision to invade Iraq, but policymakers must guard against permitting prudent caution to morph into crippling timidity. The United States, after all, is still engaged in a rare war of necessity against a lethal, elusive, and clever al Qaeda and its affiliates.

There is also the issue of what happens in Iraq after the last U.S. troops depart in 2011. Whatever occurs there will ultimately determine the success or failure of George W. Bush's great gamble in Iraq. Possible outcomes range from, on the one hand, a full-scale civil war that could dissolve Iraq as a unitary state and invite the establishment on Iraqi territory of an al Qaeda training and operating base similar to the one it enjoyed in Afghanistan prior to 9/11 to, on the other hand, a reasonably stable and politically decentralized, if not necessarily democratic, Iraq in which competing ethno-sectarian interests are accommodated primarily through bargaining rather than bombings and bullets. As of this writing, the neoconservative vision of a democratic Iraq serving as a vehicle for advancing U.S. strategic interests in the Middle East (including regime change in Tehran) and hosting U.S. military bases seems conclusively situated in the realm of fantasy.

At this juncture, it is impossible to know how Iraq will end up, but the Iraq War's continuing unpopularity and blood and treasure costs will likely rob even an unlikely favorable outcome for U.S. interests of any credible claim that the war was worth the sacrifices incurred. Most Americans have rightly concluded that the Iraq War was a horrible mistake.

———————

Weinberger proclaimed his doctrine in the wake of the Reagan administration's disastrous intervention in Lebanon (which Weinberger had opposed) and amid rising concern over possible escalation of U.S. involvement in insurgency-torn El Salvador. The announcement also targeted Weinberger's cabinet and private sector rival, Secretary of State George Shultz, who had strongly supported U.S. intervention in Lebanon and favored the direct use of U.S. force to stop the Sandinistas in Central America. Shultz was a firm believer in coercive diplomacy. More broadly, "The Uses of Military Power," Weinberger's famous National Press Club speech on November 28, 1984, reflected a growing consensus within the U.S. military leadership and the Office of the Secretary of Defense on the Vietnam War's strategic and political lessons as they were seemingly reaffirmed by the failed U.S. intervention in Lebanon in 1982–83. Those lessons boiled down to six "tests" (Weinberger's term) to be passed before the United States would commit forces abroad:

1. The United States should not commit forces to *combat* overseas unless the particular engagement or occasion is deemed vital to our national interests or that of our allies.

2. If we decide that it *is* necessary to put *combat* troops into a given situation, we should do so wholeheartedly and with the clear intention of winning.

3. If we *do* decide to commit forces to combat overseas, we should have clearly defined political and military objectives.

4. The relationship between our objectives and the forces we have committed—their size and composition—must be continually reassessed and adjusted if necessary.

5. Before the U.S. commits combat forces abroad, there must be some

reasonable assurance [that] we will have the support of the American people and their elected representatives in Congress.

6.   The commitment of U.S. forces to combat should be a last resort.[8]

Weinberger identified "gray area conflicts" as "the most likely challenge to peace," yet he warned that they "are precisely the most difficult challenges to which a democracy must respond." He further cautioned that if "we are certain that force is required in a given situation, we run the risk of inadequate national will to apply the resources needed." Weinberger went on to deplore post-Vietnam congressional intrusion in forming foreign policy but reserved his heaviest fire for those "theorists [who] argue that military force can be brought to bear in any crisis," who "are eager to advocate its use even in limited amounts simply because they believe that if there are American forces of *any* size present they will somehow solve the problem."

Weinberger decried the use of force or threatened force as a means of political coercion. As a tool of coercive diplomacy, force had obviously failed against North Vietnam, and its failure was followed by a real war. He viewed the "intermixture of diplomacy and the military" as inherently dangerous because it meant "that we should not hesitate to put a battalion or so of American forces in various places in the world where we desired . . . stability, or changes of governments or whatever else." If the enemy counter-escalated, as the Vietnamese Communists had in 1965, the United States would have to do the same. Weinberger essentially rejected force as an arm of diplomacy; rather, he saw it as a substitute for diplomacy, or something to be used only when diplomacy failed. In so doing, he implicitly rejected the Clausewitzian dictum that war is a continuation of politics by other means and denied the continuum of agreement, negotiation, threat, coercive diplomacy, and war.

The Weinberger Doctrine was carried into the George H. W. Bush administration by Gen. Colin Powell, who had served as Weinberger's military aide and had reviewed a draft of Weinberger's speech. Appointed chairman of the JCS in 1989, Powell strongly endorsed the Weinberger Doctrine, especially its commitment to winning quickly and decisively.

Though he had serious reservations about using force to expel Saddam Hussein from Kuwait (he preferred to deter an Iraqi invasion of Saudi Arabia while giving sanctions time to compel the Iraqis to quit Kuwait),[9] once President Bush made that decision, Powell orchestrated and assembled an overwhelming Coalition force in the Persian Gulf with spectacular results. As a Vietnam War veteran he passionately believed, as did many of his fellow officers who planned and executed Operation Desert Storm, that both the White House and the senior military leadership had almost criminally misused U.S. military forces in Vietnam. "War should be the politics of last resort," he wrote in his bestselling memoir. "And when we go to war we should have a purpose that our people understand and support; we should mobilize the country's resources to fulfill that mission and then go on to win. In Vietnam, we entered a half-hearted war, with much of the nation opposed or indifferent, while a small fraction carried the burden."[10] In a speech at the Vietnam Veterans Memorial shortly after the Gulf War's conclusion, Powell enunciated the doctrine that subsequently bore his name: "If in the end war becomes necessary, as it clearly did in Operation Desert Storm, you must do it right. You've got to be decisive. You've got to go in massively. You've got to be wise and fight in a way that keeps casualties to a minimum. And you've got to go in to win."[11]

Both Weinberger and Powell believed the use of force should be highly restricted. It should be avoided in situations where political restrictions threaten to impede its effective use, where a clear and quick military win is not attainable, and where public and congressional opinion is indifferent or hostile to the purpose for which force is being employed. For Powell, winning meant going in with crushing force, getting the job done quickly, and getting out cleanly—i.e., without postwar political obligations that might compel recommitting U.S. forces in less than ideal circumstances. Having a clear exit strategy was as important as having a clear entry strategy. The Gulf War was the obvious model. The United States went in big on behalf of limited, achievable objectives; won quickly and cheaply; and departed the scene. It was a short, popular, U.N.-sanctioned war that claimed the lives of only

148 Americans. It was a war that seemingly cured the United States of the Vietnam syndrome.

Powell made avoiding another Vietnam his life's mission—a tragic irony given his subsequent failure as secretary of state to dissuade George W. Bush from invading Iraq. He writes,

> Many of my generation, the captains, majors, and lieutenant colonels seasoned in that war, vowed when our turn came to call the shots, we would not quietly acquiesce in half-hearted warfare for half-baked reasons that the American people could not understand or support. If we could make good on that promise to ourselves, to the civilian leadership, and to the country, then the sacrifices of Vietnam would not have been in vain.

Powell believed the greatest fault of the senior military leadership was its failure "to talk straight to its political superiors or to itself. The top leadership never went in to the Secretary of Defense or the President and said, 'This war is unwinnable the way we are fighting it.'"[12]

In 1992, after Bill Clinton was elected president but before his inauguration, Powell wrote an article for *Foreign Affairs* in which he elliptically cautioned his audience, presumably including the president-elect, against repeating the Vietnam War's mistakes in the former Yugoslavia. He condemned gradualism and warned against "send[ing] military forces into a crisis with an unclear mission they cannot accomplish." He noted that "military force is not always the right answer" but urged that "when we do use it, we should not be equivocal; we should win and win decisively." He further warned that an intervention's objectives must be clear and achievable. He also claimed that the George H. W. Bush administration called off the Gulf War when U.S. objectives had been achieved and immediately vacated Iraqi territory because the only alternative would have been "the inevitable follow-up" of "major occupation forces in Iraq for years to come and a complex American proconsulship in Baghdad."[13]

Powell returned to this point in his memoir. He argued that it was not in America's interest to destroy or weaken Iraq to the point where Iran and Syria were not constrained by it.

> It would not contribute to the stability we want in the Middle East to have Iraq fragmented into separate Sunni, Shia, and Kurd political entities. The only way to have avoided this outcome was to have undertaken a largely U.S. conquest and occupation of a remote nation of twenty million people. I don't think this is what the American people signed up for.

He added that "it is naïve . . . to think that if Saddam had fallen, he would necessarily have been replaced by a Jeffersonian in some sort of desert democracy where people read *The Federalist Papers* along with the Koran."[14]

The Clinton administration inherited Powell as the JCS chairman, but there is no evidence that either the new president or his foreign policy principals had much use for the Weinberger-Powell Doctrine or for Powell himself, who not only made his opposition to any U.S. military intervention in the crumbling Yugoslavian state very clear but also was a potential, future Republican presidential candidate. On the contrary, the administration displayed a propensity to use force for coercive purposes in circumstances quite the opposite of those prescribed by the Weinberger-Powell Doctrine. U.S. military action was undertaken in Somalia, Haiti, Bosnia, and Serbia in the absence of either manifestly vital interests or assured public and congressional support. In all cases force was applied in an atmosphere of agonizing indecision, and in the case of the Balkans it was minimally employed. In the war over Kosovo, the result was a major mismatch between the immediate political objective sought (a cessation of Serbian ethnic cleansing) and the military means employed (airpower unsupported by ground force action).[15] Indeed, indecision, hesitation, and casualty phobia were hallmarks of the Clinton administration's approach to using force, with force protection becoming an obsession to the point of trumping any other mission.[16] Led by a president for whom the Vietnam War was the primary foreign policy referent experience, the Vietnam syndrome remained alive and well in Clinton's first term.

As we have seen, hesitation, indecision, and casualty phobia were notably absent in the George W. Bush administration's approach to its war with Iraq. The president and his foreign policy principals, with the prominent exception of Secretary of State Colin Powell, seemed positively eager for a war to bring down Saddam Hussein even though administration spokesmen, when pressed, grudgingly conceded that Iraq had nothing to do with the al Qaeda attacks of 9/11. The administration believed, or at least wanted to believe, that the Baathist regime in Baghdad had chemical and biological weapons, was on the verge of acquiring nuclear weapons, and was prepared to transfer WMDs to terrorist organizations and to even use them directly against the United States or its Middle Eastern allies. The White House portrayed Hussein as an undeterrable madman who had to be removed before he acquired nuclear weapons.

But the objectives of Operation Iraqi Freedom were not confined to Iraq's disarmament and Hussein's removal. A stable democracy that would serve as a model for the rest of the Middle East was supposed to be established in Iraq. How the administration believed such a revolutionary political objective could and would be achieved in a Middle Eastern "Yugoslavia" of deep sectarian divisions and a history of nothing but tyrannical rule remains unclear. The neoconservatives who supplied the intellectual rationale for the Iraq War apparently believed that democracy would naturally arise once the Baathist regime had been destroyed.

What *is* clear is that OIF violated key tenets of the Weinberger-Powell Doctrine. First, Saddam Hussein in 2003 arguably threatened no vital U.S. interest. He was effectively contained and deterred, his conventional military forces were a shambles, and there was little evidence that he was on the verge of acquiring nuclear weapons. That he did not have any WMDs misses the point: even had he possessed nuclear weapons, there is no convincing evidence that he would have been undeterrable. As Condoleezza Rice had written in a 2000 article in *Foreign Affairs,* with respect to Iraq and other rogue states, "the first line of defense should be a clear and classical statement of deterrence—if they do acquire WMD, their weapons will be unusable because any attempt to use them will bring national obliteration." She also said that rogue states "were living on borrowed time" and that "there should be no sense of panic about them."[17] Moreover, no expert on Hussein and his Baathist regime believed that he would transfer WMDs to any organization he could not control, especially to a terrorist organization that regarded the Iraqi dictator as a secular "apostate," and even were he prepared to do so, he could never be sure that such a transfer would escape American detection and retaliation.[18] Thus, a moral and even a legal case could have been made for OIF but not a strategic one. Indeed, some have argued that by providing a new recruiting and training ground for al Qaeda and other Islamic terrorist organizations and by creating breathtaking new opportunities for advancing Iran's imperial and ideological ambitions in the Persian Gulf, the U.S. invasion and occupation of Iraq have established a new threat to vital U.S. security interests where none had existed before.[19]

Second, it is clear, at least to almost every observer without a vested interest in defending the administration's implementation of OIF, that the amount of force employed in OIF was insufficient to establish and maintain the stability necessary to create a new political order in Iraq. Believing that relatively small, "transformed" forces could accomplish America's ends in Iraq, the administration simply ignored Powell's injunction to go in overwhelmingly and decisively and Weinberger's warning to continually reassess the relationship between objectives and the committed force. It also rejected advice from military professionals, such as U.S. Army chief of staff Gen. Eric Shinseki, that Phase IV operations in Iraq might require two or even three times the force actually committed. The Defense Department's civilian leadership apparently could not imagine that it would require more force to stabilize post-Baathist Iraq than it would to defeat the Baathist regime. Even as the unexpected insurgency arose and sectarian violence spread, it conducted no serious reassessment of force size. Only after Robert

Gates replaced Donald Rumsfeld as secretary of defense in late 2006 did President Bush announce a modest increase in U.S. force deployments to stabilize Baghdad.

Powell himself was in a most unenviable position. He was a realist secretary of state serving a neoconservative, idealist foreign policy that was propelling the United States into precisely the kind of political-military endgame in Iraq that both he, as JCS chairman, and President George H. W. Bush had emphatically rejected in 1991. The 9/11 attacks did not convince Powell that Saddam Hussein posed an unacceptable threat to the United States; moreover, he believed that Iraq was contained and containable.[20] He did not believe the attacks had suddenly established Iraq's conversion to a democracy as a vital U.S. interest. And as planning for OIF proceeded, Powell became increasingly concerned over what he regarded as an undersized invasion force. He later recalled that he was "always uneasy about the low numbers.... [The Pentagon's civilian leaders] were making up for mass with technology and speed and cleverness and special operations," assuming that they could repeat in Iraq what they had accomplished in Afghanistan.[21] He made several telephone calls to CENTCOM commander Gen. Tommy Franks, "questioning the force numbers and the length of the supply and communications lines."[22]

Powell later remembered telling the president before he launched OIF,

> When you hit this thing, it's like a crystal glass . . . it's going to shatter. There will be no government. There will be civil disorder. . . .
> I said to him, "You break it, you own it. You're going to own it. You're not going to have a government . . . not a civil society. You'll have twenty-five million Iraqis standing around looking at each other."[23]

Though it is far from self-evident that an invasion force several hundred thousand strong would have succeeded in establishing the stability prerequisite for Iraq's political reconstruction,[24] no OIF issue has drawn more fire from war opponents and proponents alike than the issue of *under*whelming force.

In the Gulf War of 1991 an attacking force three times the size of the OIF force was employed to achieve the limited objective of driving Iraqi forces out of tiny Kuwait; however, twelve years later, a comparatively small force was employed on behalf of the much more ambitious objective of seizing control of all of Iraq (a country about the size of California) and providing the security necessary for that country's political transformation. The result in 1991 was a quick and cheap victory. The result in 2003 was the beginning of a costly and unpopular eight-year war (assuming the departure of all U.S. troops by the end of 2011) that could prompt Iraq's political disintegration.

Third, although the doctrine required reasonable assurance of public and congressional support for the use of force, whatever might have attended the run-up of OIF has long since evaporated. Failure to discover either Iraqi WMDs or a collaborative relationship between Saddam Hussein and al Qaeda, the rise of an unexpected insurgency and ethno-sectarian violence, and the evident inability of the Bush administration to bring the war to a satisfactory conclusion more than six years after it launched OIF have combined to steadily sap public and congressional support for a war that most Americans now believe was a mistake. The November 2006 congressional elections, in which the Democrats regained control of both the House and the Senate, were widely regarded as a referendum on the Bush administration's handling of the Iraq War. In the 2008 elections, which were dominated by economic issues, the Democrats increased their margins in both chambers and saw their nominee, Senator Barack Obama, elected to the presidency.

Comparisons with the unpopular Korean and Vietnam wars are revealing. According to an assessment published in December 2005 by John Mueller, an expert in wartime American opinion, "The only thing remarkable about the current war in Iraq is how precipitously American public support has dropped off. Casualty for casualty, support has declined far more quickly than it did during either the Korean War or the Vietnam War. And if history is any indication, there is little the Bush administration can do to reverse this decline."[25] Mueller was pessimistic about prospects for U.S. success in Iraq, as was a National Intelligence Estimate (NIE) issued in January 2007. "In effect, the United States created an instant failed state [in Iraq], and clambering out of that condition would be difficult in the best of circumstances," contended Mueller.[26] A key judgment of the NIE was that "Iraqi society's growing polarization, the persistent weakness of the security forces and the state in general, and all sides' ready recourse to violence are collectively driving an increase in communal and insurgent violence and political extremism." The NIE further judged that "the term 'civil war' accurately describes key elements of the Iraqi conflict, including the hardening of ethno-sectarian identities, a sea change in the character of the violence, ethno-sectarian mobilization, and population displacements."[27]

In late October 2008, Iraq War expert Anthony H. Cordesman observed that al Qaeda's apparent defeat in Iraq and the decline in insurgent violence following al Qaeda's alienation of key Sunni Arab tribal leaders in Anbar Province did not constitute a U.S. victory in any grand strategic sense.

> History provides countless warnings that states as divided and weak as Iraq is today rarely become stable—much less stable, liberal democracies—without a long series of power struggles. Iraq may well retain many elements of democracy, but it will not be a transformational example or model to anyone. Iraq faces a decade or more of painful adjustments and power struggles among Arabs, Kurds and other minorities.

Cordesman added: "Al Qeada may be largely defeated [in Iraq], but it did not exist [there] before the U.S. invasion, and Islamic extremism and violence will be stronger as a result of the war."[28]

Mueller also predicted the emergence of an "Iraq syndrome":

> In the wake of the wars in Korea and Vietnam, the American public developed a strong aversion to embarking on such ventures again. A similar sentiment—an "Iraq syndrome"—seems to be developing now, and it will have important consequences for U.S. foreign policy for years after the last American battalion leaves Iraqi soil. . . .

[T]here will likely be growing skepticism about various key notions: that the United States should take unilateral military action to correct situations or overthrow regimes it considers reprehensible but that provide no immediate threat to it, that it can and should forcibly bring democracy to other nations not now so blessed, that it has the duty to rid the world of evil, that having by far the largest defense budget in the world is necessary and broadly beneficial, [and] that international cooperation is only of limited value. . . . The United States may also become more inclined to seek international cooperation, sometimes showing even signs of humility.[29]

But the Iraq War's impact is likely to extend well beyond a sharp diminution of neoconservative influence on U.S. foreign policy, especially given the financial and credit crisis of 2008–2009 and Senator Barack Obama's defeat of Senator John McCain for the presidency. Domestic economic turmoil has traditionally depressed the American electorate's appetite for expensive overseas adventures, and McCain, a staunch supporter of the Iraq War, was clearly the neoconservatives' candidate (neoconservatives figured prominently among his campaign's senior foreign policy advisers). It is possible, perhaps probable, that neoconservatism—an elitist philosophy that never appreciated the limits of American public tolerance for costly foreign policy activism, especially the kind of activism that serves up bloody, failed military interventions—will be replaced by a return to the realist approach to foreign policy that characterized the Nixon and George H. W. Bush administrations. If so, interests, not values, will become the primary driver for considerations of threatened and actual use of force, and the Iraq War will cast a dark shadow over any presidential contemplation of major war. Presidents will find it much more difficult to sell any military action that conceivably could entrap the United States in a foreign internal war. Almost certainly, as there was in the decades after Vietnam, there will be an extreme reluctance to commit U.S. ground forces to combat and a corollary emphasis on substituting local surrogates for U.S. soldiers and Marines. There will be renewed focus on training and equipping foreigners (and private military companies) to do our ground fighting for us. As was the case with the Nixon Doctrine, endangered allies and friends will be expected to bear the main burden of ground combat while the United States plays naval and air support roles. Indeed, there may well be a U.S. budgetary reemphasis of air and naval power at the expense of ground power, though present plans call for expanding the U.S. Army and Marines Corps by a total of 92,000 personnel, an expansion to be taken in significant measure out of the hides of the U.S. Air Force and Navy.[30]

This realignment may be a mistake. But for the Iraq War, there would be no need for larger U.S. ground forces, and the planned increases in the ground forces' budgets could be applied to the overdue recapitalization of the navy and air force. Indeed, post–Iraq War ground force requirements, especially requirements for heavy armored and mechanized infantry forces, may be considerably less than were the prewar requirements. The primary rationale for those forces disappeared with the Soviet Union and the shift of the Korean military balance against the north in terms of Pyongyang's capacity to reunify Korea by force (and even feed its people). Heavy ground forces would be of little or no utility in a war with China, and a war to block Iranian acquisition of nuclear weapons almost certainly would be waged by naval, air, and (if on the ground) special operations forces.

The solution to the severely stressed U.S. Army and Marine Corps is the termination of American military involvement in the Iraq War, an event now scheduled to occur by the end of 2011. Expanding the U.S. Army and Marine Corps by 92,000 people on the eve of an era in which the White House and Capitol Hill are likely to be exceptionally skittish about authorizing major ground combat operations makes no long-term strategic sense. Effective counterinsurgency is a voracious consumer of ground troops, and what are the chances of the United States, in the wake of the Iraq War, jumping into another large counterinsurgent war? (The United States and its NATO allies will remain involved in counterinsurgency operations in Afghanistan, a relatively small war that many Americans still regard as legitimate because of

Afghanistan's manifest connection with the 9/11 attacks. U.S. peak military stength in Iraq exceeded 170,000 troops. As of the late summer of 2009, U.S. forces in Afghanistan were building to a total of 68,000 troops.) The army has traditionally despised the counterinsurgency mission; it refused to practice it in Vietnam and dropped any interest in it after that war.[31] And what are the odds that it will stay interested in the mission once it leaves Iraq and Afghanistan? That a small number of gifted Iraq War veterans embraced the mission and developed an impressive new field manual on counterinsurgency is certainly no guarantee of persistent institutional army interest beyond the end of the Iraq War. Indeed, a strong case can be made that America's strategic culture is so hostile to the requirements of successful counterinsurgency that the United States should adopt a policy of deliberate avoidance of counterinsurgent interventions.[32]

Whether the Iraq War will prompt a future secretary of defense—or president—to proclaim a new, more restrictive use-of-force doctrine remains to be seen. Such a doctrine almost certainly would look back to the tenets of the Weinberger-Powell Doctrine. Its influence, however, would be problematic. Presidents might listen to public opinion, but they are free to disregard professional military judgments on when and how to use force. Recall that Bill Clinton led a reluctant military into politically messy interventions in Somalia, Haiti, and the Balkans. Secretaries of defense are also free to ignore military advice, as Robert McNamara and Donald Rumsfeld were notorious for doing.

More to the point, a close examination of the Weinberger-Powell Doctrine reveals key weaknesses. The first is the absence of any operational definition of "vital interest." Vital means life sustaining, and the further the discussion ranges from the protection of the American homeland the more contentious it becomes. Making matters worse is the presidential addiction to selling all wars as vital. Every major U.S. combat intervention overseas since 1945 has been attended by White House declarations concerning threatened vital interests. Presidents are politically compelled to bill wars of choice as wars of necessity, even though every war the United States has waged since

V-J Day, with the sole exception of the war against al Qaeda, has been a war of choice. Additionally, one of the hallmarks of being a great power is a willingness to fight for less than vital interests. Most wars that engage a great power's participation are wars fought with limited forces, for limited objectives, on foreign territory, and against enemies who pose no threat to the great power's homeland. Great powers have waged such wars to acquire and defend colonial possessions, punish aggression, suppress rebellion, halt genocide, overthrow foreign governments, protect economic investments, and maintain their reputations for using force.

Second, while clear military and political aims are indispensable to successful military intervention, they certainly offer no guarantee of success. War aims are moreover hostage to the course of hostilities. More often than not, states end wars with different or additional aims to the ones with which they started. (This adjustment is certainly true for the losers.) Only rarely do prewar exit strategies get implemented. The United States fought the last two years of the Korean War to prevent the forcible repatriation of Chinese Communist prisoners of war, a war aim it could not possibly have foreseen when Truman decided to fight in Korea. In circumstances involving multiple war aims, success may attend some while eluding others. What does victory in Iraq mean? Elimination of the Baathist regime? Establishment of a stable democracy? Prevention of Iraq's ethno-sectarian disintegration? Withdrawal of U.S. forces? Simply declaring success? (The Nixon administration cut American losses in Indochina by negotiating a "peace with honor," but it set up South Vietnam for its inevitable conquest by North Vietnam.)

Third, there are extraordinary circumstances in which war should be an early rather than a last resort. Surely, the great strategic lesson of the 1930s is that early military action is far more preferable than a last-resort use of force against that rare, powerful enemy who is both politically unappeasable and militarily undeterrable. War against Iraq in 2003 would have been strategically justifiable had Iraq been as powerful as Nazi Germany and had Saddam Hussein been undeterred by America's conventional military power and nuclear arsenal. War, moreover, is not the only use of military power.

The mere presence of force can effectively deter, and threatened force can forestall its actual use. To view the use of force as a substitute for diplomacy is to see military victory as the object of war rather than the achievement of the political ends for which war is waged. Frederick the Great got it right: "Diplomacy without arms is music without instruments."[33]

Fourth, assured public support at the beginning of an overseas military intervention can weaken or even evaporate in the event of a military stalemate or defeat. Public support for war was strong at the beginning of the Korean, Vietnam, and Iraq conflicts, but it declined dramatically over time as American casualties continued to be incurred without any apparent progress toward a satisfactory conclusion of hostilities. Sustaining American domestic political support for a war is possible as long as public opinion continues to regard the stakes at hand as worth fighting for and as long as it is persuaded that military action is moving toward fulfilling the war's objectives. Support is endangered when public opinion begins to perceive that the war's costs outweigh the value of its intended benefits. The American body politic has limited tolerance for prolonged, costly, indecisive wars, and that is precisely why such wars are the preferred choices of America's enemies.

Now to the fifth and perhaps most important point: a massive, rapid, and decisive use of force is rare except against the weakest and dumbest of enemies. Its use was unusual even in the age of great power warfare. Not even Germany's spectacular operational campaigns against France and the Low Countries in 1940 and against the Soviet Union in 1941 delivered strategic victory. Massive, rapid, and decisive use of force is virtually impossible in a world of limited and politically messy wars, especially in a global environment in which non-state enemies practice protracted irregular warfare to negate the potential effectiveness of America's conventional military supremacy. No sane enemy of the United States is going to set himself up for the kind of defeat the United States inflicted on the Iraqi army in Kuwait in 1991.

The Chinese in Korea, the Vietnamese Communists in Indochina, the Sunni Arab insurgents in Iraq, and al Qaeda and its affiliates worldwide all have one thing in common: they understood and understand that they could not and cannot defeat the United States militarily, but crushing America's political will is possible via the combination of time and unconventional violence. The fate of American interventions in Vietnam, Lebanon, Somalia, and Iraq validates the continuing utility of protracted irregular warfare against the United States. Historian Geoffrey Perret believes that the

> age of armed intervention is over for the United States. Unable to play its ace—the ability to fight and win a major war—it will no longer be feared. No developing country needs nuclear weapons now to defeat the United States. The distribution of assault weapons and explosives and the creation of an embryonic network of insurgents will do the job at much lower cost.[34]

British Gen. Rupert Smith (Ret.), a veteran of protracted wars against irregular enemies, goes further:

> War no longer exists. Confrontation, conflict and combat un-doubtedly exist all around the world—most noticeably, but not only, in Iraq, Afghanistan, the Democratic Republic of the Congo and the Palestinian territories—and states still have armed forces which they use as a symbol of power. Nonetheless, war as cognitively known to most non-combatants, war as a battle in a field between men and machinery, war as a massive deciding event in a dispute in international affairs: such war no longer exists.[35]

The Weinberger-Powell Doctrine is a nostalgic yearning for the days when wars were wars (and men were men); when states fought each other force on force in open battle; when progress could be measured by divisions destroyed, factories bombed, and territory taken; and when the enemy's unconditional surrender could be sought and obtained. It has very limited relevance in a world in which intrastate wars and transnational terrorism have replaced interstate warfare as the primary threats to U.S. security. America's very acquisition of conventional military supremacy has become its biggest disadvantage by compelling America's enemies to embrace strategies and tactics that will deny that supremacy any decisive effectiveness. As Adrian Lewis has observed in his magisterial *The American Culture of War: The History of U.S. Military Force from World War II to Operation Iraqi Freedom*,

> Weinberger's theory . . . postulated a black and white world with nothing in between. There were only two conditions—war and peace, victory or defeat. Hence, given the logic of this position, the Eighth Army in Korea would have had to complete the destruction of the Chinese People's Volunteer Army in North Korea, and advanced to the Yalu, and to do this America would have had to use nuclear weapons. . . . The Weinberger doctrine meant no war or more total war.[36]

(And, in fact, Weinberger believed that President Truman was "seriously wrong . . . to limit General Douglas MacArthur's freedom of movement in Korea" and to reprimand the general for "going too far.")[37]

The doctrine is also a recipe and an excuse for inaction. Colin Powell opposed both U.S. wars against Iraq and both interventions in the former Yugoslavia because in his view they entailed the risk of bogging down his cherished U.S. Army in another Vietnam. He had no such reservations about U.S. intervention in Panama to overthrow Manuel Noriega's regime in 1989–90. Panama was a tiny, defenseless banana republic; overwhelming force was available; and the intervention passed all of the Weinberger tests, with protecting U.S. military personnel and their families in Panama from further murder and physical harassment by Noriega's goons forming an arguably vital interest. The problem of course is that the United States cannot restrict its use of force to bashing only helpless enemies. If it could, war itself would be virtually risk free. The United States cannot pick and choose its enemies; but in wars of choice, if not those of necessity, it must pick and choose if, when, where, and how it will use force.

The experience of the Iraq War almost certainly will diminish America's appetite for the kind of interventionist military activism that has characterized post–Cold War U.S. foreign policy, especially that during the Clinton and George W. Bush administrations. One hopes it will also alert future presidents and other foreign policy decision makers to the limits of America's military power, especially when it comes to effecting fundamental political change abroad. The United States is hardly the first great power to incur the penalties of military overconfidence, and it must recognize how truly unique the circumstances were that delivered America's total victory of 1945 and the subsequent political transformation of Germany and Japan. What has happened to the United States in Iraq mandates choosing greater caution and selectivity in using force as well as paying greater attention to the potential unintended repercussions of military action. The Iraq War has revealed the dangers of putting threats in the worst light while underestimating intervention's costs and consequences.

Future enemies undoubtedly will attempt to lure the United States into fighting the kind of indecisive, protracted, and politically messy wars into which it stumbled in Vietnam and Iraq. But if such wars are wars of choice rather than wars of necessity for the United States, it should think more than twice before entering them.

Notes

Chapter 1. Introduction: A Mysterious War

1. Robert Draper, *Dead Certain: The Presidency of George W. Bush* (New York: Free Press, 2007), 174.
2. Melvin A. Goodman, *Failure of Intelligence: The Decline and Fall of the CIA* (New York: Rowman and Littlefield, 2008), 222, 223.
3. America's defeat in Vietnam was a political one. The Vietnamese Communists were never in a position to defeat U.S. military forces in Indochina, but they did succeed in defeating the political objective for which the United States fought—the preservation of an independent, non-Communist South Vietnam.
4. Joseph J. Collins, *Choosing War: The Decision to Invade Iraq and Its Aftermath* (Washington, D.C.: Institute for National Strategic Studies, National Defense University, April 2008).
5. Shu Guang Zhang, *Deterrence and Strategic Culture: Chinese-American Confrontations, 1949–1958* (Ithaca, NY: Cornell University Press, 1992), 84.
6. Quoted in Rosemary Foot, *The Wrong War: American Policy and the Dimensions of the Korean Conflict, 1950–1953* (Ithaca, NY: Cornell University Press, 1985), 81.
7. Quoted in Jean Edward Smith, *FDR* (New York: Random House, 2007), 518.
8. John G. Stoessinger, *Why Nations Go to War,* 7th ed. (New York: St. Martin's Press, 1998), 71.
9. See Eliot Cohen and John Gooch, *Military Misfortunes: The Anatomy of Failure in War* (New York: Free Press, 1990), 175–82.
10. Quoted in Clay Blair, *The Forgotten War: America in Korea, 1950–1953* (New York: Times Books, 1987), 348.
11. Ibid., 349.
12. David Halberstam, *The Coldest Winter: America and the Korean War* (New York: Hyperion, 2007), 323.
13. Ibid., 369.

14. For an assessment of the reasons for U.S. military intervention in Vietnam, see Jeffrey Record, *The Wrong War: Why We Lost in Vietnam* (Annapolis, MD: Naval Institute Press, 1998), 1–28.

15. President Eisenhower's remarks at the Governors' Conference, August 4, 1953, excerpted in *The Pentagon Papers: The Defense Department History of United States Decisionmaking on Vietnam*, Senator Gravel ed. (Boston: Beacon Press, 1971), 1:592.

16. "Eisenhower Explains the Domino Theory," excerpt from President Dwight Eisenhower's press conference of April 7, 1954, http://www.richmond.edu/~ebolt/history398/DominoTheory.html.

17. See Jeffrey Record, *Making War, Thinking History: Munich, Vietnam, and Presidential Uses of Force from Korea to Kosovo* (Annapolis, MD: Naval Institute Press, 2002), 55–64.

18. Interview with Secretary Rusk and Secretary McNamara on CBS Television News, August 9, 1965, published as "Political and Military Aspects of U.S. Policy in Vietnam" in *Department of State Bulletin* 53, no. 1366 (August 30, 1965): 342.

19. Robert S. McNamara with Brian VanDeMark, *In Retrospect: The Tragedy and Lessons of Vietnam* (New York: Random House, 1995), 39.

20. See Jeffrey Record and W. Andrew Terrill, *Iraq and Vietnam: Differences, Similarities, and Insights* (Carlisle, PA: Strategic Studies Institute, U.S. Army War College, May 2004), 13.

21. Quoted in George McT. Kahin, *Intervention: How America Became Involved in Vietnam* (New York: Alfred A. Knopf, 1986), 249.

22. Quoted in Tom Wells, *The War Within: America's Battle over Vietnam* (New York: Henry Holt, 1994), 99.

23. Dean Rusk with Richard Rusk and Dan Papp, *As I Saw It* (New York: W. W. Norton, 1990), 472.

24. William Westmoreland interview with Tom Wells, in Wells, *The War Within*, 99.

25. William C. Westmoreland, *A Soldier Reports* (Garden City, NY: Doubleday, 1976), 306.

26. Robert L. Beisner, *Dean Acheson: A Life in the Cold War* (New York: Oxford University Press, 2006), 620.

27. Ibid., 399, 401.

28. Gary R. Hess, *Presidential Decisions for War: Korea, Vietnam, and the Persian Gulf* (Baltimore, MD: Johns Hopkins University Press, 2001), 44.

29. Dean Acheson, *Present at the Creation: My Years at the State Department* (New York: W. W. Norton and Company, 1969), 445.

30. Hess, *Presidential Decisions for War*, 44.

31. Ibid., 44–45.

32. Ibid., 45.

33. See Acheson, *Present at the Creation*, 445–55, and George F. Kennan, *Memoirs 1950–1963* (Boston: Little, Brown and Company, 1972), 23–24. In his memoirs, Nitze states that the "principal flaw" in the argument for invading North Korea was that "it failed to take into account the possibility that China, the Soviet Union, or both might intervene if our forces moved too close to

their borders. It seemed to me that rather than risk widening the war, which might well result from crossing the 38th Parallel, we should consolidate what we had gained by the Inchon victory and seek peace on terms that would guarantee the security of the South Korean regime. If this could be done, we would avoid the necessity of having to keep troops in Korea after the peace." Paul H. Nitze, with Ann M. Smith and Steven L. Rearden, *From Hiroshima to Glasnost: At the Center of Decision—a Memoir* (New York: Grove Weidenfeld, 1989), 107.

34. Quoted in Doris Kearns, *Lyndon Johnson and the American Dream* (New York: Harper & Row, 1976), 252.
35. Quoted in ibid., 252.
36. George Packer, *The Assassins' Gate: America in Iraq* (New York: Farrar, Straus, and Giroux, 2005), 46.
37. John J. Mearsheimer and Stephen Walt, *The Israel Lobby and U.S. Foreign Policy* (New York: Farrar, Straus, and Giroux, 2007), 229.
38. Brent Scowcroft, "Don't Attack Saddam," *Wall Street Journal,* August 15, 2002.
39. Steven Metz, "Iraq and the Evolution of American Strategy," in *Presidential Policies and the Road to the Second Iraq War: From Forty One to Forty Three,* ed. John Davis (Burlington, VT: Ashgate, 2006), 259–60.
40. Jacob Weisberg, *The Bush Tragedy* (New York: Random House, 2008), 205, 202.
41. Ibid., 205.
42. See Jeffrey Record, "The Limits and Temptations of America's Conventional Military Primacy," *Survival* 47, no. 1 (Spring 2005): 33–50.
43. John Quincy Adams, "Warning against the Search for 'Monsters to Destroy,' 1821," http://www.mtholyoke.edu/acad/intrel/jqadams.htm.

Chapter 2. The Neoconservative Imprint

1. James Mann, *Rise of the Vulcans: The History of Bush's War Cabinet* (New York: Viking, 2004), 52.
2. Frances Fukuyama, *America at the Crossroads: Democracy, Power, and the Neoconservative Legacy* (New Haven, CT: Yale University Press, 2006), 36.
3. The pre-9/11 momentum for war with Iraq is traced and analyzed in great detail in Davis, *Presidential Policies.*
4. Douglas J. Feith, *War and Decision: Inside the Pentagon at the Dawn of the War on Terrorism* (New York: HarperCollins, 2008), 9, 48.
5. Ibid., 49–50.
6. See John Davis, "The Ideology of War: The Neoconservatives and the Hijacking of U.S. Policy in Iraq," in Davis, *Presidential Policies,* 34–49.
7. President George W. Bush, "The Remarks Prior to Discussion with President Alvaro Uribe of Colombia and an Exchange with Reporters," the Oval Office, September 25, 2002, http://www.gpo.gov/fdsys/pkg/WCPD-2002-09-30/pdf/WCPD-2002-09-30-Pg1618.pdf.
8. Richard A. Clarke, *Against All Enemies: Inside America's War on Terror* (New York: Free Press, 2004), 244.
9. The neoconservatives' philosophy and the profound influence of key neo-conservatives and their thinking on President George W. Bush and his foreign

policy are detailed in Mann, *The Rise of the Vulcans*; Stefan Halper and Jonathan Clarke, *America Alone: The Neo-Conservatives and the Global Order* (New York: Cambridge University Press, 2004); Murray Friedman, *The Neoconservative Revolution: Jewish Intellectuals and the Shaping of Public Policy* (New York: Cambridge University Press, 2005); Gary Dorrien's *The Neoconservative Mind: Politics, Culture, and the War of Ideology* (Philadelphia, PA: Temple University Press, 1993) and *Imperial Designs: Neoconservatism and the New Pax Americana* (New York: Routledge, 2004); Jacob Heilbrunn, *They Knew They Were Right: The Rise of the Neocons* (New York: Doubleday, 2008); and John Ehrman, *The Rise of Neoconservatism: Intellectuals and Foreign Affairs* (New Haven, CT: Yale University Press, 1995). Also see Joshua Muravchik, "The Past, Present, and Future of Neoconservatism," *Commentary* 124, no. 3 (October 2007): 19–29.

10. Alan Weisman, *Prince of Darkness, Richard Perle: The Kingdom, the Power and the End of Empire in America* (New York: Union Square Press, 2007), 3.

11. Halper and Clarke, *America Alone*, 4, 206 (emphasis in original). Quotation from Lawrence Kaplan and William Kristol, *The War over Iraq: Saddam's Tyranny and America's Mission* (San Francisco: Encounter Books, 2003), vii–viii.

12. Andrew J. Bacevich, *The New American Militarism: How Americans Are Seduced by War* (New York: Oxford University Press, 2005), 73.

13. See Jeffrey Record, *The Specter of Munich: Reconsidering the Lessons of Appeasing Hitler* (Washington, D.C.: Potomac Books, 2006), especially 111–15; and "Retiring Hitler and 'Appeasement' from the National Security Debate," *Parameters* 38, no. 2 (Summer 2008): 91–101.

14. Bacevich, *The New American Militarism*, 75.

15. Ibid., 76.

16. Ibid., 77.

17. Ibid.

18. See James Mann, *The Rebellion of Ronald Reagan: A History of the End of the Cold War* (New York: Viking, 2009).

19. Edward Rhodes, "The Imperial Logic of Bush's Liberal Agenda," *Survival* 35, no. 1 (Spring 2003): 133, 137

20. "Text of the President's Speech at West Point," *New York Times*, June 1, 2002, http://www.nytimes.com/2002/06/01/international/02PTEX-WEB.html.

21. *National Security Strategy of the United States of America* (Washington, D.C.: The White House, September 17, 2002), iii.

22. See, for examples, Zalmay Khalilzad, *From Containment to Global Leadership: America and the World After the Cold War* (Santa Monica, CA: Rand, 1995); Joshua Muravchick, *The Imperative of American Leadership: A Challenge to Neo-Isolationism* (Washington, D.C.: American Enterprise Press, 1996); and David Wurmser, *Tyranny's Ally: America's Failure to Defeat Saddam Hussein* (Washington, D.C.: American Enterprise Institute Press, 1999).

23. Charles Krauthammer, "The Bush Doctrine," *Weekly Standard* 6, no. 36 (June 4, 2001).

24. Philip Stephens, "Present at the Destruction of the World's Partnership," *Financial Times*, March 7, 2003.

25. Project for a New American Century, "Statement of Principles," June 3, 1997, http://www.newamericancentury.org/statementofprinciples.htm.

26. Robert Kagan and William Kristol, "National Interest and Global Responsibility," in *Present Dangers: Crisis and Opportunity in American Foreign and Defense Policy,* edited by Kagan and Kristol (San Francisco: Encounter Books, 2000), 4.

27. Ibid., 6–7.

28. Ibid., 9, 13–14, 16–17.

29. Ibid., 17–18.

30. Wurmser, *Tyranny's Ally,* 39.

31. Kagan and Kristol, "National Interest and Global Responsibility," 23–24.

32. Paul Wolfowitz, "Statesmanship in the New Century," in Kagan and Kristol, *Present Dangers,* 325, 319, and 320.

33. Kaplan and Kristol, *The War over Iraq,* 99.

34. Bill Keller, "The Sunshine Warrior," *New York Times Magazine,* September 22, 2002, 51.

35. Richard Perle, "Why the West Must Strike First against Saddam Hussein," *London Daily Telegraph,* August 9, 2002.

36. Quoted in Heilbrunn, *They Knew They Were Right,* 265.

37. Tom Barry, "A Strategy Foretold," *Foreign Policy in Focus,* October 2002, 1–3.

38. Arguably the most important national security policy document of the Cold War was diplomat George F. Kennan's "Long Telegram" of February 22, 1946, from the American embassy in Moscow to the U.S. Treasury Department. He subsequently published a reedited version of it as "The Sources of Soviet Conduct" under the pseudonym "X" in the July 1947 issue of *Foreign Affairs.* Kennan's assessment of how the Soviets viewed themselves and the international community and how the United States should respond to Soviet behavior became the policy foundation of the U.S. containment strategy regarding the Soviets' expanding power and influence for the next forty years.

39. Kaplan and Kristol, *The War over Iraq,* 71.

40. Robert S. Litwak, *Regime Change: U.S. Strategy through the Prism of 9/11* (Washington, D.C.: Woodrow Wilson Center Press, 2008), 25.

41. Kaplan and Kristol, *The War over Iraq,* 72.

42. International Institute for Strategic Studies, *Strategic Survey 2002–2003: An Evaluation and Forecast of World Affairs* (London: International Institute for Strategic Studies, 2003), 177.

43. David Frum, *The Right Man: The Surprise Presidency of George W. Bush* (New York: Random House, 2003), 231.

44. Clarke, *Against All Enemies,* 30.

45. Julian Borger, "Interview: Richard Clarke," *Guardian* (London), March 23, 2004.

46. Clarke, *Against All Enemies,* 32.

47. Kenneth Pollack, *The Threatening Storm: The Case for Invading Iraq* (New York: Random House, 2002), 105.

48. Clarke, *Against All Enemies,* 265.

49. Bob Woodward, *Bush at War* (New York: Simon & Schuster, 2002), 49.

50. Ibid.
51. Clarke, *Against All Enemies,* 30–31.
52. Karen DeYoung, *Soldier: The Life of Colin Powell* (New York: Alfred A. Knopf, 2006), 349.
53. Woodward, *Bush at War,* 83–85.
54. Emphasis added. Signers of the letter included William Kristol, William J. Bennett, Eliot Cohen, Midge Decter, Francis Fukuyama, Reuel Marc Gerecht, Donald Kagan, Robert Kagan, Jeane Kirkpatrick, Charles Krauthammer, Richard Perle, Norman Podhoretz, Gary Schmitt, and Leon Wieseltier. Entitled "Toward a Comprehensive Strategy," the letter can be accessed on the *National Review* website: http://www.nationalreview.com/document/document092101b.shtml.
55. Michael Elliott and James Carney, "First Stop, Iraq," *Time,* March 22, 2003.
56. Elisabeth Bumiller, *Condoleezza Rice: An American Life* (New York: Random House, 2007), 185.
57. Quentin Peel, Robert Graham, James Harding, and Judy Dempsey, "War in Iraq: How the Die Was Cast before Transatlantic Diplomacy Failed," *Financial Times,* May 27, 2003.
58. *National Security Strategy* (2002), 13. For a convenient compilation of key Bush speeches on foreign policy from September 11, 2001, through his "Mission Accomplished" appearance on the USS *Abraham Lincoln* on May 1, 2003, see George W. Bush, *"We Will Prevail": President George W. Bush on War Terrorism, and Freedom* (New York: Continuum, 2003).
59. *National Security Strategy,* iv.
60. Ibid., 1, 3.
61. Ibid., iv.
62. Ibid.
63. Ibid., 14.
64. Ibid.
65. Ibid., 15.
66. Ibid., 29.
67. Ibid., 30.
68. Ibid., 27.

Chapter 3. Bogus Assumptions, Wishful Thinking

1. Excerpted in Bush, *We Will Prevail,* 184.
2. Robert Dreyfuss and Jason Vest, "The Lie Factory," *Mother Jones,* January–February 2004.
3. "Vice President Speaks at VFW 103rd National Convention," August 26, 2002, http://www.georgewbush-whitehouse.archives.gov/news/releases/2002/08/20020826.html.
4. All quotations from Bush's Cincinnati speech are taken from "Excerpted Remarks by the President from Speech at the Cincinnati Museum Center, Cincinnati, Ohio, October 7, 2002," in *We Will Prevail,* 192–200.
5. Noah Feldman, *What We Owe Iraq: War and the Ethics of Nation Building* (Princeton: Princeton University Press, 2004), 19.

6. Stephen Holmes, *The Matador's Cape: America's Reckless Response to Terror* (New York: Cambridge University Press, 2007), 108.

7. Mark Clodfelter, *The Limits of Air Power: The American Bombing of North Vietnam* (New York: Free Press, 1989), 40, 47–48.

8. See ibid., 117–46, 203–10.

9. Donald Rumsfeld, "Testimony on Iraq," Hearing before the Senate Armed Services Committee, Washington, D.C., July 9, 2003, www.defenselink.mil/speeches/2003/sp20030709-secdef0364.html.

10. Feith, *War and Decision*, 215.

11. Ibid., 64 (emphasis added).

12. Ibid., 225.

13. Ibid., 215.

14. Richard Perle, "Ambushed on the Potomac," *The National Interest Online*, January 21, 2009, 5, http://www.nationalinterest.org/PrinterFriendly.aspx?id=20486 (emphasis added).

15. Richard K. Betts, *Enemies of Intelligence: Knowledge and Power in American National Security* (New York: Columbia University Press, 2007), 118.

16. For a comprehensive account of the Bush administration's deliberate deception on the issues of Iraq's alleged alliance with al Qaeda and its possession of WMDs, including a robust nuclear weapons program, see Russ Hoyle, *Going to War: How Misinformation, Disinformation, and Arrogance Led America into Iraq* (New York: St. Martin's Press, 2008).

17. James P. Pfiffner, "Did President Bush Mislead the Country in His Arguments for War with Iraq?" *Presidential Studies Quarterly* 34, no. 1 (March 2004): 25–26.

18. Chaim Kaufmann, "Threat Inflation and the Failure of the Marketplace of Ideas: The Selling of the Iraq War," *International Security* 29, no. 1 (Summer 2004): 9.

19. "Secretary Wolfowitz Interview with Sam Tannenhaus," *Vanity Fair*, May 9, 2003, http://www.defenselink.mil/transcripts/transcript.asx?transcriptid=2549.

20. Joseph Cirincione, Jessica T. Matthews, and George Perkovich with Alexis Orton, *WMD in Iraq: Evidence and Implications* (Washington, D.C.: Carnegie Endowment for International Peace, January 2004), 7.

21. John Prados, *Hoodwinked: The Documents That Reveal How Bush Sold Us a War* (New York: New Press, 2004), xi–xii. For other assessments of the Bush administration's deliberate inflation of the Iraqi threat, see Paul Pillar, "Intelligence, Policy, and the War in Iraq," *Foreign Affairs* 85, no. 2 (March–April 2006): 15–27; John J. Mearsheimer and Stephen M. Walt, "An Unnecessary War," *Foreign Policy*, no. 134 (January–February 2002): 51–59; Craig R. Whitney, ed., *The WMD Mirage: Iraq's Decade of Deception and America's False Premise for War* (New York: Public Affairs, 2005); and Michael Isikoff and David Corn, *Hubris: The Inside Story of Spin, Scandal, and the Selling of the Iraq War* (New York: Crown Publishers, 2006).

22. Pillar, "Intelligence, Policy, and the War in Iraq," 18.

23. Ibid.

24. Ibid., 19.

25. Ibid., 20–21.

26. Caitlin A. Johnson, "Transcript: President Bush, Part 2: Couric's Interview with President Bush," CBS News, September 6, 2006, 1, http://www.cbsnews.com/stories/2006/09/06/five_years/main1980074.shtml.

27. Weisberg, *The Bush Tragedy*, 188–94.

28. Scott McClellan, *What Happened: Inside the Bush White House and Washington's Culture of Deception* (New York: Public Affairs, 2008), 111–12.

29. Richard N. Haass, *The Opportunity: America's Moment to Alter History's Course* (New York: Public Affairs, 2005), 185.

30. Mohamed ElBaradei, "The Status of Nuclear Inspections in Iraq," United Nations Security Council, January 27, 2003, excerpted in Hoyle, *Going to War*, 310.

31. Steven Metz, *Iraq and the Evolution of American Strategy* (Washington, D.C.: Potomac Books, 2008), 117.

32. Trita Parsi, *Treacherous Alliance: The Secret Dealings of Israel, Iran, and the U.S.* (New Haven, CT: Yale University Press, 2007), 270–71.

33. Adam Cobb, "A Strategic Assessment of Iraq," *Civil War* 9, no. 1 (March 2007): 35.

34. Litwak, *Regime Change*, 304.

35. Ibid., 162.

36. Scowcroft, "Don't Attack Saddam."

37. Daniel Benjamin and Steven Simon, *The Age of Sacred Terror* (New York: Random House, 2002), 254.

38. *Final Report of the National Commission on Terrorist Attacks upon the United States*, authorized edition (New York: W. W. Norton, 2005), 66.

39. Kevin M. Woods with James Lacey, *Iraqi Perspectives Report: Saddam and Terrorism: Emerging Insights from Captured Iraqi Documents* (redacted) (Washington, D.C.: Institute for Defense Analyses, November, 2007), 1: ES-1, ES-1-2.

40. See Graham Allison, *Nuclear Terrorism: The Ultimate Preventable Catastrophe* (New York: Times Books, 2004), 61–86; and Joseph Cirincione, *Bomb Scare: The History and Future of Nuclear Weapons* (New York: Columbia University Press, 2007), 89–102.

41. Allison, *Nuclear Terrorism*, 67–74; and Cirincione, *Bomb Scare*, 92–93.

42. Quoted in Joseph Cirincione, Jon B. Wolfsthal, and Miriam Rajkumar, *Deadly Arsenals: Nuclear, Biological, and Chemical Threats*, 2nd ed. (Washington, D.C.: Carnegie Endowment for International Peace, 2005), 132.

43. Allison, *Nuclear Terrorism*, 74–78; and Cirincione, *Bomb Scare*, 94.

44. Cirincione, *Bomb Scare*, 91.

45. See Douglas Jehl, "Pentagon Reportedly Skewed CIA's View of Qaeda Tie," *New York Times*, October 22, 2004; Jeffrey Goldberg, "A Little Learning: What Douglas Feith Knew, and When He Knew It," *New Yorker*, May 9, 2005; David S. Cloud and Mark Mazzetti, "Prewar Intelligence Unit at Pentagon Is Criticized," *New York Times*, February 7, 2007; and Daniel Benjamin, "Feith-Based Intelligence," *Washington Post*, March 8, 2008.

46. Quoted in Kaufmann, "Threat Inflation," 25 (text and note 87).

47. Hans Blix, *Disarming Iraq* (New York: Pantheon, 2004), 3.

48. Ibid., 156.
49. Hoyle, *Going to War,* 349–51.
50. Ibid., 349–50; Bob Woodward, *State of Denial* (New York: Simon & Schuster, 2006), 92–103; and Jeff Stein, "Army General Tells a Little-Known Tale of Pre-War Intelligence on Iraq," *CQ.com,* October 20, 2006, http://public .cq.com/public/20061020_homeland.html.
51. Barton Gellman, "U.S. Has Not Inspected Iraqi Nuclear Facility," *Washington Post,* April 25, 2003. Also see Gellman, "Seven Nuclear Sites Looted," *Washington Post,* May 10, 2003.
52. Cirincione, Wolfsthal, and Rajkumar, *Deadly Arsenals,* 342.
53. Michael R. Gordon and Bernard E. Trainor, *Cobra II: The Inside Story of the Invasion and Occupation of Iraq* (New York: Pantheon Books, 2006), 503–4. Also see 78–83; and Woodward, *State of Denial,* 92–96 and 100–3.
54. Donald Rumsfeld, "Secretary Rumsfeld's Remarks on ABC 'This Week' with George Stephanopoulos," Department of Defense news transcript, March 30, 2003, http://www.defenselink.mil/transcripts/transcript.aspx?transcript id=2185.
55. See Kevin M Woods and others, *The Iraqi Perspectives Report: Saddam's Senior Leadership on Operation Iraqi Freedom from the Official U.S. Joint Forces Command Report* (Annapolis, MD: Naval Institute Press, 2006), xvii–36.
56. Quoted in DeYoung, *Soldier,* 376.
57. Gen. Anthony Zinni, "The 10 Mistakes," speech to the Center for Defense Information, Washington, D.C., May 26, 2004. Reprinted in http://dir.salon. com/story/news/feature/2004/05/26/zinni/index.html.
58. Suicide bombing was a post-invasion phenomenon. Prior to April 2003, there had never been a suicide bombing in Iraq. See Robert A. Pape, *Dying to Win: The Logic of Suicide Terrorism* (New York: Random House, 2005), 245–46. The Baathist regime monopolized terrorism in Iraq, and Saddam Hussein, for all his brutality and paranoia, ran a stable, secular regime that formed a significant barrier against the expansion of Iranian power and influence in the Middle East.
59. For a comprehensive assessment of the present insurgency in Afghanistan and a critique of NATO's counterinsurgency effort, see Antonio Giustozzi, *Koran, Kalashnikov, and Laptop: The Neo-Taliban Insurgency in Afghanistan* (New York: Columbia University Press, 2008).
60. Litwak, *Regime Change,* 287.
61. Cited in Bradley Martin, *Under the Loving Care of the Fatherly Leader: North Korea and the Kim Dynasty* (New York: St. Martin's Press, 2004), 676.
62. Andrew J. Bacevich, "Gulliver at Bay: The Paradox of the Imperial Presidency," in *Iraq and the Lessons of Vietnam: How Not to Learn from the Past,* eds. Lloyd C. Gardner and Marilyn B. Young (New York: New Press, 2007), 127.
63. See Jeffrey Record, *Dark Victory: America's Second War against Iraq* (Annapolis, MD: Naval Institute Press, 2004), 64–89.
64. Quoted in Draper, *Dead Certain,* 178.
65. Quoted in ibid., 189.

66. Holmes, *The Matador's Cape*, 125.
67. Fukuyama, *America at the Crossroads*, 116.
68. Danielle Pletka, "There's No Freedom Gene," *New York Times*, March 16, 2008.

Chapter 4. The Reasons Why

1. Quoted in Hanna Batatu, *The Old Social Classes and the Revolutionary Movements in Iraq: A Study of Iraq's Oldest Landed and Commercial Classes and of Its Communists, Ba'thists, and Free Officers* (Princeton, NJ: Princeton University Press, 1978), 25.
2. William Kristol, "Testimony," Senate Foreign Relations Committee, February 7, 2002, www.newamericancentury.org/defense-20020207.htm.
3. Andrew Cockburn, *Rumsfeld: His Rise, Fall, and Catastrophic Legacy* (New York: Scribner, 2007), 170.
4. Both quotes are in Draper, *Dead Certain*, 173.
5. Quoted in Craig Unger, *The Fall of the House of Bush* (New York: Scribner, 2007), 264.
6. The alleged assassination attempt on George H. W. Bush in Kuwait is surrounded by considerable uncertainty. According to W. Andrew Terrill, one of the U.S. Army's leading experts on Iraq, "It is at least possible that the Kuwaitis used captured smugglers to fake the incident because they were worried about a faltering U.S. commitment to Kuwait's defense by the new American president, Bill Clinton." Terrill, in correspondence with the author, July 7, 2008.
7. Kaplan and Kristol, *The War over Iraq*, 37.
8. Reuel Marc Gerecht, "A Cowering Superpower," *Weekly Standard* 6, no. 43 (July 30, 2001).
9. Christian Alfonsi, *Circle in the Sand: Why We Went Back to Iraq* (New York: Doubleday, 2006), 411.
10. William Kristol and Robert Kagan, "Introduction: National Interest and Global Responsibility," in Kristol and Kagan, *Present Dangers*, 4.
11. Hoyle, *Going to War*, 33.
12. David Frum and Richard Perle, *An End to Evil: How to Win the War on Terror* (New York: Random House, 2003), 17.
13. For an analysis of the Vietnam syndrome's impact on U.S. decision making in the 1990s regarding the Balkans, see Jeffrey Record, *Serbia and Vietnam: A Preliminary Comparison of U.S. Decisions to Use Force*, Occasional Paper no. 8 (Maxwell Air Force Base, AL: Center for Strategy and Technology, Air War College, May 1999).
14. Quoted in Weisman, *Prince of Darkness*, 146.
15. Richard A. Clarke, *Your Government Failed You: Breaking the Cycle of National Security Disasters* (New York: HarperCollins, 2008), 266.
16. Richard Haass, *War of Necessity, War of Choice: A Memoir of Two Iraq Wars* (New York: Simon and Schuster, 2009), 234–35.
17. Quoted in James Carney and John F. Dickerson, "Inside the War Room," *Time*, December 31, 2001–January 7, 2002, 116.

18. "President Bush Discusses Global War on Terror," Wardman Park Marriott Hotel, Washington, D.C., September 26, 2006, http://docs.google.com/gvie w?a=v&q=cache:3Da3UV5YSJMJ:merln.ndu.edu/archivepdf/afghanistan/ WH/20060929-3.pdf+"President+Bush+at+Wardman+Park+Marriott+Hotel ,&hl=en&gl=us.

19. "Vice President's Remarks to Marines at Camp Lejeune, N.C.," October 3, 2005, http://merln.ndu.edu/archivepdf/iraq/WH/20051003-4.pdf.

20. Quoted in Jim Rutenberg, "In Farewell, Rumsfeld Warns Weakness Is 'Provocative,'" *New York Times*, December 16, 2006.

21. Philip Shenon, *The Commission: The Uncensored History of the 9/11 Investigation* (New York: Twelve, 2008), 316.

22. See Norman Cigar, "Iraq's Strategic Mindset and the Gulf War; Blueprint for Defeat," *Journal of Strategic Studies* 15, no. 1 (March 1992): 1–29; and Jeffrey Record, "Defeating Desert Storm (and Why Saddam Didn't)," *Comparative Strategy* 12, no. 2 (1993): 125–50.

23. Woods, *The Iraqi Perspectives Report*, xvii.

24. Kaplan and Kristol, *The War over Iraq*, 112.

25. Quoted in James Gerstenzang, "Bush Says Iraq Exit Would Bolster Iran," *Los Angeles Times*, October 4, 2007.

26. See Jeffrey Record, *Nuclear Deterrence, Preventive War, and Counterproliferation* (Washington, D.C.: Cato Institute, July 2004).

27. *The National Security Strategy* (2002), 15.

28. "Text of the President's Speech at West Point," *New York Times*, June 1, 2002, http://www.nytimes.com/2002/06/01/international/02PTEX-WEB.html.

29. See Record, *Dark Victory*, 33–34.

30. "Text of the President's Speech at West Point."

31. See Jeffrey Record, "Threat Confusion and Its Penalties," *Survival* 46, no. 2 (Summer 2004): 51–72.

32. Quoted in Scott Sagan, "The Perils of Proliferation: Organization Theory, Deterrence Theory, and the Spread of Nuclear Weapons," *International Security* 18, no. 4 (Spring 1994): 78.

33. *The National Security Strategy* (2002), 27, 30.

34. Frum and Perle, *An End to Evil*, 33.

35. See Jeffrey Record, "Back to the Weinberger-Powell Doctrine?" *Strategic Studies Quarterly* 1, no. 1 (Fall 2007): 79–95.

36. Zbigniew Brzezinski, "George Bush's Suicidal Statecraft," *International Herald Tribune*, October 13, 2005.

37. Fareed Zakaria, *The Post-American World* (New York: W. W. Norton, 2008), 235.

38. Ray Takeyh, "Iran's New Iraq" *Middle East Journal* 62, no. 1 (Winter 2008): 20.

39. Ibid., 13, 30.

40. Parsi, *Treacherous Alliance*, 278.

41. Christopher J. Fettweis, *Losing Hurts Twice as Bad: The Four Stages to Moving Beyond Iraq* (New York: W. W. Norton, 2008), 123.

42. Peter Galbraith, "The Victor?" in *The Consequences to Come: American Power after Bush*, ed. Robert B. Silvers (New York: New York Review Books, 2008), 64.

43. Thomas Powers, "Iran: The Threat," *New York Review of Books*, July 17, 2008, 9.

44. Robert Kagan, *The Return of History and the End of Dreams* (New York: Alfred A. Knopf, 2008), 46–47.

45. Ibid., 47.

46. Ibid., 47–48.

47. See Akbar Ganji, "The Latter-Day Sultan: Powers and Politics in Iran," *Foreign Affairs* 87, no. 6 (November–December 2008): 45–66.

48. George Packer, "Dreaming of Democracy," *New York Times Magazine*, March 2, 2003, 49.

49. Frum, *The Right Man*, 196.

50. Glenn Kessler, *The Confidante: Condoleezza Rice and the Creation of the Bush Legacy* (New York: St. Martin's Press, 2007), 91.

51. Condoleezza Rice, "Transforming the Middle East," *Washington Post*, August 7, 2003.

52. Quoted in Kessler, *The Confidante*, 98.

53. Bumiller, *Condoleezza Rice*, xxiv.

54. McClellan, *What Happened*, 243.

55. Ibid., 128.

56. Ibid., 145.

57. See Ivo H. Daalder and James M. Lindsay, *America Unbound: The Bush Revolution in Foreign Policy* (Washington, D.C.: Brookings Institution, 2003), 15.

58. "Vice President Speaks at VFW."

59. Feith, *War and Decision*, 475, 476 (emphasis in original).

60. Douglas J. Feith, "How Bush Sold the War," *Wall Street Journal*, May 27, 2008.

61. McClellan, *What Happened*, 131.

62. Ibid., 128–29.

63. "Bush Speech on Iraq: 'Saddam Hussein and His Sons Must Leave,'" *New York Times*, March 18, 2003.

64. "Bush: 'We Will Do What Is Necessary.' Transcript of President George W. Bush's Address to the Nation, September 7, 2003," *Washington Post*, September 8, 2003.

65. *The National Security Strategy of the United States of America* (Washington, D.C.: The White House, March 2006), 1. On March 12, 1947, in response to a Communist insurgency in Greece and to Soviet pressure on Turkey for political concessions, President Truman declared to a joint session of Congress that "it must be the policy of the United States to support free peoples who are resisting subjugation by armed minorities or by outside pressures." Quoted in Richard Crockatt, *The Fifty Years War: The United States and the Soviet Union in World Politics, 1941–1991* (New York: Routledge, 1995), 73.

66. Fred Kaplan, *Daydream Believers: How a Few Grand Ideas Wrecked American Power* (New York: John Wiley and Sons, 2008), 175–76.

67. "In the President's Words: 'Free People Will Keep the Peace of the World,'" Transcript of President Bush's speech to the American Enterprise Institute, Washington, D.C., February 26, 2003, in *New York Times*, February 27, 2003.

68. John Dower, *Embracing Defeat: Japan in the Wake of World War II* (New York: W. W. Norton, 1999), 204.

69. See William Manchester, *American Caesar: Douglas MacArthur, 1880–1964* (Boston: Little, Brown), 459–544; Herbert Bix, *Hirohito and the Making of Modern Japan* (New York: HarperCollins, 2000), 533–44; and David M. Edelstein, *Occupational Hazards: Success and Failure in Military Occupation* (Ithaca, NY: Cornell University Press, 2008), 122–35.

70. Conrad C. Crane and W. Andrew Terrill, *Reconstructing Iraq: Insights, Challenges, and Missions for Military Forces in a Post-Conflict Scenario* (Carlisle, PA: Strategic Studies Institute, U.S. Army War College, February 2003), 15.

71. James Webb, "Heading for Trouble," *Washington Post*, September 4, 2002.

72. Marjorie Connelly, "Sinking Views of the United States," *New York Times*, March 23, 2003.

73. Fouad Ajami, *The Foreigner's Gift: The Americans, the Arabs, and the Iraqis in Iraq* (New York: Free Press, 2006), 67.

74. See Frum and Perle, *An End to Evil*, 129–42.

75. See Robert Baer, "The Fall of the House of Saud," *Atlantic Monthly* 291, no. 40 (May 2003): 53–62.

76. Kaplan and Kristol, *The War over Iraq*, 99–100 (emphasis added).

77. Bacevich, *The New American Militarism*, 127–28.

78. See Weisman, *Prince of Darkness*, 175–78.

79. See Aram Roston, *The Man Who Pushed America to War: The Extraordinary Life, Adventures, and Obsessions of Ahmad Chalabi* (New York; Nation Books, 2008); Jane Mayer, "The Manipulator," *New Yorker*, June 7, 2004; John Dizard, "How Ahmed Chalabi Conned the Neocons," *Financial Times*, May 4, 2004; and Robert Dreyfuss, "Tinker, Tailor, Neocon, Spy," *American Prospect*, November 18, 2002.

80. Mayer, "The Manipulator," 51.

81. Dizard, "How Ahmed Chalabi Conned the Neocons."

82. See Halper and Clarke, *America Alone*, 104–8; and Dorrien, *Imperial Designs*, 195–98.

83. Heilbrunn, *They Knew They Were Right*, 10.

84. Dorrien, *Imperial Designs*, 203–4.

85. Parsi, *Treacherous Alliance*, 239–41,

86. Quoted in "Gates Revives Old Military Axiom: 'Never Fight Unless You Have To,'" http://ebird.afis.mil/ebfiles/e20080422595686.html.

87. Dale R. Herspring, *Rumsfeld's Wars: The Arrogance of Power* (Lawrence: University Press of Kansas, 2008), 31.

88. Ibid., 71.

89. Thomas E. Ricks, *Fiasco: The American Military Adventure in Iraq* (New York: Penguin, 2006), 102.

90. Gordon and Trainor, *Cobra II*, 53.

91. Kaplan, *Daydream Believers*, 159.

92. Ibid., 153.

93. Heilbrunn, *They Knew They Were Right*, 231.

94. "DoD News Briefing—Secretary Rumsfeld and Gen. Myers," official Department of Defense transcript, April 11, 2003, http://www.defenselink.mil/transcripts/transcript/aspx?transcripted=2367.

95. Interview with George Packer, reprinted in Charles H. Ferguson, *No End in Sight: Iraq's Descent into Chaos* (New York: Public Affairs, 2008), 136.

96. Ricardo S. Sanchez with Donald T. Phillips, *Wiser in Battle: A Soldier's Story* (New York: HarperCollins, 2008), 171.

97. Ibid., 168–69.

98. Ibid., 169.

99. Gordon and Trainor, *Cobra II*, 503.

100. See Record, *Dark Victory*, 85–89.

101. Bacevich, "Gulliver at Bay," 132.

102. Colin S. Gray, "The American Way of War: Critique and Implications," in *Rethinking the Principles of War*, ed. Anthony D. McIvor (Annapolis, MD: Naval Institute Press, 2005), 27–28.

103. Ibid., 31.

104. Antulio J. Echevarria, *Toward an American Way of War* (Carlisle, PA: Strategic Studies Institute, U.S. Army War College, March 2004), 10, 16.

105. Frederick W. Kagan, "War and Aftermath," *Policy Review* 120 (August–September 2003), 27.

106. Donald Rumsfeld, "Defending Ourselves: Why Should We Attack Iraq?" Opening statement before the Senate Armed Services Committee, September 19, 2002, reprinted in *Vital Speeches of the Day* 68, no. 24 (October 1, 2002): 770–74.

107. Frederick W. Kagan, *Finding the Target: The Transformation of American Military Policy* (New York: Encounter Books, 2006), 346.

108. Stephen Biddle et al., *Toppling Saddam: Iraq and American Military Transformation* (Carlisle, PA: Strategic Studies Institute, U.S. Army War College, April 2004), v.

109. See Jane Mayer, *The Dark Side: The Inside Story of How the War on Terror Turned into a War on American Ideals* (New York: Doubleday, 2008).

110. Quoted from the Nixon-Frost interview, republished in the *New York Times*, May 20, 1977.

111. Charlie Savage, *Takeover: The Return of the Imperial Presidency and the Subversion of American Democracy* (New York: Little, Brown, 2007), 8–9.

112. See John P. MacKenzie, *Absolute Power: How the Unitary Executive Theory Is Undermining the Constitution* (New York: Century Foundation Press, 2008).

113. See Savage, *Takeover*, 54–57, 59–61.

114. WGBH Educational Foundation, "Cheney in His Own Words," in "The Dark Side," *Frontline*, Public Broadcasting Service, posted June 20, 2006, http://www.pbs.org/wgbh/pages/frontline/drakside/themes/ownwords.html.

115. See Unger, *The Fall of the House of Bush*, 181–214.

116. See Barton Gellmann, *Angler: The Cheney Vice Presidency* (New York: Penguin, 2008).

117. Hoyle, *Going to War*, 60.

118. See Jack Goldsmith, *The Terror Presidency: Law and Judgment Inside the Bush Administration* (New York: W. W. Norton, 2007), 177–216.

119. Ibid., 212.

120. Arthur M. Schlesinger, Jr., *The Imperial Presidency* (Boston: Houghton Mifflin, 1973), 326.

121. Goldsmith, *The Terror Presidency,* 215.

122. Peter Singer, *The President of Good and Evil: The Ethics of George W. Bush* (New York: Dutton, 2004), 1.

123. Ibid., 212.

124. Glenn Greenwald, *A Tragic Legacy: How a Good vs. Evil Mentality Destroyed the Bush Presidency* (New York: Crown Publishers, 2007), xii.

125. Quoted in Unger, *The Fall of the House of Bush,* 160.

126. Quoted in Greenwald, *The President of Good and Evil,* 63.

127. Quoted in ibid., 61.

128. "Remarks by the President from Speech at National Day of Prayer and Remembrance Ceremony," Washington, D.C., September 14, 2001, excerpted in Bush, *We Will Prevail,* 6.

129. "Presidential Radio Address to the Nation," September 15, 2001, excerpted in ibid, 8.

130. "Remarks by the President from Speech at the Islamic Center of Washington, D.C.," September 17, 2001, excerpted in ibid., 9.

131. "Remarks by the President from Speech to Employees at the Federal Bureau of Investigation," Washington, D.C., September 25, 2001, excerpted in ibid., 22.

132. "Remarks by the President from Speech to Employees of the Central Intelligence Agency," September 26, 2001, excerpted in ibid., 24.

133. "Remarks by the President from Speech to the Employees of the Department of Labor," October 4, 2001, excerpted in ibid., 29, 30.

134. "Remarks by the President from Speech Unveiling 'Most Wanted' Terrorist List," FBI Headquarters, Washington, D.C., October 10, 2001, excerpted in ibid., 39.

135. "Remarks by the President from Speech at the Department of Defense Service of Remembrance," October 11, 2001, excerpted in ibid., 40.

136. "Remarks by the President from Speech to Military Personnel at Travis Air Force Base," October 17, 2001, excerpted in ibid., 46.

137. "Remarks by the President from Speech to the Warsaw Conference," Warsaw, Poland, November 6, 2001, excerpted in ibid, 59.

138. "Remarks by the President from Speech to the Veterans Day Prayer Breakfast," New York City, November 11, 2001, excerpted in ibid., 73.

139. "Remarks by the President from Speech to Military Personnel," Fort Campbell, Kentucky, November 21, 2001, excerpted in ibid., 74, 75.

140. "Remarks by the President from Speech to the U.S. Attorneys Conference," Washington, D.C., November 29, 2001, excerpted in ibid., 78.

141. "Remarks by the President from Speech Commemorating Pearl Harbor Day," aboard the USS *Enterprise,* Norfolk, Virginia, December 7, 2001, excerpted in ibid., 86.

142. "Remarks by the President from Speech to the New York City Police Department Personnel," New York City, February 6, 2002, excerpted in ibid., 117.

143. "Remarks by the President from Speech to Military Personnel in Anchorage, Alaska," February 16, 2002, excerpted in ibid., 122.

144. "Remarks by the President from Speech at the Graduation Exercises of the United States Military Academy," West Point, New York, June 1, 2002, excerpted in ibid., 161.

145. Fukuyama, *America at the Crossroads*, 60–61.

146. Weisberg, *The Bush Tragedy*, 206–7.

147. C. E. Callwell, *Small Wars: Their Principles and Practice*, 3rd ed. (Lincoln: University of Nebraska Press, 1996), 21.

148. Begin was a member of the Irgun, a Jewish terrorist group, and led the Irgun's 1946 bombing attack on the British administrative headquarters at the King David Hotel in Jerusalem in which ninety-three people were killed, including seventeen Jewish civilians. Shamir was a leader of the even more notorious Stern Gang and participated in the assassinations of British and UN officials. Both Begin and Shamir once proudly referred to themselves as "terrorists."

149. Walter Laqueur, *The New Terrorism: Fanaticism and the Arms of Mass Destruction* (New York: Oxford University Press, 1999), 8.

150. Quoted in P. H. Gordon and Jeremy Shapiro, *Allies at War: America, Europe, and the Crisis over Iraq* (New York: McGraw-Hill, 2004), 61.

151. James J. Sheehan, *Where Have All the Soldiers Gone? The Transformation of Modern Europe* (Boston: Houghton Mifflin, 2008), 211.

152. Metz, *Iraq and the Evolution of American Strategy*, 107–8, 117.

153. Kaufmann, "Threat Inflation," 6.

154. Ron Suskind, *The One Percent Doctrine: Deep Inside America's Pursuit of Its Enemies since 9/11* (New York: Simon & Schuster, 2006), 214.

155. John Darwin, *After Tamerlane: The Global History of Empire Since 1405* (New York: Bloomsbury Press, 2008), 482.

156. Fukuyama, *America at the Crossroads*, 111.

157. Ibid., 112.

158. Ibid.

159. Ibid., 113.

160. Ferguson, *No End in Sight*, 402.

161. U.S. Congress, Joint Committee on the Investigation of the Pearl Harbor Attack, "Appendix A. Prior Investigations Concerning the Pearl Harbor Attack," in *Investigation of the Pearl Harbor Attack Report*, 79th Cong., 2d sess., document 244 (Washington, D.C.: U.S. Government Printing Office, 1946), 1, http://www.ibiblio.org/pha/pha/congress/app-a.html. The Roberts Commission consisted of Justice Roberts, two retired U.S. Navy admirals, and two retired U.S. Army generals.

162. U.S. Congress, *Investigation of the Pearl Harbor Attack*, 2, 10, http://www.ibiblio.org/pha/pha/congress/part_0.html. All told, there were eight separate official investigations of the Pearl Harbor attack. (See U.S. Congress, "Appendix A. Prior Investigations," 1–4.)

Chapter 5. Consequences: An Iraq Syndrome?

1. "Gates Revives Old Military Axiom."

2. John Mueller, "The Iraq Syndrome," *Foreign Affairs* 84, no. 6 November–December 2005: 44.

3. Timothy Noah, "Dick Cheney, Dove," *Slate,* October 16, 2002, http://www. slate.com/?id=2072609.

4. Ibid.

5. George Bush and Brent Scowcroft, *A World Transformed* (New York: Alfred A. Knopf, 1998), 464, 489 (emphasis added).

6. For a comprehensive assessment of why military occupations succeed or fail, see Edelstein, *Occupational Hazards.*

7. See Andrew Mack, "Why Big Nations Lose Small Wars: The Politics of Asymmetric Conflict," *World Politics* 27, no. 2, January 1975: 175–200; Gil Merom, *How Democracies Lose Small Wars: State, Society, and the Failures of France in Algeria, Israel in Lebanon, and the United States in Vietnam* (New York: Cambridge University Press, 2003); Ivan Arreguin-Toft, *How the Weak Win Wars: A Theory of Asymmetric Conflict* (New York: Cambridge University Press, 2005); and Jeffrey Record, *Beating Goliath: Why Insurgencies Win* (Washington, D.C.: Potomac Books, 2007).

8. Excerpts from the Weinberger speech appearing in the above and following paragraphs are drawn from "The Uses of Military Power," a speech before the National Press Club, Washington, D.C., November 28, 1984, and reprinted in Michael I. Handel, *Masters of War: Classical Strategic Thought* (Portland, OR: Frank Cass, 2001), 329–35 (emphasis in original).

9. See DeYoung, *Soldier,* 194–201.

10. Colin Powell, with Joseph E. Persico, *My American Journey* (New York: Random House, 1995), 148.

11. Colin Powell, speech at the Vietnam Veterans Memorial, May 27, 1991, quoted in DeYoung, *Soldier,* 210.

12. Powell, *My American Journey,* 149.

13. Colin Powell, "U.S. Forces: Challenges Ahead," *Foreign Affairs* 71 (Winter 1992–93), 38, 39, 40.

14. Powell, *My American Journey,* 527.

15. See Record, *Serbia and Vietnam.*

16. See Jeffrey Record, "Force Protection Fetishism: Sources, Consequences, and (?) Solutions," *Aerospace Power Journal,* Summer 2000, 4–11.

17. Condoleezza Rice, "Promoting the National Interest," *Foreign Affairs* 79, no. 1 (January–February 2000): 61.

18. See Record, *Dark Victory,* 45–63.

19. See Clarke, *Against All Enemies;* Michael Scheuer, *Imperial Hubris: Why the West Is Losing the War on Terror* (Washington, D.C.: Potomac Books, 2004); and Daniel Benjamin and Steven Simon, *The Next Attack: The Failure of the War on Terror and a Strategy for Getting It Right* (New York: Henry Holt, 2005).

20. Quoted in DeYoung, *Soldier,* 376.

21. Interview with Karen DeYoung, quoted in ibid., 394.

22. DeYoung, *Soldier,* 426.

23. Interview with Karen DeYoung, quoted in DeYoung, *Soldier,* 401–2.

24. See David C. Hendrickson and Robert W. Tucker, *Revisions in Need of Revising: What Went Wrong in the Iraq War* (Carlisle, PA: Strategic Studies Institute, December 2005); and Benjamin H. Friedman, Harvey M. Sapolsky,

and Christopher Preble, *Learning the Right Lessons from Iraq* (Washington, D.C.: Cato Institute, February 13, 2008).

25. Mueller, "The Iraq Syndrome," 44.

26. Ibid., 50.

27. Office of the Director of National Intelligence, "Prospects for Iraq's Stability: A Challenging Road Ahead," *National Intelligence Estimate* (Washington, D.C.: National Intelligence Council, January 2007).

28. Anthony H. Cordesman, "Success in Iraq Hinges on More than Troops, Costs," *Washington Times*, October 29, 2008.

29. Mueller, "The Iraq Syndrome," 44, 53–54.

30. The proposed fiscal year 2008 defense budget increases the proportion of overall defense spending that would go to the army from 25.4 percent to 27 percent and the Marine Corps from 3.7 percent to 4.3 percent while lowering that for the navy from 25.5 percent to 24.8 percent and the air force from 29.7 percent to 28.2 percent. See Ann Scott Tyson, "Bush's Defense Budget Biggest Since Reagan Era," *Washington Post*, February 6, 2007.

31. See Andrew Krepinevich, *The Army and Vietnam* (Baltimore, MD: Johns Hopkins University Press, 1986).

32. See Jeffrey Record, *The American Way of War: Cultural Barriers to Successful Counterinsurgency*, Cato Institute Policy Analysis Paper no. 577 (Washington, D.C.: Cato Institute, September 1, 2006).

33. Quoted in Robert Debs Heinl, Jr., *Dictionary of Military and Naval Quotations* (Annapolis, MD: Naval Institute Press, 1966), 88.

34. Geoffrey Perret, *Commander in Chief: How Truman, Johnson, and Bush Turned a Presidential Power into a Threat to America's Future* (New York: Farrar, Straus, and Giroux, 2007), 389.

35. Gen. Rupert Smith, *The Utility of Force: The Art of War in the Modern World* (New York: Alfred A. Knopf, 2007), 3.

36. Adrian R. Lewis, *The American Culture of War: The History of U.S. Military Force from World War II to Operation Iraqi Freedom* (New York: Routledge, 2007), 309.

37. Caspar W. Weinberger, *Fighting for Peace: Seven Critical Years in the Pentagon* (New York: Warner Books, 1990), 8.

Bibliography

Acheson, Dean. *Present at the Creation: My Years at the State Department*. New York: W. W. Norton, 1969.

Adams, John Quincy. "Warning against the Search for 'Monsters to Destroy,' 1821." http://www.mtholyoke.edu/acad/intrel/jqadams.htm.

Ajami, Fouad. *The Foreigner's Gift: The Americans, the Arabs, and the Iraqis in Iraq*. New York: Free Press, 2006.

Alfonsi, Christian. *Circle in the Sand: Why We Went Back to Iraq*. New York: Doubleday, 2006.

Allison, Graham. *Nuclear Terrorism: The Ultimate Preventable Catastrophe*. New York: Times Books, 2004.

Arreguin-Toft, Ivan. *How the Weak Win Wars: A Theory of Asymmetric Conflict*. New York: Cambridge University Press, 2005.

Bacevich, Andrew J. "Gulliver at Bay: The Paradox of the Imperial Presidency." In *Iraq and the Lessons of Vietnam: How Not to Learn from the Past*, edited by Lloyd C. Gardner and Marilyn B. Young. New York: New Press, 2007.

———. *The New American Militarism: How Americans Are Seduced by War*. New York: Oxford University Press, 2005.

Baer, Robert. "The Fall of the House of Saud." *Atlantic Monthly* 291, no. 40 (May 2003): 53–62.

Barry, Tom. "A Strategy Foretold." *Foreign Policy in Focus*, October 2002, 1–3.

Batatu, Hanna. *The Old Social Classes and the Revolutionary Movements in Iraq: A Study of Iraq's Oldest Landed and Commercial Classes and of Its Communists, Ba'thists, and Free Officers*. Princeton, NJ: Princeton University Press, 1978.

Beisner, Robert L. *Dean Acheson: A Life in the Cold War*. New York: Oxford University Press, 2006.

Benjamin, Daniel. "Feith-Based Intelligence." *Washington Post*, March 8, 2007.

Benjamin, Daniel, and Steven Simon. *The Age of Sacred Terror*. New York: Random House, 2002.

————. *The Next Attack: The Failure of the War on Terror and a Strategy for Getting It Right* (New York: Henry Holt, 2005).

Betts, Richard K. *Enemies of Intelligence: Knowledge and Power in American National Security.* New York: Columbia University Press, 2007.

Biddle, Stephen, James Embrey, Edward Filiberti, Stephen Kidder, Steven Metz, Ivan C. Oelrich, and Richard Shelton. *Toppling Saddam: Iraq and American Military Transformation.* Carlisle, PA: Strategic Studies Institute, U.S. Army War College, April 2004.

Bix, Herbert P. *Hirohito and the Making of Modern Japan.* New York: HarperCollins, 2000.

Blair, Clay. *The Forgotten War: America in Korea, 1950–1953.* New York: Times Books, 1987.

Blix, Hans. *Disarming Iraq.* New York: Pantheon, 2004.

Borger, Julian. "Interview with Richard Clarke." *Guardian* (London), March 23, 2004.

Brzezinski, Zbigniew. "George Bush's Suicidal Statecraft." *International Herald Tribune,* October 13, 2005.

Bumiller, Elisabeth. *Condoleezza Rice: An American Life.* New York: Random House, 2007.

Bush, George, and Brent Scowcroft. *A World Transformed.* New York: Alfred A. Knopf, 1998.

Bush, George W. *The National Security Strategy of the United States of America.* Washington, D.C.: The White House, September 17, 2002.

————. *The National Security Strategy of the United States of America.* Washington, D.C.: The White House, March 2006.

————. "Presidential Radio Address to the Nation, September 15, 2001." In *We Will Prevail: President George W. Bush on War, Terrorism, and Freedom,* 8. New York: Continuum, 2003.

————. "Remarks by President Bush and President Alvaro Uribe of Columbia in a Photo Opportunity." The Oval Office, September 25, 2002. www.whitehouse. gov/news/releases/2002/09/20020925-1html.

————. "Remarks by the President from Speech at National Day of Prayer and Remembrance Ceremony," the National Cathedral, Washington, D.C., September 14, 2001. Excerpted in *We Will Prevail,* 5–7.

————. "Remarks by the President from Speech at the Department of Defense Service of Remembrance," October 11, 2001, Washington, D.C. Excerpted in *We Will Prevail,* 39–42.

————. "Remarks by the President from Speech at the Graduation Exercises of the United States Military Academy," West Point, New York, June 1, 2002. Excerpted in *We Will Prevail,* 158–168.

————. "Remarks by the President from Speech at the Islamic Center of Washington, D.C.," September 17, 2001. Excerpted in *We Will Prevail,* 9–10.

————. "Remarks by the President from Speech Commemorating Pearl Harbor Day, aboard the USS *Enterprise,*" Norfolk, Virginia, December 7, 2001. Excerpted in *We Will Prevail,* 84–87.

————. "Remarks by the President from Speech to Employees at the Federal Bureau of Investigation," Washington, D.C., September 25, 2001. Excerpted in *We Will Prevail,* 22–24.

————. "Remarks by the President from Speech to Employees of the Central Intelligence Agency," September 26, 2001. Excerpted in *We Will Prevail*, 24.

————. "Remarks by the President from Speech to Military Personnel at Travis Air Force Base, California," October 17, 2001. Excerpted in *We Will Prevail*, 46–48.

————. "Remarks by the President from Speech to Military Personnel, Fort Campbell, Kentucky," November 12, 2001. Excerpted in *We Will Prevail*, 74–76.

————. "Remarks by the President from Speech to Military Personnel in Anchorage, Alaska," February 16, 2002. Excerpted in *We Will Prevail*, 120–123.

————. "Remarks by the President from Speech to the Employees of the Department of Labor," Washington, D.C., October 4, 2001. Excerpted in *We Will Prevail*, 29–31.

————. "Remarks by the President from Speech to the New York City Police Department Personnel," New City, February 6, 2002. Excerpted in *We Will Prevail*, 113–118.

————. "Remarks by the President from Speech to the Warsaw Conference, Warsaw, Poland," November 6, 2001. Excerpted in *We Will Prevail*, 58–60.

————. "Remarks by the President from Speech to U.S. Attorneys Conference," Washington, D.C., November 29, 2001. Excerpted in *We Will Prevail*, 78–81.

————. "Remarks by the President from Speech to Veterans Day Prayer Breakfast, New York City," November 11, 2001." Excerpted in *We Will Prevail*, 72–74.

————. "Remarks by the President from Speech Unveiling 'Most Wanted' Terrorist List, FBI Headquarters," Washington, D.C., October 10, 2001. Excerpted in *We Will Prevail*, 38–39.

"Bush Speech on Iraq: 'Saddam Hussein and His Sons Must Leave.'" *New York Times*, March 18, 2003.

"Bush: 'We Will Do What Is Necessary.' Transcript of President George W. Bush's Address to the Nation, September 7, 2003." *Washington Post*, September 8, 2003.

Callwell, C. E. *Small Wars: Their Principles and Practice*. 3rd ed. Lincoln: University of Nebraska Press, 1996.

Carney, James, and John F. Dickerson. "Inside the War Room." *Time*, December 31, 2001–January 7, 2002, 112–21.

Cigar, Norman. "Iraq's Strategic Mindset and the Gulf War: Blueprint for Defeat." *Journal of Strategic Studies* 15, no. 1 (March 1992): 1–29.

Cirincione, Joseph. *Bomb Scare: The History and Future of Nuclear Weapons*. New York: Columbia University Press, 2007.

Cirincione, Joseph, Jessica T. Mathews, and George Perkovich. *WMD in Iraq: Evidence and Implications*. With Alex Orton. Washington, D.C.: Carnegie Endowment for International Peace, January 2004.

Cirincione, Joseph, Jon B. Wolfstahl, and Miriam Rajkumar. *Deadly Arsenals: Nuclear, Biological, and Chemical Threats*. 2nd ed. Washington, D.C.: Carnegie Endowment for International Peace, 2005.

Clarke, Richard A. *Against All Enemies: Inside America's War on Terror*. New York: Free Press, 2004.

————. *Your Government Failed You: Breaking the Cycle of National Security Disasters*. New York: HarperCollins, 2008.

Clodfelter, Mark. *The Limits of Air Power: The American Bombing of North Vietnam*. New York: Free Press, 1989.

Cloud, David S., and Marek Mazzetti. "Prewar Intelligence Unit at Pentagon Is Criticized." *New York Times*, February 9, 2007.

Cobb, Adam. "A Strategic Assessment of Iraq." *Civil Wars* 9, no. 1 (March 2007): 32–60.

Cockburn, Andrew. *Rumsfeld: His Rise, Fall, and Catastrophic Legacy* (New York: Scribner, 2007), 170.

Cohen, Eliot, and John Gooch. *Military Misfortunes: The Anatomy of Failure in War*. New York: Free Press, 1990.

Collins, Joseph J. *Choosing War: The Decision to Invade Iraq and Its Aftermath*. Washington, D.C.: Institute for National Strategic Studies, National Defense University, April 2008.

Condoleezza Rice, "Transforming the Middle East," *Washington Post*, August 7, 2003.

Connelly, Marjorie. "The World: Sinking Views of the United States." *New York Times*, March 23, 2003.

Cordesman, Anthony H. "Success in Iraq Hinges on More than Troops, Costs." *Washington Times*, October 29, 2008.

Crane, Conrad C., and W. Andrew Terrill. *Reconstructing Iraq: Insights, Challenges, and Missions for Military Forces in a Post-Conflict Scenario*. Carlisle, PA: Strategic Studies Institute, U.S. Army War College, February 2003.

Crockatt, Richard. *The Fifty Years War: The United States and the Soviet Union in World Politics, 1941–1991*. New York: Routledge, 1995.

Daalder, Ivo H., and James M. Lindsay. *America Unbound: The Bush Revolution in Foreign Policy*. Washington, D.C.: Brookings Institution, 2003.

Darwin, John. *After Tamerlane: The Global History of Empire since 1405*. New York: Bloomsbury Press, 2008.

Davis, John. "The Ideology of War: The Neoconservatives and the Hijacking of U.S. Policy in Iraq." In *Presidential Policies and the Road to the Second Iraq War: From Forty One to Forty Three*, edited by John Davis. Burlington, VT: Ashgate, 2006.

DeYoung, Karen. *Soldier: The Life of Colin Powell*. New York: Alfred A. Knopf, 2006.

Dizard, John. "How Ahmed Chalabi Conned the Neocons." *Financial Times*, May 4, 2004.

Dorrien, Gary. *Imperial Designs: Neoconservatism and the New Pax Americana*. New York: Routledge, 2004.

———. *The Neoconservative Mind: Politics, Culture, and the War of Ideology*. Philadelphia, PA: Temple University, 1993.

Dower, John. *Embracing Defeat: Japan in the Wake of World War II*. New York: W. W. Norton, 1999.

Draper, Robert. *Dead Certain: The Presidency of George W. Bush*. New York: Free Press, 2007.

Dreyfuss, Robert. "Tinker, Tailor, Neocon, Spy." *American Prospect*, November 18, 2002.

Dreyfuss, Robert, and Jason Vest. "The Lie Factory." *Mother Jones*, January–February 2004.

Echevarria, Antulio J. *Toward an American Way of War*. Carlisle, PA: Strategic Studies Institute, U.S. Army War College, March 2004.

Edelstein, David M. *Occupational Hazards: Success and Failure in Military Occupation.* Ithaca, NY: Cornell University Press, 2008.

Ehrman, John. *The Rise of Neoconservatism: Intellectuals and Foreign Affairs.* New Haven, CT: Yale University Press, 1995.

"Eisenhower Explains the Domino Theory." Excerpt from President Dwight Eisenhower's press conference, April 7, 1954. http://www.richmond.edu/~ebolt/history398/DominoTheory.html.

Elliott, Michael, and James Carney. "First Stop, Iraq." *Time*, March 22, 2003.

Feith, Douglas J. "How Bush Sold the War." *Wall Street Journal*, May 27, 2008.

———. *War and Decision: Inside the Pentagon at the Dawn of the War on Terror.* New York: HarperCollins, 2008.

Feldman, Noah. *What We Owe Iraq: War and the Ethics of Nation Building.* Princeton, NJ: Princeton University Press, 2004.

Ferguson, Charles H. *No End in Sight: Iraq's Descent into Chaos.* New York: Public Affairs, 2008.

Fettweis, Christopher J. *Losing Hurts Twice as Bad: The Four Stages to Moving Beyond Iraq.* New York: W. W. Norton, 2008.

Final Report of the National Commission on Terrorist Attacks upon the United States. Authorized edition. New York: W. W. Norton, 2005.

Foot, Rosemary. *The Wrong War: American Policy and the Dimensions of the Korean Conflict, 1950–1953.* Ithaca, NY: Cornell University Press, 1985.

Friedman, Benjamin H., Harvey M. Sapolsky, and Christopher Preble. *Learning the Right Lessons from Iraq.* Washington, D.C.: Cato Institute, February 13, 2008.

Friedman, Murray. *The Neoconservative Revolution: Jewish Intellectuals and the Shaping of Public Policy.* New York: Cambridge University Press, 2005.

Frum, David. *The Right Man: The Surprise Presidency of George W. Bush.* New York: Random House, 2003.

Frum, David, and Richard Perle. *An End to Evil: How to Win the War on Terror.* New York: Random House, 2003.

Fukuyama, Frances. *America at the Crossroads: Democracy, Power, and the Neoconservative Legacy.* New Haven, CT: Yale University Press, 2006.

Galbraith, Peter. "The Victor?" In *The Consequences to Come: American Power after Bush,* edited by Robert B. Silvers. New York: New York Review Books, 2008, 59–76.

Ganji, Akbar. "The Latter-Day Sultan: Power and Politics in Iran." *Foreign Affairs* 87, no. 6 (November–December 2008): 44–66.

Gellman, Barton. *Angler: The Cheney Vice Presidency.* New York: Penguin, 2008.

———. "Seven Nuclear Sites Looted." *Washington Post*, May 10, 2003.

———. "U.S. Has Not Inspected Iraqi Nuclear Facility." *Washington Post*, April 25, 2003.

Gerecht, Reuel Marc. "A Cowering Superpower." *Weekly Standard* 6, no. 43 (July 30, 2001): 26–29.

Gerstenzang, James. "Bush Says Iraq Exit Would Bolster Iran." *Los Angeles Times,* October 4, 2007.

Giustozzi, Antonio. *Koran, Kalashnikov, and Laptop: The Neo-Taliban Insurgency in Afghanistan.* New York: Columbia University Press, 2008.

Goldberg, Jeffrey. "A Little Learning: What Douglas Feith Knew, and When He Knew It." *New Yorker,* May 9, 2005.

Goldsmith, Jack. *The Terror Presidency: Law and Judgment inside the Bush Administration.* New York: W. W. Norton, 2007.

Goodman, Melvin A. *Failure of Intelligence: The Decline and Fall of the CIA.* New York: Rowman and Littlefield, 2008.

Gordon, Michael R., and Bernard E. Trainor. *Cobra II: The Inside Story of the Invasion and Occupation of Iraq.* New York: Pantheon Books, 2006.

Gordon, P. H., and Jeremy Shapiro. *Allies at War: America, Europe, and the Crisis over Iraq.* New York: McGraw-Hill, 2004.

Gray, Colin S. "The American Way of War: Critique and Implications." In *Rethinking the Principles of War,* edited by Anthony D. McIvor, 13–40. Annapolis, MD: Naval Institute Press, 2005.

Greenwald, Glenn. *A Tragic Legacy: How a Good vs. Evil Mentality Destroyed the Bush Presidency.* New York: Crown Publishers, 2007.

Haass, Richard N. *The Opportunity: America's Moment to Alter History's Course.* New York: Public Affairs, 2005.

———. *War of Necessity, War of Choice: A Memoir of Two Iraq Wars.* New York: Simon and Schuster, 2009.

Halberstam, David. *The Coldest Winter: America and the Korean War.* New York: Hyperion, 2007.

Halper, Stefan, and Jonathan Clarke. *America Alone: The Neo-Conservatives and the Global Order.* New York: Cambridge University Press, 2004.

Heilbrunn, Jacob. *They Knew They Were Right: The Rise of the Neocons.* New York: Doubleday, 2008.

Heinl, Robert Debs, Jr. *Dictionary of Military and Naval Quotations.* Annapolis, MD: Naval Institute Press, 1966.

Hendrickson, David C., and Robert W. Tucker. *Revisions in Need of Revising: What Went Wrong in the Iraq War.* Carlisle, PA: Strategic Studies Institute, U.S. Army War College, December 2005.

Hess, Gary. *Presidential Decisions for War: Korea, Vietnam, and the Persian Gulf.* Baltimore, MD: Johns Hopkins University Press, 2001.

Holmes, Stephen. *The Matador's Cape: America's Reckless Response to Terror.* New York: Cambridge University Press, 2007.

Hoyle, Russ. *Going to War: How Misinformation, Disinformation, and Arrogance Led America into Iraq.* New York: St. Martin's Press, 2008.

"In the President's Words: 'Free People Will Keep the Peace of the World.'"Transcript of President Bush's speech to the American Enterprise Institute, Washington, D.C., February 26, 2003. Printed in *New York Times,* February 27, 2003.

International Institute for Strategic Studies. *Strategic Survey 2002–2003: An Evaluation and Forecast of World Affairs.* London: International Institute for Strategic Studies, 2003.

Isikoff, Michael, and David Corn. *Hubris: The Inside Story of Spin, Scandal, and the Selling of the Iraq War.* New York: Crown Publishers, 2006.

Jehl, Douglas. "Pentagon Reportedly Skewed CIA's View of Qaeda Tie." *New York Times,* October 22, 2004.

Johnson, Caitlin A. "Transcript: President Bush, Part 2; Couric's Interview with

President Bush." CBS News, September 6, 2006. http://www.cbsnews.com/stories/2006/09/06/five_years/main1980074.shtml.

Kagan, Frederick W. *Finding the Target: The Transformation of American Military Policy.* New York: Encounter Books, 2006.

———. "War and Aftermath." *Policy Review* 120 (August–September 2003): 3–27.

Kagan, Robert. *The Return of History and the End of Dreams.* New York: Alfred A. Knopf, 2008.

Kagan, Robert, and William Kristol. "National Interest and Global Responsibility." In *Present Dangers: Crisis and Opportunity in American Foreign and Defense Policy,* edited by Robert Kagan and William Kristol, 3–24. San Francisco: Encounter Books, 2000.

Kahin, George McT. *Intervention: How America Became Involved in Vietnam.* New York: Alfred A. Knopf, 1986.

Kaplan, Fred. *Daydream Believers: How a Few Grand Ideas Wrecked American Power.* New York: John Wiley and Sons, 2008.

Kaplan, Lawrence, and William Kristol. *The War Over Iraq: Saddam's Tyranny and America's Mission.* San Francisco: Encounter Books, 2003.

Kaufmann, Chaim. "Threat Inflation and the Failure of the Marketplace of Ideas: The Selling of the Iraq War." *International Security* 29, no. 1 (Summer 2004): 5–48.

Kearns, Doris. *Lyndon Johnson and the American Dream.* New York: Harper & Row, 1976.

Keller, Bill. "The Sunshine Warrior." *New York Times Magazine,* September 22, 2002, 108.

Kennan, George F. *Memoirs 1950–1963.* Boston: Little, Brown and Company, 1972.

Kessler, Glenn. *The Confidante: Condoleezza Rice and the Creation of the Bush Legacy.* New York: St. Martin's Press, 2007.

Khalilzad, Zalmay. *From Containment to Global Leadership: America and the World after the Cold War.* Santa Monica, CA: Rand, 1995.

Krauthammer, Charles. "The Bush Doctrine." *Weekly Standard* 6, no. 36 (June 4, 2001): 21–25.

Krepinevich, Andrew. *The Army and Vietnam.* Baltimore, MD: Johns Hopkins University Press, 1986.

Kristol, William. "Testimony." Senate Foreign Relations Committee, February 7, 2002. www.newamericancentury.org/defense-20020207.htm.

Kristol, William, and others. "Toward a Comprehensive Strategy: A Letter to the President." *National Review Online,* September 20, 2001. http://www.nationalreview.com/document/document092101b.shtml.

Laqueur, Walter. *The New Terrorism: Fanaticism and the Arms of Mass Destruction.* New York: Oxford University Press, 1999.

Lewis, Adrian R. *The American Culture of War: The History of U.S. Military Force from World War II to Operation Iraqi Freedom.* New York: Routledge, 2007.

Litwak, Robert S. *Regime Change: U.S. Strategy through the Prism of 9/11.* Washington, D.C.: Woodrow Wilson Center Press, 2007.

Mack, Andrew. "Why Big Nations Lose Small Wars: The Politics of Asymmetric Conflict." *World Politics* 27, no. 2 (January 1975): 175–200.

MacKenzie, John P. *Absolute Power: How the Unitary Executive Theory Is Undermining the Constitution.* New York: Century Foundation Press, 2008.

Manchester, William. *American Caesar: Douglas MacArthur, 1880–1964.* Boston: Little, Brown, 1978.

Mann, James. *The Rebellion of Ronald Reagan: A History of the End of the Cold War.* New York: Viking, 2009.

———. *Rise of the Vulcans: The History of Bush's War Cabinet.* New York: Viking, 2004.

Martin, Bradley. *Under the Loving Care of the Fatherly Leader: North Korea and the Kim Dynasty.* New York: St. Martin's Press, 2004.

Mayer, Jane. *The Dark Side: The Inside Story of How the War on Terror Turned into a War on American Ideals.* New York: Doubleday, 2008.

———. "The Manipulator." *New Yorker,* June 7, 2004, 48–72.

McClellan, Scott. *What Happened: Inside the Bush White House and Washington's Culture of Deception.* New York: Public Affairs, 2008.

McNamara, Robert S. *In Retrospect: The Tragedy and Lessons of Vietnam.* With Brian VanDeMark. New York: Random House, 1995.

Mearsheimer, John J., and Stephen Walt. *The Israel Lobby and U.S. Foreign Policy.* New York: Farrar, Straus, and Giroux, 2007.

———. "An Unnecessary War." *Foreign Policy,* no. 134 (January–February 2003): 51–59.

Merom, Gil. *How Democracies Lose Small Wars: State, Society, and the Failures of France in Algeria, Israel in Lebanon, and the United States in Vietnam.* New: York: Cambridge University Press, 2003.

Metz, Steven. *Iraq and the Evolution of American Strategy.* Washington, D.C.: Potomac Books, 2008.

Mueller, John. "The Iraq Syndrome." *Foreign Affairs* 84, no. 6 (November–December 2005): 44–54.

Muravchik, Joshua. *The Imperative of American Leadership: A Challenge to Neo-Isolationism.* Washington, D.C.: American Enterprise Institute Press, 1996.

———. "The Past, Present, and Future of Neoconservatism." *Commentary* 124, no. 3 (October 2007): 19–29.

Nitze, Paul H. *From Hiroshima to Glasnost: At the Center of Decision—a Memoir.* With Ann M. Smith and Steven L. Rearden. New York: Grove Weidenfield, 1989.

Office of the Director of National Intelligence. "Prospects for Iraq's Stability: A Challenging Road Ahead." National Intelligence Estimate. Washington, D.C.: National Intelligence Council, January 2007.

Packer, George. *The Assassins' Gate: America in Iraq.* New York: Farrar, Straus, and Giroux, 2007.

———. "Dreaming of Democracy." *New York Times Magazine,* March 2, 2003, 44–49, 60, 90, and 104.

Pape, Robert A. *Dying to Win: The Logic of Suicide Terrorism.* New York: Random House, 2005.

Parsi, Trita. *Treacherous Alliance: The Secret Dealings of Israel, Iran, and the U.S.* New Haven, CT: Yale University Press, 2007.

Peel, Quentin, Robert Graham, James Harding, and Judy Dempsey. "War In Iraq: How The Die Was Cast before Transatlantic Diplomacy Failed." *Financial Times,* May 27, 2003.

The Pentagon Papers: The Defense Department History of United States Decisionmaking on Vietnam. Senator Gravel edition. Boston: Beacon Press, 1971.

Perle, Richard. "Ambushed on the Potomac." *The National Interest Online,* January 21, 2009. http://nationalinterest.org/PrinterFriendly.aspx?id=20486.

———. "Why the West Must Strike First against Saddam Hussein." *London Daily Telegraph,* August 9, 2002.

Perret, Geoffrey. *Commander in Chief: How Truman, Johnson, and Bush Turned a Presidential Power into a Threat to America's Future.* New York: Farrar, Straus, and Giroux, 2007.

Pfiffner, James P. "Did President Bush Mislead the Country in His Arguments for War with Iraq?" *Presidential Studies Quarterly* 34, no. 1 (March 2004): 25–46.

Pillar, Paul. "Intelligence, Policy, and the War in Iraq." *Foreign Affairs* 85, no. 2 (March–April 2006): 15–27.

Pletka, Danielle. "There's No Freedom Gene." *New York Times,* March 16, 2008.

"Political and Military Aspects of U.S. Policy in Vietnam." *Department of State Bulletin* 53, no. 1366 (August 30, 1965): 342–56.

Pollack, Kenneth. *The Threatening Storm: The Case for Invading Iraq.* New York: Random House, 2002.

Powell, Colin. *My American Journey.* With Joseph E. Persico. New York: Random House, 1995.

———. "U.S. Forces: Challenges Ahead." *Foreign Affairs* 71 (Winter 1992–93): 32–45.

Powers, Thomas. "Iran: The Threat." *New York Review of Books,* July 17, 2008, 9–11.

Prados, John. *Hoodwinked: The Documents That Reveal How Bush Sold Us a War.* New York: New Press, 2004.

"President Bush Discusses Global War on Terror." Wardman Park Marriott Hotel, Washington, D.C., September 26, 2006. http://docs.google.com/gview?a=v&q=cache:3Da3UV5YSJMJ:merln.ndu.edu/archivepdf/afghanistan/WH/20060929-3.pdf+"President+Bush+at+Wardman+Park+Marriott+Hotel,&hl=en&gl=us.

Project for the New American Century. "Statement of Principles," June 3, 1997. http://www.newamericancentury.org/statementofprinciples.htm.

Record, Jeffrey. *The American Way of War: Cultural Barriers to Successful Counterinsurgency.* Cato Institute Policy Analysis Paper no. 577. Washington, D.C.: Cato Institute, September 1, 2006.

———. "Back to the Weinberger-Powell Doctrine?" *Strategic Studies Quarterly* 1, no. 1 (Fall 2007): 79–95.

———. *Beating Goliath: Why Insurgencies Win.* Washington, D.C.: Potomac Books, 2007.

———. *Dark Victory: America's Second War against Iraq.* Annapolis, MD: Naval Institute Press, 2004.

———. "Defeating Desert Storm (and Why Saddam Didn't)." *Comparative Strategy* 12, no. 2 (April–June 1993): 125–40.

———. "Force Protection Fetishism: Sources, Consequences, and (?) Solutions." *Aerospace Power Journal,* Summer 2001, 4–11.

———. "The Limits and Temptations of America's Conventional Military Primacy." *Survival* 47, no. 1 (Spring 2005): 33–50.

———. *Making War, Thinking History: Munich, Vietnam, and Presidential Uses of Force from Korea to Kosovo.* Annapolis, MD: Naval Institute Press, 2002.

———. *Nuclear Deterrence, Preventive War, and Counterproliferation.* Washington, D.C.: Cato Institute, July 2004.

————. "Retiring Hitler and 'Appeasement' from the National Security Debate." *Parameters* 38, no. 2 (Summer 2008): 91–101.

————. *Serbia and Vietnam: A Preliminary Comparison of U.S. Decisions to Use Force.* Occasional Paper no. 8. Maxwell Air Force Base, AL: Center for Strategy and Technology, Air War College, May 1999.

————. *The Specter of Munich: Reconsidering the Lessons of Appeasing Hitler.* Washington, D.C.: Potomac Books, 2006.

————. "Threat Confusion and Its Penalties." *Survival* 46, no. 2 (Summer 2004): 51–72.

————. *The Wrong War: Why We Lost in Vietnam.* Annapolis, MD: Naval Institute Press, 1998.

Record, Jeffrey, and W. Andrew Terrill. *Iraq and Vietnam: Differences, Similarities, and Insights.* Carlisle, PA: Strategic Studies Institute, U.S. Army War College, May 2004.

Rhodes, Edward. "The Imperial Logic of Bush's Liberal Agenda." *Survival* 35, no. 1 (Spring 2005): 131–54.

Rice, Condoleezza. "Promoting the National Interest." *Foreign Affairs* 79, no. 1 (January–February 2000): 45–62.

Ricks, Thomas E. *Fiasco: The American Military Adventure in Iraq.* New York: Penguin, 2006.

Roston, Aram. *The Man Who Pushed America to War: The Extraordinary Life, Adventures, and Obsessions of Ahmad Chalabi.* New York: Nation Books, 2008.

Rumsfeld, Donald H. "Defending Ourselves: Why Should We Attack Iraq?" Opening Statement before the Senate Armed Services Committee, September 19, 2002. Reprinted in *Vital Speeches of the Day* 68, no. 24 (October 1, 2002): 770–74.

————. "Secretary Rumsfeld Remarks on ABC 'This Week with George Stephanopoulos.'" Department of Defense news transcript, March 30, 2003. http://www.defenselink.mil/transcripts/transcript.aspx?transcriptid=2185.

————. "Testimony on Iraq." Hearing before the Senate Armed Services Committee, Washington, D.C., July 9, 2003. www.defenselink.mil/speeches/2003/sp20030709-secdef0364.html.

————. "DoD News Briefing—Secretary Rumsfeld and Gen. Myers." Official Department of Defense transcript, April 11, 2003. http://www.defenselink .mil/transcripts/transcript.aspx?transcripted=2367.

Rusk, Dean. *As I Saw It.* With Richard Rusk and Dan Papp. New York: W. W. Norton, 1990.

Rutenberg, Jim. "In Farewell, Rumsfeld Warns 'Weakness Is 'Provocative.'" *New York Times,* December 16, 2006.

Sagan, Scott. "The Perils of Proliferation: Organization Theory, Deterrence Theory, and the Spread of Nuclear Weapons." *International Security* 18, no. 4 (Spring 1994): 66–107.

Sanchez, Ricardo S. *Wiser in Battle: A Soldier's Story.* With Donald T. Phillips. New York: HarperCollins, 2008.

Savage, Charlie. *Takeover: The Return of the Imperial Presidency and the Subversion of American Democracy.* New York: Little, Brown, 2007.

Scheuer, Michael. *Imperial Hubris: Why the West Is Losing the War on Terror.* Washington, D.C.: Potomac Books, 2004.

Schlesinger, Arthur, M., Jr. *The Imperial Presidency*. Boston: Houghton Mifflin, 1973.

Scowcroft, Brent. "Don't Attack Saddam." *Wall Street Journal*, August 15, 2002.

"Secretary Wolfowitz Interview with Sam Tannenhaus." *Vanity Fair*, May 9, 2003. http://www.defenselink.mil/transcripts/transcript.aspx?transcriptid=2594.

Sheehan, James J. *Where Have All the Soldiers Gone? The Transformation of Modern Europe*. Boston: Houghton Mifflin, 2008.

Shenon, Philip. *The Commission: The Uncensored History of the 9/11 Investigation*. New York: Twelve, 2008.

Singer, Peter. *The President of Good and Evil: The Ethics of George W. Bush*. New York: Dutton, 2004.

Smith, Jean Edward. *FDR*. New York: Random House, 2007.

Smith, Gen. Rupert. *The Utility of Force: The Art of War in the Modern World*. New York: Alfred A. Knopf, 2007.

Stein, Jeff. "Army General Tells a Little-Known Tale of Pre-War Intelligence on Iraq." *CQ.com*, October 20, 2006. http://public.cq.com/public/20061020_home land.html.

Stephens, Philip. "Present at the Destruction of the World's Partnership." *Financial Times*, March 7, 2003.

Stoessinger, John G. *Why Nations Go to War*. 7th ed. New York: St. Martin's Press, 1998.

Suskind, Ron. *The One Percent Doctrine: Deep Inside America's Pursuit of Its Enemies since 9/11*. New York: Simon & Schuster, 2006.

Takeyh, Ray. "Iran's New Iraq." *Middle East Journal* 62, no. 1 (Winter 2008): 13–30.

"Text of the President's Speech at West Point." *New York Times*, June 1, 2002. http://www.nytimes.com/2002/06/01/international/02PTEX-WEB.html.

Tyson, Ann Scott. "Bush's Defense Budget Biggest since Reagan Era." *Washington Post*, February 6, 2007.

Unger, Craig. *The Fall of the House of Bush*. New York: Scribner, 2007.

U.S. Congress. Joint Committee on the Investigation of the Pearl Harbor Attack. "Appendix A. Prior Investigations Concerning the Pearl Harbor Attack." *Investigation of the Pearl Harbor Attack Report*. 79th Cong., 2d sess., document 244. Washington, D.C.: U.S. Government Printing Office, 1946. http://www .ibiblio.org/pha/pha/congress/app-a.html.

"Vice President Speaks at VFW 103rd National Convention," August 26, 2002. http://georgewbush-whitehouse.archives.gov/news/releases/2002/08/20020826.html.

"Vice President's Remarks to Marines at Camp Lejeune, N.C.," October 3, 2005. http://merln.ndu.edu/archivepdf/iraq/WH/20051003-4.pdf.

Webb, James. "Heading for Trouble." *Washington Post*, September 4, 2002.

Weinberger, Caspar W. *Fighting for Peace: Seven Critical Years in the Pentagon*. New York: Warner Books, 1990.

———. "The Uses of Military Power." Speech before the National Press Club, Washington, D.C., November 28, 1984. Reprinted in Michael I. Handel, *Masters of War: Classical Strategic Thought*. Portland, OR: Frank Cass, 2001, 329–35.

Weisberg, Jacob. *The Bush Tragedy*. New York: Random House, 2008.

Weisman, Alan. *Prince of Darkness, Richard Perle: The Kingdom, the Power, and the End of Empire in America*. New York: Union Square Press, 2007.

Wells, Tom. *The War Within: America's Battle over Vietnam.* New York: Henry Holt, 1994.

Westmoreland, William C. *A Soldier Reports.* Garden City, NY: Doubleday, 1976.

WGBH Educational Foundation. "Cheney in His Own Words." In "The Dark Side," *Frontline.* Public Broadcasting Service, posted June 20, 2006. http://www.pbs.org/wgbh/pages/frontline/darkside/themes/ownwords.html.

Whitney, Craig R., ed. *The WMD Mirage: Iraq's Decade of Deception and America's False Premise for War.* New York: Public Affairs. 2005.

Wolfowitz, Paul. "Statesmanship in the New Century." In Kagan and Kristol, *Present Dangers,* 307–336.

Woods, Kevin M. *Iraqi Perspectives Report: Saddam and Terrorism: Emerging Insights from Captured Iraqi Documents.* Vol. 1 (redacted). With James Lacey. Washington, D.C.: Institute for Defense Analyses, November 2007.

Woods, Kevin M., Michael R. Peace, Mark E. Stout, Williamson Murray, and James G. Lacey. *The Iraqi Perspectives Report: Saddam's Senior Leadership on Operation Iraqi Freedom from the Official U.S. Joint Forces Command.* Annapolis, MD: Naval Institute Press, 2006.

Woodward, Bob. *Bush at War.* New York: Simon & Schuster, 2002.

———. *State of Denial.* New York: Simon & Schuster, 2006.

Wurmser, David. *Tyranny's Ally: America's Failure to Defeat Saddam Hussein.* Washington, D.C.: American Enterprise Institute Press, 1999.

Zakaria, Fareed. *The Post-American World.* New York: W. W. Norton, 2008.

Zhang, Shu Guang. *Deterrence and Strategic Culture: Chinese-American Confrontations, 1949–1958.* Ithaca, NY: Cornell University Press, 1992.

Zinni, Anthony. "The Ten Mistakes." Speech to the Center for Defense Information, Washington, D.C., May 26, 2004. Reprinted in http://dir.salon.com/story/news/feature/2004/05/26/zinni/index,html.

Index

About the Author

Well-known defense policy critic Jeffrey Record teaches strategy at the U.S. Air Force's Air War College in Montgomery, Alabama. He received his doctorate at the Johns Hopkins School of Advanced International Studies and is the author of eight books and a dozen monographs, including: *Beating Goliath: Why Insurgencies Win*; *Dark Victory: America's Second War against Iraq*; *Making War, Thinking History: Munich, Vietnam, and Presidential Uses of Force from Korea to Kosovo*; *Hollow Victory: A Contrary View of the Gulf War*; *The Wrong War: Why We Lost in Vietnam*; and *Bounding the Global War on Terrorism*. Dr. Record has served as a pacification adviser in the Mekong Delta during the Vietnam War, as a Rockefeller Young Scholar on the Brookings Institution's Defense Analysis Staff, and as a senior fellow at the Institute for Foreign Policy Analysis, the Hudson Institute, and the BDM International Corporation. He also has extensive Capitol Hill experience, having served as a legislative assistant for national security affairs to senators Sam Nunn and Lloyd Bentsen and later as a professional staff member of the Senate Armed Services Committee. He lives in Atlanta, Georgia, with his wife, Leigh.